Approaches to Teaching Nabokov's *Lolita*

Approaches to Teaching
World Literature

Joseph Gibaldi, series editor

For a complete listing of titles,
see the last pages of this book.

Approaches to Teaching Nabokov's *Lolita*

Edited by

Zoran Kuzmanovich

and

Galya Diment

The Modern Language Association of America
New York   2008

For information about obtaining permission to reprint material from MLA book publications, send your request by mail (see address below), e-mail (permissions@mla.org), or fax (646 458-0030).

Library of Congress Cataloging-in-Publication Data

Approaches to teaching Nabokov's Lolita /
edited by Zoran Kuzmanovich and Galya Diment.
p. cm. — (Approaches to teaching world literature)
Includes bibliographical references and index.
ISBN: 978-0-87352-942-6 (hardcover : alk. paper)
ISBN: 978-0-87352-943-3 (pbk. : alk. paper)
1. Nabokov, Vladimir Vladimirovich, 1899–1977. Lolita.
2. Nabokov, Vladimir Vladimirovich, 1899–1977. —Study and teaching.
I. Kuzmanovich, Zoran, 1955–
II. Diment, Galya.
PS3527.A15A67   2008
813'.54—dc22   2007049237
ISSN 1059-1133

Cover illustration of the paperback edition: *Mystery and Melancholy of a Street*, by Giorgio de Chirico. 1914. Oil on canvas. Private collection. © 2008 Artists Rights Society, New York, and SIAE, Rome

Printed on recycled paper

Published by The Modern Language Association of America
26 Broadway, New York, New York 10004-1789
www.mla.org

To our friend and mentor, Professor D. Barton Johnson,
whose early critical work on Nabokov helped establish
what could be said about Lolita *in the classroom.*

Zoran
&
Galya

CONTENTS

Literary, Generic, and Cultural Contexts

Precursors and Causes

Teaching the Russian Roots of *Lolita*

Teaching *Lolita* from an American Perspective

Philosophical, Ethical, and Ideological Approaches

PREFACE TO THE SERIES

In *The Art of Teaching* Gilbert Highet wrote, "Bad teaching wastes a great deal of effort, and spoils many lives which might have been full of energy and happiness." All too many teachers have failed in their work, Highet argued, simply "because they have not thought about it." We hope that the Approaches to Teaching World Literature series, sponsored by the Modern Language Association's Publications Committee, will not only improve the craft—as well as the art—of teaching but also encourage serious and continuing discussion of the aims and methods of teaching literature.

The principal objective of the series is to collect within each volume different points of view on teaching a specific literary work, a literary tradition, or a writer widely taught at the undergraduate level. The preparation of each volume begins with a wide-ranging survey of instructors, thus enabling us to include in the volume the philosophies and approaches, thoughts and methods of scores of experienced teachers. The result is a sourcebook of material, information, and ideas on teaching the subject of the volume to undergraduates.

The series is intended to serve nonspecialists as well as specialists, inexperienced as well as experienced teachers, graduate students who wish to learn effective ways of teaching as well as senior professors who wish to compare their own approaches with the approaches of colleagues in other schools. Of course, no volume in the series can ever substitute for erudition, intelligence, creativity, and sensitivity in teaching. We hope merely that each book will point readers in useful directions; at most each will offer only a first step in the long journey to successful teaching.

Joseph Gibaldi
Series Editor

PREFACE TO THE VOLUME

Lolita usually lands near the top of lists devoted to ranking the best books of the last century, yet its particular mix of complex narrative strategies, ornate allusive prose, and troublesome subject matter continues to produce outcries. The novel, rejected by a publisher's reader with the recommendation "this book should be buried under a stone for a thousand years" (Henderson and Bernard 239), more than fifty years after its publication still invites editorial pieces with titles such as "Why This Loathsome *Lolita* Must Be Banished." The author of the piece blames *Lolita* for "the creation of a climate of opinion which saw all sexual inhibitions as bad in themselves, and in which the idea that there was any such thing as sexual deviancy was itself part of a culture which had to be destroyed" (Oddie).

As readers and writers, we would like to believe that a single book can indeed have that kind of power, but the realist in us knows that a single book does not change a culture unless that culture is ripe for a change. *Lolita*'s place in the larger culture has been the subject of many public debates; *Lolita*'s place on the syllabus, on the other hand, does not seem to have produced much controversy. The syllabus makers seem less concerned with *Lolita* as a culture-poisoning tract than with ways of making this rich book accessible to their students (despite their frustration with students who may not be up to the intellectual labor the book demands and with their own occasional inability to convert their love of Nabokov's chocolate mousse prose into food for student thought).

We attempt to address this problem in both the "Materials" and "Approaches" sections of this volume. In "Materials" we present a biographical chronology, reflect briefly on Nabokov as a teacher, trace *Lolita*'s precursors, and outline its curious publication history. In addition, we provide a summary of the critical studies recommended by the respondents to the MLA survey of *Lolita* instructors. Finally, we include descriptive listings of reference works on *Lolita* and textual and audiovisual materials relevant to the teaching of the novel. In "Approaches" instructors reflect on the best ways to illuminate the novel's ethical quandaries and pass on its textual intricacies and contextual linkages. The breadth and inventiveness of these essays make it clear that banishing *Lolita* or burying it under a stone for a thousand years is no longer an option.

ZK
GD

Part One

MATERIALS

Chronology

"Neither in environment nor in heredity can I find the exact instrument that fashioned me, the anonymous roller that pressed upon my life a certain intricate watermark whose unique design becomes visible when the lamp of art is made to shine through life's foolscap" (*Speak* 25). Thus Vladimir Nabokov explains the way his art and his life illuminate each other. I doubt that he intended the crafty explanation as an invitation to find under the reflecting ripples of his fiction autobiographical fact. Because he said that he based *Lolita* on a theme that was "so distant, so remote" from his own psyche (*Strong Opinions* 15) and because chronologies reckon with time, heredity, and environment, trying to create a Nabokov chronology that may prove useful for reading *Lolita* is a little like consulting an oracle bone. In my previous attempts at ritual divination to reveal the "intricate watermark" (Kuzmanovich, "Strong Opinions"), I found that all hermeneutic effort spent on the task simply reduced the number of connections one could make between Nabokov's life and the most useful ways of reading and teaching his books. Whatever "unique design" one imagines encompassing both Nabokov's life and his fiction (exile, Romantic, modernist, moralist, metafictionist, etc.), the singleness of the design inevitably reduces the playful complexity that should attend any serious reading of Nabokov's most controversial work. Even to get at the usual first item on a writer's chronology, his birth, we must set aside the turtle plastrons, ox scapulae, and other materials of competing calendars. Because Europe's nineteenth-century New Style Gregorian Calendar ran twelve days ahead of Russia's Old Style Julian one, to which the twentieth century added an extra day, Vladimir Vladimirovich Nabokov was born on 10 or 22 April in 1899 but (after 1900) on 23 April 1899. To simplify the matter, I provide only the twentieth-century New Style dates here. I rely heavily on the chronology Brian Boyd prepared for the Library of America (V. Nabokov, *Novels* 837–68) and on Michael Juliar's descriptive bibliography of Nabokov's works.

1899	Vladimir Vladimirovich Nabokov is born (23 April) to Elena Ivanovna Nabokov (née Rukavishnikov) and Vladimir Dmitrievich Nabokov, a distinguished jurist and editor, in Saint Petersburg.
1900	Brother Sergey is born.
1902	The first of many British governesses arrives. Vladimir and Sergey start to learn English.
1903	Sister Olga is born.
1906	Sister Elena is born. The sisters are raised in a separate part of the household.
1908	Nabokov's father is imprisoned for three months as punishment for signing the Vyborg Manifesto, which called on people to oppose

the policies of the tsarist government by committing acts of civil disobedience.

1911   Nabokov enters the Tenishev School. Brother Kirill is born.

1914   Nabokov writes his first poem.

1916   His mother's brother, Vasily Rukavishnikov, bequeaths his estate to Nabokov. Nabokov has his first book of poetry, *Stikhi* (*Poems* [1959]), privately published in Saint Petersburg.

1917–18   After the February Revolution Nabokov's father is appointed head of chancellery in the provisional government. Following the October Revolution the Nabokovs flee to Crimea. They settle near Yalta. V. D. Nabokov is named minister of justice of the Crimean regional government.

1919   With Bolsheviks on the verge of taking over Crimea, the entire Nabokov family leaves for Sebastopol and then London. Vladimir and Sergey attend Cambridge University, Trinity College, and Oxford University, respectively.

1920   The rest of the Nabokov family moves to Berlin, where job prospects appear to be better than in England. There, Nabokov's father edits the newspaper *Rul'* ("The Rudder"). Sergey transfers to Cambridge University, Christ College.

1922   While trying to prevent the assassination of the politician Paul Miliukov, Nabokov's father is fatally shot. Nabokov receives his BA (in French and Russian) with Second Class Honors from Cambridge. He moves to Berlin, becomes engaged to Svetlana Siewert, and begins translating into Russian Lewis Carroll's *Alice's Adventures in Wonderland*. The Berlin publishing firm Gamayun brings out Nabokov's book *Grozd'* ("The Cluster"), a collection of thirty-six poems.

1923   Because of the bleak economic prospects for Nabokov and his family, the Siewert family break off their daughter's engagement to Nabokov. With his sisters, Elena and Olga, and his brother Kirill, Nabokov's mother moves to Prague, where she collects a small government pension as the widow of V. D. Nabokov. At a charity costume ball in Berlin Nabokov meets his future wife, Véra Evseevna Slonim, daughter of a Jewish businessman.

Nabokov publishes another poetry collection, *Gornyi put'* ("The Empyrean Path" [Berlin: Grani]), and the play *Skital'tsy* ("The Wanderers" [Berlin: Grani]), "a supposed translation of the first act of a play by the nonexistent English author 'Vivian Calmbrood.'" Other publications, all in *Rul'*, include the verse play *Smert'* ("Death"), *Dedushka* ("The Grandad"), *Agasfer* ("The Wandering Jew"), and excerpts from another verse play, *Tragediia gospodina Morna* ("The Tragedy of Mister Morn"). His translation of *Alice's Adventures in Wonderland* (*Ania v strane chudes*) also appears.

1924	Needing money, Nabokov composes poems, short stories, cabaret scenarios, chess problems, and crossword puzzles. He also gives lessons in tennis, boxing, French, and English.
1925	Nabokov marries Véra Slonim.
1926	Nabokov publishes his first novel, *Mashen'ka* (*Mary* [1970]), and has his play *Chelovek iz SSSR* (*The Man from the USSR* [1984]) produced in Berlin by a Russian émigré theater. Only the first act is published in *Rul'*.
1928	*Korol', dama, valet* (Berlin: Slovo; *King, Queen, Knave* [1968]) is published. Leaving a party at the Nabokovs, Yuly Aikhenvald, the first critic to recognize Nabokov as a major talent, is killed by a streetcar.
1929	The Nabokovs travel to the eastern Pyrenees to hunt butterflies. Slovo publishes *Vozvrashchenie Chorba* ("The Return of Chorb"), a collection mainly of stories and poems in Russian. Many of the *Chorba* pieces had already appeared in *Rul'*. *Zashchita Luzhina* is published (Berlin: Slovo; *The Defense* [1964]).
1930	*Sogliadatai* (*The Eye* [1965]), a short novel, is published in issue 44 of *Sovremennye zapiski* ("Contemporary Annals").
1931	*Podvig* (*Glory* [1963]) is serialized in *Sovremennye zapiski*, issues 45–48, and released in book form a year later (also by Sovremennye zapiski), establishing a pattern for Nabokov's novels in Russian.
1932	*Kamera obskura* (*Laughter in the Dark* [1938]) is serialized in *Sovremennye zapiski*, issues 49–52.
1933	Book form of *Kamera obskura* appears.
1934	*Otchaianie* (*Despair* [1937]) is published in *Sovremennye zapiski*, issues 54–56. Birth of Dmitri, the Nabokovs' only child.
1936	Publication in book form of *Otchaianie* (Berlin: Petropolis). Publication in *Sovremennye zapiski*, issues 58–60, of *Priglashenie na kazn'* (*Invitation to a Beheading* [1959]). Véra's Jewishness causes her to lose her job.
1937	The family leaves Germany for Paris to avoid further interference from the Nazi regime. Nabokov has an affair with Irina Guadinini, gets psoriasis, falls into near suicidal depression, ends the affair, and tells his wife about it. The complete versions of the first two chapters of *Dar* (*The Gift* [1961]) and the first part of the third appear in *Sovremennye zapiski*, issues 63–65. He gives readings, one of which is attended by James Joyce, and writes in French an essay on Aleksandr Pushkin, "Pouchkine, ou le vrai et le vraisemblable."
1938	Two of Nabokov's plays are produced in Russian in Paris: *Sobytie* ("The Event") and *Izobretenie Val'sa* (*The Waltz Invention* [1966]). *Russkie zapiski* ("Russian Annals") publishes *Sobytie* in issue 4 and

then *Izobretenie Val'sa* in issue 11. The remaining text of *Dar's* chapter 3 is published in *Sovremennye zapiski*, issue 66. Because the journal would not publish chapter 4, the biography of the Russian critic and political activist Nikolai Chernyshevsky, *Sovremennye zapiski*, issue 67, carried only the fifth and last chapter of *Dar*. Book form of *Priglashenie na kazn'* is published in Paris by Dom Knigi. Book form of *Sogliadatai* (short novel, along with twelve stories in Russian) is published in Paris by Russkie Zapiski.

1939   Nabokov writes in French "Mademoiselle O." He works on completing *The Real Life of Sebastian Knight* in English and *Volshebnik* (*The Enchanter* [1986]) in Russian, another road sign on the path to *Lolita* that would be published only posthumously. His mother dies in Prague.

1940   Once again hearing the sound of fast-approaching Nazi boots, the Nabokovs leave for the United States on board the *Champlain*. Nabokov works on lepidoptery at the Museum of Natural History in New York. His cousin Nicolas Nabokov arranges a meeting with Edmund Wilson, the acting literary editor for the *New Republic*. Wilson in turn introduces Nabokov to the *New Yorker* and *Atlantic Monthly*.

1941   Nabokov's first English novel, *The Real Life of Sebastian Knight* (Norfolk: New Directions), appears, drawing decent reviews but generating miserable sales. Nabokov privately tutors students in Russian, teaches at Stanford University during the summer, and receives an appointment as resident lecturer in comparative literature at Wellesley College.

1942   Nabokov begins research at Harvard University's Museum of Comparative Zoology. He prepares to write a book on Gogol while teaching Russian literature at Wellesley.

1943   Nabokov teaches, translates, works on lepidoptery, and has his upper teeth removed and replaced with a dental plate. He begins publishing stories in *Atlantic Monthly*. *Nikolai Gogol* is published by New Directions.

1945   Nabokov learns that his brother Sergey died in a Nazi concentration camp. The Nabokovs become American citizens. *Three Russian Poets* (Norfolk: New Directions) is published. The three poets Nabokov chose to translate are Pushkin, Mikhail Lermontov, and Fedor Tiutchev.

1947   *Bend Sinister* (New York: Holt) and *Nine Stories* (New Directions) are published.

1948   Nabokov is named professor of Russian and European literature at Cornell University. The family moves to Ithaca, New York, and takes on a lodger to offset rent and Dmitri's tuition costs. Nabokov suffers from a broken blood vessel in his lung but with Véra's help continues teaching and composing his autobiography.

1950	Nabokov suffers from intercostal neuralgia. He begins "Kingdom by the Sea," the book that will become *Lolita*.
1951	Nabokov publishes the first American version of the autobiography, *Conclusive Evidence* (New York: Harper). In England, the book's title is *Speak, Memory*.
1953	Nabokov continues writing *Lolita* and begins research for his monumentally annotated translation of *Eugene Onegin*.
1954	American publishers turn down *Lolita*. Nabokov tells Wilson (who read only the first half of the book) that *Lolita* is "a highly moral affair" (*Dear Bunny* 331). He starts publishing stories about the Russian émigré professor Timofey Pnin in the *New Yorker*.
1955	*Lolita* is published in Paris by Olympia Press. Graham Greene names it one of the best three books of the year.
1956	*Lolita* is banned in France. Nabokov writes "On a Book Entitled *Lolita*" for the *Anchor Review*. For his Russian readers Nabokov publishes *Vesna v Fial'te* (New York: Chekhov).
1957	Publication of *Pnin* (Garden City: Doubleday). A sizable excerpt from *Lolita*, with Nabokov's afterword, appears in the *Anchor Review*.
1958	Putnam publishes *Lolita* in the United States. Doubleday publishes a short story collection, *Nabokov's Dozen*.
1959	Nabokov leaves his teaching post at Cornell and is replaced by the novelist Herbert Gold. He begins translating his Russian-language works for publication in English.
1960	Nabokov writes and rewrites the *Lolita* screenplay for Stanley Kubrick's film. Kubrick uses less of it than Nabokov had hoped for, but Nabokov keeps his disappointment to himself.
1961	Nabokov and Véra settle in the Montreux Palace Hotel in Montreux, Switzerland.
1962	*Pale Fire* is published (New York: Putnam). Kubrick's *Lolita* is released, starring James Mason, Shelley Winters, Peter Sellers, and Sue Lyon. Nabokov's picture graces the cover of *Newsweek*.
1964	Nabokov's translation, with commentary, of Pushkin's *Eugene Onegin* (Princeton: Princeton UP–Bollingen) receives a harsh review from Wilson and sparks several rounds of literary pugilism between the two men on the editorial pages of major journals.
1965	Fearing hack translators, Nabokov completes his own translation of *Lolita* into Russian.
1969	Nabokov's new publisher, McGraw-Hill, publishes *Ada, or Ardor: A Family Chronicle*. Nabokov appears on the cover of *Time* as the grand old man of American letters.
1971	*Lolita, My Love*, the musical version of *Lolita*, by John Barry and Alan Jay Lerner, is not well received in Boston and Philadelphia

and dies a quick death. The musical includes lyrics such as "In the broken-promise land of fifteen / Tears that fell upon the sand still are seen."

1972   *Transparent Things* is published (New York: McGraw).

1973   McGraw-Hill publishes "*A Russian Beauty*" *and Other Stories* and *Strong Opinions* (a collection of Nabokov interviews, criticism, essays, and letters).

1974   McGraw-Hill publishes *Lolita: A Screenplay* and *Look at the Harlequins.*

1975   "*Tyrants Destroyed*" *and Other Stories* is published (New York: McGraw).

1976   "*Details of a Sunset*" *and Other Stories* is published (New York: McGraw). Nabokov works on *The Original of Laura* but is prevented from finishing it by physical ailments and medical complications after a fall.

1977   Nabokov dies 2 July in a hospital in Lausanne, where he was being treated for fever and bronchial congestion. He is cremated, and his ashes are interred in Clarens cemetery. His tombstone reads, "Vladimir Nabokov, écrivain."

1981   Edward Albee's play version of *Lolita*, directed by Frank Dunlop, debuts on Broadway. Despite its stars Donald Sutherland, Ian Richardson, and Blanche Baker, as well as Albee's addition of "A Certain Gentleman" narrator, the play is not well received and closes quickly.

1991   Véra Nabokov dies.

1997   Major American studios and distributors refuse to release Adrian Lyne's film version of *Lolita*. In 1998 it is shown on Showtime, and the Samuel Goldwyn Company releases it in New York and Los Angeles theaters later that year.

Nabokov as Teacher

Nabokov made his entry into American academia as a substitute teacher (for Mark Aldanov, who did not want the post) in summer 1940 by way of Stanford University, where he seems to have taught primarily drama. It is not clear how much that experience had to do with Nabokov's ceasing to write plays. Although Nabokov did not care for teaching (it struck him as the manifest neglect of his own writing), by now even the bricks in the Cornell University sidewalks must remember that Nabokov gave his first lecture in 1951 for Literature 311-312, a modestly enrolled course on the masters of European fiction, and that the course would go on to become a student favorite by the time Nabokov left teaching, Cornell, Ithaca, and America. In other words, though teaching delayed the completion of his own books, Nabokov was a terrific teacher. His comments on *Madame Bovary, Bleak House, Mansfield Park, Ulysses, The Metamorphosis, The Strange Case of Dr. Jekyll and Mr. Hyde*, and *Swann's Way* have now been collected in *Lectures on Literature*, as have his *Lectures on Russian Literature* and *Lectures on* Don Quixote.

All three volumes of lectures are united by two central dogmas: "Style and structure are the essence of a book" and "[G]reat ideas are hogwash" (*Lectures on Literature* xxiii). Nabokov's students were required to learn the precise arrangements of objects in space and to be able to map the movements of the characters within the space of the stories. Anecdotes abound, and though it may be apocryphal, my favorite is the one about a Literature 311 student who ignored a high fever and several other ailments to come to Nabokov's lectures because, as she put it, "I felt he could teach me how to read. I believed he could give me something that would last all my life—and it did" (V. Nabokov, *Lectures on Literature* xxiii). I fervently hope that this book helps our students catch the kind of fever that sends them to our classes where they learn how to read. For life.

Publication History

Even before Nabokov began work on what he would eventually deem a "time-bomb" in a letter to James Laughlin (*Vladimir Nabokov* 144), *Lolita* had had an interesting though intermittent gestational history. Embryonic themes and motifs of what we now cannot separate from *Lolita*'s own texture could be found among Nabokov's earlier works, from his 1928 poem "Lilith" to his 1951 autobiography *Conclusive Evidence* (*Speak, Memory* in the revised edition [1966]), which preceded *Lolita* in publication but parts of which were written concurrently. After "Lilith" forevisions of *Lolita* can be glimpsed in Nabokov's Russian works of the 1930s *Kamera obskura* (*Laughter in the Dark*), *Dar* (*The Gift*), and *Volshebnik* (*The Enchanter*).

In his note to "Lilith," Nabokov warned "intelligent readers" to "abstain from examining this impersonal fantasy for any links" with his later fiction. "Lilith" is a startling poetic vision of a man, killed the night before, who at first thinks that he is in Paradise reliving "the springtime" of his life on Earth when a girl, an "unforgotten child" with "pert glee," invites him to her abode. When he is "at half the distance / to rapture," she suddenly disappears, and he finds himself outside alone with his "pummeled lust" and a jeering crowd of "goat-hoofed" youngsters. Humbert would later appropriate this troubled vision of Lilith for the allegorical depiction of his own sexual heaven and hell: "Humbert was perfectly capable of intercourse with Eve, but it was Lilith he longed for" (20). In *The Gift*, the stepfather of the protagonist's girlfriend dreams of a very *Lolita*-like plotline for a novel:

> Ah, if only I had a tick or two, what a novel I'd whip off! From real life. Imagine this kind of thing: an old dog—but still in his prime, fiery, thirsting for happiness—gets to know a widow, and she has a daughter, still quite a little girl . . . when nothing is formed yet but already she has a way of walking that drives you out of your mind. . . . What to do? Well, not long thinking, he ups and marries the widow.   (198)

In *Conclusive Evidence*, Nabokov introduced his own adolescent passion, "Colette," who just happens to have a number of affinities with Humbert's "little Annabel" (11).

But it was *The Enchanter*, which Nabokov himself described as "the first little throb of *Lolita*" ("On a Book" 311), that came the closest to anticipating Nabokov's future masterpiece. In it Nabokov seems to follow the outline suggested by the stepfather from *The Gift* and has a forty-year-old man, identified only as "a jeweler," marry a sick woman with the express purpose of gaining access to her twelve-year-old daughter, whom he first sees as a nameless schoolgirl on roller skates. There are many more intimations of *Lolita* here, but there are also substantial differences. Although the mother dies in convenient haste and the jeweler becomes solely responsible for a stepdaughter whom he, like Humbert, immediately whisks off to a hotel, this stepfather is not destined to enjoy his nymphet for long. Instead, horrified by her reaction to his sexual arousal, he rushes out in a Charlotte-like fashion and, also like Charlotte, is killed by an oncoming vehicle.

While this part of *Lolita*'s prehistory is fairly straightforward, the novel's publication history is long and twisted, knotted by rejections, police raids, and protracted contractual foot-dragging. Begun in 1950 as "The Kingdom by the Sea" and completed in 1953, *Lolita* could not find an American publisher. After Doubleday; Farrar, Straus; New Directions; Simon and Schuster; and Viking all rejected the novel, it was published in Paris by Maurice Girodias of Olympia Press. Although Girodias was also publishing Samuel Beckett, J. P. Dunleavy, Jean Genet, and William S. Burroughs, his financial support for their literary projects seems to have been generated by the publication of many books such as *The Sexual Life of Robinson Crusoe* and *Tender Thighs* in Olympia's Traveller's Companion series. As Nabokov understood the contract, he was assigned ten percent royalty on the first ten thousand sales and twelve percent after that, with payments to be made quarterly. *Lolita* was released in the Traveller's Companion series as a paperbound two-volume set on 15 September 1955. The book sold reasonably well but did not seem to attract much critical attention until 25 December 1955, when Graham Greene, writing in the London *Sunday Times*, recommended *Lolita* to his readers and provoked the first of many outbursts that would make *Lolita* into a cause célèbre. John Gordon, a columnist for the *Sunday Express,* responded with the accusation that *Lolita* was nothing but "unrestrained pornography." Greene responded in turn with an ironic poke at Gordon's presumptions ("John Gordon"), and *Lolita* was quickly on its way to becoming a landmark in the battles over censorship. Noting that "My poor *Lolita* is having a tough time," Nabokov even violated his policy of never thanking reviewers by sending Greene an inscribed first edition of *Lolita* in gratitude for Greene's "courageous support" (McCrum 53).

The incident that would eventually lead to *Lolita's* publication in the United States involved a raid on the offices of Olympia Press by the Parisian police. The raid resulted in an injunction against the selling of twenty-five Olympia titles, *Lolita* among them. The complaint had been lodged by the British Home Office, whose officials asked the French authorities to ban the sale of *Lolita,* apparently hoping that the ban would spare British citizens the embarrassment of having copies of the faded hunter green Travellers Series *Lolita* confiscated by British Customs ("Ban"). Girodias, the owner of Olympia Press, responded by publishing an anticensorship pamphlet. He tried to enlist Nabokov's help in defending *Lolita,* but Nabokov realized that he could not really defend *Lolita* without defending the other banned books. He refused to cooperate with Girodias, who in Nabokov's view was invoking Nabokov's status as a professor at Cornell to have the ban lifted. After the ban was reported in the United States press and intellectuals on both sides of the Atlantic joined the fray, a number of United States publishing houses developed an interest in publishing *Lolita,* especially since the United States customs did not seem to consider the book obscene. Doubleday allowed the second issue of its *Anchor Review* for 1957 to publish generous excerpts from *Lolita,* with an introduction by F. W. Dupee and Nabokov's conclusion of sorts, "On a Book Entitled *Lolita*," the now standard afterword to *Lolita.* Although the *Anchor Review's* partial publication had demonstrated *Lolita's* nonpornographic nature, Girodias's demands for uncustomarily high royalties discouraged some American publishers from entering the bidding process and thus further delayed *Lolita's* publication in the United States. Only when Nabokov threatened to pull out of the contract because of Olympia's irregular payment of royalties did Girodias relent and agree to split with Nabokov the fifteen percent royalty Putnam was offering. On 18 August 1958, Putnam published the full text of *Lolita,* with Nabokov's afterword. But one cloud still remained on *Lolita's* horizon—the suspicion that the novel was mainly a succès de scandale and not a major work of art. Preparing the American public for the United States publication of *Lolita* and reflecting on the already turbulent aftermath of *Lolita's* 1955 publication in France, Alfred Alvarez offered the readers of *Partisan Review* this snide mixture of hyperbole, consolation, and prophecy:

> I doubt if any book since the King James Bible has been more eagerly awaited and so avidly discussed. . . . It has been brought up by the M.P.s in

the House of Commons and by the police in Bow Street Station; by critics, lawyers, aficionados of all banned books, defenders of public morality and by the usual letter-writing cranks. . . . Even the gutter press has been on to it. . . . When the thing is finally published in the spring—if despite all the goings on it is published, it will almost certainly be an anti-climax. It would take a work a good deal more substantial than poor *Lolita* to stand the strain.   (288–89)

Though I have done my best to locate them, I have been unable to find any letters to the editor crafted by "the usual letter-writing cranks" detailing their reactions to the publication of the King James Bible, especially its early books. Even after its United States publication, in England *Lolita* still seemed more interesting as a means of provocation than as a literary masterpiece. In the *Spectator* for 6 November 1959, Kingsley Amis published a not particularly favorable review of *Lolita* that begins in the same tone, with the same set of allusions, and with the same targets as Alvarez's reflection:

Few books published in this country since the King James Bible can have set up more eager expectation than "Lolita," nor, on the other hand, can any work have been much better known in advance to its potential audience. The interest of this first British issue, indeed, is likely to be less in what the thing is actually like—you and I had already got hold of it somehow, hadn't we?—than in what "they" will say about it. "They" in this case covers a far wider spectrum than usual . . . the couple of hundred thousand people in Britain who have, or can scrounge, access to some public medium. It is encouraging to see all this concern for a book of serious literary pretension, even if some of the concern, while serious enough, is not literary.

While Amis made it clear that he was tired of *Lolita* because it was less interesting for what it said or how it said it than for what others said about it, "poor *Lolita*" not only withstood the initial strain Alvarez and Amis were worried about but also aged rather well. Though fifty years may not be long enough for a book to achieve literary majority, *Lolita*—with translations into more than two dozen languages and sales of over fifteen million copies—seems to be doing fine in print, in the canon, and on the syllabus.

Editions

Those who responded to our survey list four editions of *Lolita* that serve their purposes. Here we mention some advantages and disadvantages of these editions and focus on what teachers like or dislike about them. The edition cited by this volume's contributors is the one most of the survey participants prefer—the relatively inexpensive Random House–Vintage International paperback edition, which has a new cover (a close-up of half of a woman's glossy mouth) to mark the fiftieth anniversary of *Lolita's* publication. Gone are the awkwardly posed legs of the pleated-skirt bobby-soxer. They have joined Random House's backlot of *Lolita* covers, where the little girl with a bicycle keeps company with Sue Lyon, the Lolita of Kubrick's 1962 movie version, complete with her heart-shaped sunglasses and a glossy lollipop. The main advantage of the Vintage volume is that it follows the pagination of the Putnam-published *Lolita* and thus makes it easier to find referenced passages. Luckily, *Amazon* has made the Vintage *Lolita* searchable online. Also searchable is the front matter of *Annotated* Lolita, edited by Alfred Appel, Jr. While the volume's 148 pages of intricate and exhaustive notes in rather small font are not searchable, the print version of *Annotated* Lolita is the second choice recommended by teachers of the novel. Brian Boyd used only thirteen pages of annotations for his edition of *Lolita*, the first text in the second volume of the Library of America Nabokov series, *Novels, 1955–1962*, a hardbound volume that, along with *Lolita*, *Pnin*, and *Pale Fire*, includes Nabokov's screenplay of *Lolita*. (Nabokov had prepared the screenplay in 1960, but Kubrick did not use much of it. As Boyd tell us, Harris-Kubrick Productions held on to the screenplay until 1971, when it allowed Nabokov to publish it.) In addition to its four-in-one format, the main advantage of this scholarly edition is that it incorporates all corrections and revisions to *Lolita* since Nabokov sent the corrected Olympia Press proofs to Putnam. Respondents list as the only drawback to this text the fact that it does not follow the Putnam pagination. While all three Library of America Nabokov volumes are searchable on Amazon, the error rate is unacceptably high. The font used for the volumes, coupled with the thinness of their pages, creates a nightmarish task for the scanner. Scholars using the Amazon search engine find themselves in the situation of Thomas Pynchon's Mucho Maas, who, to overcome the distorting noise introduced by the very process of radio transmissions, must announce the name of his wife Oedipa Mass as Edna Mosh. To get "bepearled" out of Amazon's volume, users must take into account the errors introduced during optical character recognition and search for "bcpeirlcd." In the United Kingdom, the most readily available edition seems to be the Everyman's Library hardback, whose introduction is by Martin Amis. A word of warning goes out to the teachers who request this edition. There are at least some copies of the Everyman's *Lolita* in which Amis's introduction replaces John Ray's. While instructors' desk copies are unlikely to still contain that mistake, students who shop for secondhand copies may protest that there is no John Ray, Jr., in their copies of the book. Finally, a respondent warns against using the Berkeley paperback edition of *Lolita* because of its extraordinarily fragile binding.

Further Reading for Students

Almost a third of the survey respondents reported that they shy away from assigning secondary reading, mainly because of *Lolita*'s complexity and because they prefer to base their teaching on the unmediated student responses. Those who do assign secondary reading single out a small set of Nabokov must-reads and critical essays: chapter 11 of *Speak, Memory* (the poetry-writing chapter); his essay on inspiration from *Lectures on Literature;* and his interview with Gold (reprinted in *Strong Opinions* 93–107). There is little agreement on what critical essays to assign, so here we simply list each of the suggested essays and quote the most suggestive passage from the essay.

Lionel Trilling's "The Last Lover: Vladimir Nabokov's *Lolita*" was the first serious discussion of the book to call *Lolita* a love story. Trilling was also the first to discuss the discomfort of doing so: "[O]ur response to the situation Mr. Nabokov presents is that of shock. And we find ourselves the more shocked when we realize that, in the course of reading the novel, we have come virtually to condone the violation it presents" (93). Compared with Trilling, who invoked the courtly love traditions of the Middle Ages, John Hollander in "The Perilous Magic of Nymphets" drew a somewhat narrower sweep: "*Lolita*, if it is about anything, '*really*,' is the record of Mr. Nabokov's love affair with the romantic novel" (557). In his afterword to *Lolita* Nabokov responded, obliquely as always, by proclaiming that the "substitution 'English language' for 'romantic novel' would make this elegant formula more correct" ("On a Book" 316). Appel's "*Lolita*: The Springboard of Parody" connected Nabokov's treatment of his characters with Plato's dialogues as a way of theorizing Humbert's crime against Lolita:

> By "solipsizing" Lolita, Humbert condemns her to the solitary confinement of his obsessional shadowland. "She had entered my world, black and umber Humberland," says Humbert (168), who, by choosing to chase figurative shadows that play on the walls of his "cave," upends Plato's famous allegory.   (109)

Thomas R. Frosch, in "Parody and Authenticity in *Lolita*," extends Hollander's claim and modifies Appel's work to demonstrate that Nabokov's "swerving" from the "dead seriousness of typical romance" into parody is the enabling moment of both the plot and style of *Lolita*: "Nabokov must kill off a bad romantic and a bad artist in Humbert in order for his own brand of enchantment to exist" (185).

The rhetorical zigzags of Nabokov's "swerving" are analyzed by Nomi Tamir-Ghez in "The Art of Persuasion in Nabokov's *Lolita*." Sensing that Frosch's notions of rhetorical swerving and Trilling's notions of moral condoning were connected, Tamir-Ghez starts with a detailed description of the rhetorical devices Nabokov loaned to Humbert and on the basis of that description argues that Humbert "does not, in effect, have an unlimited control over the rhetorical resources" but in the end still "wins us over" ("Art" 18, 35). Richard Rorty's "The Barber of Kasbeam: Nabokov on Cruelty" is a philosopher's foray into literary criticism. Rorty's pragmatic conclusions regarding the ethical effects of reading divide narratives into two kinds:

> Fiction like that of Dickens, Olive Schreiner, or Richard Wright gives us the details about kinds of suffering being endured by people to whom we have previously not attended. Fiction like that of Choderlos de Laclos, Henry James, or Nabokov gives us the details about what sorts of cruelty we ourselves are capable of, and thereby lets us redescribe ourselves.
>
> (xvi)

In the inaugural issue of *Nabokov Studies* (1994), Leona Toker, a Nabokov scholar trained in philosophy, responded with "Liberal Ironists and the 'Gaudily Painted Savage': On Richard Rorty's Reading of Vladimir Nabokov." Protesting Rorty's occasional confusion of cruelty with callousness and the aesthetics that attend such confusion, Toker points out that a utopia filled with systematic-thinking self-redescribing liberal ironists is a less likely outcome of living out Nabokov's imaginings than a state of mind dominated by "religious experience" defined as "intuitions that defy the strictures of the intellect" (198, 206).

Linda S. Kauffman's "Framing Lolita: Is There a Woman in the Text?" changed the terms of the debate about *Lolita*'s rhetoric: "*Lolita* is not about love but about incest, which is a betrayal of trust, a violation of love." Starting with Trilling, Kauffman asks herself, "How have critics managed so consistently to confuse love with incest in this novel?" (152 [1993]), and finds that the textual dynamic of *Lolita* "mimes" a "bundle of relations between men" (155 [1993]). *Lolita* is thus a male-inflected textual bundle whose "[a]esthetic form distances us from Lolita's pain" (160 [1993]). Only partly responding to Kauffman, Sarah Herbold, in her essay "Reflections on Modernism: *Lolita* and Political Engagement; or, How the Left and the Right Both Have It Wrong," refuses the seductions of Humbert's narration as well as the easy dichotomy of male and female, victimizer and victim, the political and the aesthetic. Herbold finds "swerving" and "collusion" of Humbert's rhetoric both disturbing and invigorating:

> *Lolita* forces us to experience the shock of seeing in the textual mirror our own visages, distorted by laughter, fury, concupiscence, disgust, and tears. We must see ourselves flailing in the double grip of the law and narrative desire. We have nowhere to turn—except, like Humbert, to take pity on our own pathetic and exhilarating struggle to meet the demands—and enjoy the benefits—of both. It is in this way that "the senses make sense" in *Lolita*: we are induced to carry on the mutually creative and destructive war between the aesthetic and political realms in its most exacerbated—and sexualized—form ever.
>
> (150)

Like Herbold's essay, Rachel Bowlby's *"Lolita* and the Poetry of Advertising"
is singled out by survey takers but only partially for its response to Kauffman
(although Bowlby does find Kauffman's approach to incest in *Lolita* unconvincing, because its victim/victimizer binary requires the removal of all agency from
Lolita). Finding equally unconvincing the arguments that rely on the Humbert/
Lolita pairing as a conflict of high and low culture or of poetry and consumerism, Bowlby proclaims, "It is Lolita who is the poetic reader, indifferent to things
in themselves and entranced by the words that shape them into the image of
desire which consumption then perfectly satisfies" (67). Bowlby's conclusion is
the one teachers of gender studies, cultural studies, and media studies like to have
tested by their students:

> There is no separation of form between Humbert's literary world and
> Lolita's consumerly world: the gap is rather in the incompatibility of the
> particular wishes and dreams that make them up. Lolita, "as glad as an ad"
> (170 [161 in Vintage ed.]), is the modern attraction for the literary seeker
> after the latest embodiment of youthful female perfection, but by depriv-
> ing her of her premature "girlish games" he turns her story into something
> never shown in the happy world of advertisements.   (70–71)

And, of course, however unreliable he is, Humbert is the only one telling
us *Lolita*'s story. While he certainly is willing to call attention to the ways in
which his storytelling falsifies ("I am not going very far for my pseudonyms"
[268]), it is the calendrical confusion he creates in the final paragraphs of the
novel that has generated the most sustained discussions of his unreliability
and of the implications of that unreliability for reading and teaching *Lolita*.
His claim that he "started, fifty-six days ago, to write *Lolita*, first in the psy-
chopathic ward for observation, and then in this well-heated, albeit tombal,
seclusion" (308), when held up against his report that he received Lolita's letter
on 22 September 1952 (267) and killed Quilty three days later, the morning
of 25 September (293–305), creates an unexplained gap of three days in the
light of John Ray, Jr.'s report that Humbert "died in legal captivity, of coronary
thrombosis, on November 16, 1952" (3). The gap, which puts Humbert in jail
for a crime he has not yet committed, has drawn the attention of scholars for
almost four decades. In *Keys to* Lolita, Carl Proffer dismissed it as a product
of Humbert's bad memory (125–30, 153–54). In *Autobiographical Acts: The
Changing Situation of a Literary Genre*, Elizabeth Bruss questioned whether
Humbert's reunion with Lolita or his murder of Quilty ever took place (145–
46), and Christina Tekiner, taking a hint from Bruss, declared that the events
before 22 September had "some basis in the 'reality'" of Humbert's life and that
those described as taking place after 22 September were Humbert's "fabrication"
(466). Her reading, were it substantiated textually, would make the last nine
chapters of the book take place only in Humbert's imagination, not Coalmont
or Pavor Manor. Toker, in *Nabokov: The Mystery of Literary Structures*, saw the

date mix-up as Nabokov's way of signaling Humbert's "cognitive unreliability" (211). The second volume of *Nabokov Studies* (1995) devoted a great deal of space to the disagreements among the scholars regarding the dates in *Lolita*. Using as evidence Nabokov's treatment of dates in his translation of *Lolita* into Russian, Alexander Dolinin, in "Nabokov's Time Doubling: From *The Gift* to *Lolita*," supported the Bruss-Tekiner hypothesis and concluded that at the end of *Lolita* Humbert Humbert is "at his writing desk but not in a cell awaiting trial, as he has tried to convince his gullible readers" (39). Julian W. Connolly, in "'Nature's Reality' or Humbert's 'Fancy'?: Scenes of Reunion and Murder in *Lolita*," reviewed carefully and cautiously the consequences of Bruss's and Tekiner's claims but decided against providing the surefire means for readers to separate Humbert's reports about the outside world from his obsessed imaginings. Boyd, in "'Even Homais Nods': Nabokov's Fallibility; or, How to Revise *Lolita*," adopted the Proffer approach but assigned Humbert's errors to Nabokov: "In view of Nabokov's fallibility [with dates], it seems much sounder . . . to call into question a single numeral than to doubt the detailed reality of a whole series of major scenes" (73). In the most recent examination of the calendrical discrepancy, Anthony R. Moore's "How Unreliable Is Humbert in *Lolita*?" Humbert is revealed to be two stylistically separable narrators, "the fully-grown degenerate character obsessed with pedophilia, his own glamorized leading man," and "the regenerate artist who, as we read, develops the integrated consciousness which fits him to complete the text" (72). Humbert's unreliability is one of *Lolita*'s charms, a textual dimension that invites a playful pedagogical touch and rewards individual student persistence even as it delays the Coalmont moments of "fusion" when "everything [falls] into order" (V. Nabokov, *Lolita* 272).

Further Reading for Teachers

Biographical Materials

Nabokov's autobiography *Conclusive Evidence*, revised as *Speak, Memory*, is the most common starting point for those teachers who like to begin with biographical matters. Because Nabokov's highly selective story of his life stops with 1940, no student or teacher of Nabokov can ignore Boyd's monumental, prize-winning, two-volume biography, *Vladimir Nabokov: The Russian Years* and *Vladimir Nabokov: The American Years*. His biography not only traces the background of the fatidic themes for *Speak, Memory* but also enlarges, corrects, complements, and in large measure supersedes Andrew Field's *Nabokov: His Life in Art*. Despite being largely superseded as a resource for factual information, Field's work was written during Nabokov's lifetime and thus has been subjected to Nabokov's reaction. While *Nabokov: His Life in Art* received only minor corrections from Nabokov, Field's subsequent efforts at a biography of Nabokov provoked his subject into breaking off all contact with Field and then threatening a lawsuit. Jane Grayson's recent biography, *Vladimir Nabokov*, makes up for its brevity with a surfeit of rare photographs.

Other biographical sources, notable for different reasons, include Stacy Schiff's Pulitzer Prize–winning *Véra (Mrs. Vladimir Nabokov): Portrait of a Marriage* and Zinaïda Schakovskoy's rather arch and skewed reminiscence, *V poiskakh Nabokova*, an effort to show the real Nabokov as he had presented himself through the sixty-four letters he had written to her. Because copyright laws prohibited the inclusion of those letters, the book, published two years after Nabokov's death, seems little more than an effort to provoke with its attempt to take down the reputation of the author by attacking the man. To the real and perceived provocations, Dmitri Nabokov has reacted with fierce defenses and tender reminiscences that include "A Few Things That Must Be Said on Behalf of Vladimir Nabokov," "Things I Could Have Said," "On Revisiting Father's Room" and "In Memoriam." Other reminiscences of Nabokov (see, e.g., "Remembering" and "Reminiscences") are by émigré writers (Georgy Adamovich, Nina Nikolaevna Berberova), Cornell faculty members and friends (Gold; Morris Bishop, Alison Bishop; Meyer Abrams; J. Milton Cowan; William L. Brown, Jr.; Peter Kahn; Ephim Fogel), and his students (Stephen Jan Parker, Appel, Ross Wetzsteon). A counterview to some of these warm reminiscences is Galya Diment's *Pniniad* and "Nabokov at Cornell University: A View of the Outsider." A somewhat surprising work to be listed among the biographical sources is Appel's *Nabokov's Dark Cinema*, which includes scattered but wonderful information about Nabokov and the cinema.

Nabokov's life is threaded through his art but not in predictable or easily retraceable ways. For the full range of possible approaches to Nabokov's life and art and the occasionally surprising echoes of *Lolita* in other Nabokov works, we direct you to several anthologies of critical essays. Vladimir Alexandrov's *Garland Companion to Vladimir Nabokov*, searchable on Amazon, is a good first step for anyone beginning to read or teach Nabokov. More recent collections include the two Cambridge University Press volumes edited by Connolly and the conference proceedings edited by Gavriel Shapiro (*Nabokov*) and by Grayson, Arnold McMillin, and Priscilla Meyer.

Nabokov's lifelong interest in and obsession with Lepidoptera has produced a literature of its own. Teachers of *Lolita* may wish to familiarize themselves with *Nabokov's Lepidoptera: Genres and Genera*, by Joann Karges; *Nabokov's Butterflies: Unpublished and Uncollected Writings*, edited by Boyd and Robert Michael Pyle; Kurt Johnson and Steve Coates's *Nabokov's Blues*; and Dieter E. Zimmer's informative and sumptuously illustrated *A Guide to Nabokov's Butterflies and Moths*.

Although *Strong Opinions* contains several of Nabokov's letters to editors, larger collections of Nabokov's letters include *Vladimir Nabokov: Selected*

Letters 1940–1977, edited by Dmitri Nabokov and Matthew J. Bruccoli, and *Perepiska s sestroi*, Nabokov's five-decade-long correspondence with his sister Elena Sikorskaya. Simon Karlinsky edited *Dear Bunny, Dear Volodya: The Nabokov-Wilson Letters, 1940–1971*, an exchange that shows Wilson and Nabokov disagreeing on everything from Lenin to Russian prosody but most deeply, quietly, and resolutely on *Lolita*.

Reference Works

Bibliographies of Nabokov's works include Field's *Nabokov: A Bibliography*, Michael Juliar's 780-page *Vladimir Nabokov: A Descriptive Bibliography* (and its 32-page addendum [1988]), and Zimmer's *Vladimir Nabokov: Bibliographie des Gesamtwerks*. Originally published in 1963, Zimmer's bibliography has since been expanded, translated into English, and relocated to Zembla, where, with the help of Jeff Edmunds, it remains the most accessible starting point for serious research on Nabokov. For information on Nabokov's manuscripts, one should consult Boyd's "Nabokov's Manuscripts." Stephen Jan Parker has cataloged and discussed the contents of Nabokov's library in "Nabokov in the Margins: The Montreux Books" and "Nabokov's Montreux Books: Part II."

In addition to the *MLA International Bibliography* and Parker's annual bibliography in *The Nabokovian*, studies of Nabokov's works have been cataloged by Jackson R. Bryer and Thomas J. Bergin, Jr., in "Vladimir Nabokov's Critical Reputation in English: A Note and a Checklist" and by Samuel Schuman in *Vladimir Nabokov: A Reference Guide*, now a rare book but one that is still useful for its trustworthy annotations. In "Nabokov, ou le vrai et l'invraisemblable," Edmunds reviews (in English) criticism on Nabokov's work written in French, and Nassim Balestrini reviews the materials written in German in "Nabokov Criticism in German-Speaking Countries: A Survey." The most useful tool for tracing the development of Nabokov studies and the beginning of *Lolita* studies is Norman Page's *Nabokov: The Critical Heritage*. Nancy J. Jones has supplemented the Page and Schuman surveys with one specifically devoted to *Lolita*, "Vladimir Nabokov's *Lolita*: A Survey of Scholarship and Criticism in English, 1977–95." Jones has also added to the growing field of *Lolita*'s "daughters" with *Molly*, a novel that sports a character named Richard Richard and the tagline "This radiant first novel is also a loving tribute to Vladimir Nabokov and his classic work, invoking the spirit of the legendary *Lolita*." *The Nabokovian* (edited by Parker) and *Nabokov Studies* (edited by Zoran Kuzmanovich) note and review most significant new works on Nabokov. The searchable discussion list NABOKV-L (http://listserv.ucsb.edu/lsv-cgi-bin/wa?S1=nabokv-l), created by D. Barton Johnson (now edited by Stephen Blackwell and Susan Elizabeth Sweeney), is not strictly a bibliographical source, but like Edmunds's prize-winning Web site Zembla (http://www.libraries.psu.edu/nabokov/zembla.htm), it is an invaluable electronic resource for getting one's questions about Nabokov answered.

Commentary on Lolita

Of the over 2,500 scholarly pieces written on Nabokov, roughly one-fifth are devoted to *Lolita*. Although those essays and book chapters are rich and varied in approach and viewpoint on the debates the novel has occasioned, unless one counts Azar Nafizi's memoir *Reading* Lolita *in Tehran* as a scholarly work, there are only eight book-length scholarly projects devoted to *Lolita*. They are Proffer's *Keys to* Lolita, Alexander D. Nakhimovsky and S. Paperno's *An English-Russian Dictionary of Nabokov's* Lolita, Richard Corliss's *Lolita* (a discussion of Kubrick's 1962 film), Lance Olsen's Lolita: *A Janus Text*, Maurice Couturier's *Lolita* and *V. Nabokov:* Lolita (for the Agrégation d'Anglais), Christine Raguet-Bouvart's reception study Lolita: *Un royaume au-delà des mers*, and Michael Maar's *Two Lolitas*. Maar's book, unlikely to see wide circulation, is a study of the possibility that Nabokov subliminally or "cryptomnesiacally" borrowed not just the name of his heroine but some of *Lolita's* plot from Heinz von Leichberg, a German aristocrat with Nazi sympathies. There are three collections of essays on *Lolita* and one book summarizing critical trends and reprinting largish snippets of the material that went into the making of the trends. Harold Bloom has devoted two volumes of essays to *Lolita*. *Vladimir Nabokov's* Lolita came out in the series Bloom's Modern Critical Interpretations, and *Lolita* was part of his series Major Literary Characters. Ellen Pifer, the editor of *Vladimir Nabokov's* Lolita: *A Casebook*, addressed some of the gaps left by Bloom's idiosyncratic tastes and a general distaste for Nabokov's writing, and Christine Clegg's hybrid volume, *Vladimir Nabokov,* Lolita: *A Reader's Guide to Essential Criticism*, part review and part reprint of the *Lolita* criticism, has created some new gaps by treating a very narrow band of *Lolita* criticism as essential.

Nabokov, in drawing his distinction between essential and inessential criticism, insisted that the critic or the teacher pay close attention to details of style and structure. Since all critics and teachers, regardless of their approach to *Lolita,* can profit from greater attention to style and structure, we can do no better than repeat Nabokov's admonition. To list selected criticism at this point would simply replicate the problems of selection that plague Bloom's and Clegg's works; instead, we direct readers to the *MLA International Bibliography* in its online and print forms.

Study Guides for Students

There exist several study guides to *Lolita*, four of which are available online. Though in essence a promotion for Random House Nabokov books, a brief but free and fairly interesting set of questions can be found at Random House's Web site (http://www.randomhouse.com/vintage/read/lolita/). Also free and inter-

esting is *"Lolita* A–Z," available online through Davidson College (http://www
.davidson.edu/academic/english/faculty/zk/vnaz/nabaz.htm; a print version in
article form is available from *Post Road* [Kuzmanovich et al.]). Marie Rose
Napierkowski et al. have written *Vladimir Nabokov's "Lolita": A Study Guide
from Gale's "Novels for Students."* This sixteen-page PDF document is available
for paid download from Amazon. A longer study guide, on the model of Cliffs
Notes or Monarch Notes, is available from SparkNotes, also as a paid download.
At forty-seven pages, though, the SparkNotes guide should make the unwary
student think seriously about reading the book instead. Mary Bellino's "The
Student's Nabokov" is a spirited and very thorough review of the academic gray-
market goods available to the student of Nabokov.

Audiovisual Aids

Nabokov Films

Half an Hour with Nabokov. Interview with Peter Duval Smith and Christopher
Burstall. *Bookstand.* BBC, London. July 1962. 29 mins. Filmed at Zermatt.
   Vladimir Nabokov. Interview with Robert Hughes. National Educational
Television, New York. 1965. 29 mins. Available for rental from Indiana University, ISS, Bloomington, Indiana 47405-5901 (or call 800 552-8620). Many of the
subsequent sources include footage from this interview.
   Great Writers of The Twentieth Century: Vladimir Nabokov. Clark Television
for BBC Worldwide Television, London. 1998. 52 mins. Uses footage from *Half
an Hour* and *Vladimir Nabokov.* Scenes feature Dmitri Nabokov, Allison Jolly
(the daughter of Morris Bishop, who hired Nabokov for a post at Cornell University), Girodias, Martin Amis, A. S. Byatt, and Ellendea Proffer.

Lolita Films

Lolita. Dir. Stanley Kubrick. Screenplay by Stanley Kubrick (uncredited) and
Vladimir Nabokov (credited). MGM with Seven Arts Production, 1962. 152
mins. Tagline: "How did they make a film out of *Lolita*?" In the light of Kubrick's
rewriting of Nabokov's overlong script and the censorship laws in place in 1962,
the easy answer was, "They didn't."
   Lolita. Dir. Adrian Lyne. Screenplay by Stephen Schiff (Lyne rejected
drafts by James Deardon, Harold Pinter, and David Mamet). MK Productions
(Mario Kassar and Joel B. Michaels) and Chargeurs, 1997. 137 mins. Tagline:
"A forbidden love. An unthinkable attraction. The ultimate price." Though the
film was advertised for its sex appeal, concerns about pedophilia and pornography trumped the potentially profitable titillation of nympholepsy when it came
to the actual release. The film had difficulty finding a distributor since it was

being shopped around during the investigation of the JonBenet Ramsey murder and the child murders by a Belgian pedophile. The 1996 Child Pornography Prevention Act had just been passed, and a lawyer had to be pressed into service as an editor to eliminate any scenes that suggested anything unworthy of an R rating, which the film eventually received. Some potential distributors also questioned Lyne's artistic ability and sensitivity to the subject matter. As a result, *Lolita* became the most expensive and talked-about film to be released directly to cable, with Showtime airing the movie to middling reviews.

Audio Materials

Lolita. Read by Jeremy Irons. Random, 1997. 12 hrs. (unabridged). Despite Irons's lyrical voice, my students have complained that in his reading of Lolita's speech they hear less of her desperation than in their own readings of the passages in which she calls her relationship to Humbert "incest" or threatens to tell the police that he "raped" her.

   Lolita. Read by James Mason, who played Humbert Humbert in Stanley Kubrick's film adaptation. Abridged. Audiocassette. Caedmon, 1998.

   Lolita *and Poems.* Read by Vladimir Nabokov. Audiocassette. Spoken Arts, 1980. Excerpts from the novel and a few poems. This cassette seems to be a rare find these days. Though nothing compares with Nabokov's wonderful reading of the "killing Quilty" scene, one can also listen to Nabokov intoning "The Ballad of Longwood Glen," "Exile," "A Literary Dinner," "The Refrigerator Awakes," "A Discovery," Fedor Tiutchev's "Silentium," Aleksandr Pushkin's "Exegi Monumentum," and some of his own extracts from *Pale Fire* online at Zembla (http://www.libraries.psu.edu/nabokov/realaud.htm).

   Lolita, My Love. The bootleg soundtrack of the musical. By John Barry. Lyrics by Alan Jay Lerner. Perf. Leonard Frey, Lance Westergard, Dorothy Loudon, Denise Nickerson, and John Neville. LP. Bleu Pear, 1971. These are its tracks:

1. Overture   *Orchestra*
2. Going, Going, Gone   *Leonard Frey, Lance Westergard*
3. The Same Old Song   *Dorothy Loudon, Denise Nickerson*
4. Saturday   *Denise Nickerson*
5. In the Broken Promise Land of Fifteen   *John Neville*
6. The Same Old Song (Reprise)   *Dorothy Loudon, Denise Nickerson, John Neville*
7. Dante, Petrarch and Poe   *John Neville and Guests*
8. Sur les Quais   *Dorothy Loudon*
9. Charlotte's Letter   *John Neville, Dorothy Loudon and Choir*
10. Farewell, Little Dream   *John Neville*
11. At the Bed-D-By Motel   *John Witham, Leonard Frey and Conventioneers*
12. Tell Me, Tell Me   *John Neville*

13. Buckin' for Beardsley / Beardsley School for Girls   *Students*
14. March out of My Life   *Leonard Frey*
15. The Same Old Song (Reprise)   *Denise Nickerson, John Neville*
16. All You Can Do Is Tell Me You Love Me   *Denise Nickerson*
17. How Far Is It to the Next Town   *John Neville*
18. How Far Is It to the Next Town (Reprise)   *John Neville, Denise Nickerson and Chorus*
19. Lolita   *John Neville*
20. Finale   *Chorus*

Part Two

APPROACHES

Introduction

The richness of *Lolita* invites—nay, demands—a richness of approaches to teaching and analyzing the novel. In classrooms on almost all continents and in scores of languages, *Lolita* is pursued through various pedagogical, ideological, cultural, and critical tools and angles. This volume can give but a few examples of what is happening in our global classrooms, with special attention being paid to the English-speaking academic world.

The editors' choice of three larger themes in the volume—teaching *Lolita* in specific courses; literary, generic, and cultural contexts of *Lolita* (including subsections on teaching the Russian roots of *Lolita* and teaching *Lolita* from an American perspective); and philosophical, ethical, and ideological approaches to *Lolita*—derived from the interests expressed in survey respondents' questionnaires, the abstracts submitted to us, and our own editorial intuition about what would do the novel the most justice in a fairly short volume.

The focus was also guided by our own practices of teaching *Lolita*. In our classrooms, we teach *Lolita* without trying to favor a particular critical theory or ideological angle. We aim to provide students with the tools to help them understand their own reading habits and approaches. To prevent students from falling into platitudes, we ask that they define *love*, *lust*, *incest*, and *child abuse*; to widen their knowledge of the contexts and subtexts in which "hurricane Lolita" landed, we insist that they figure out the relevance of nineteenth-century Romantic literature and of 1950s childlike sex symbols; to teach them to read closely and coherently and to appreciate Nabokov's meticulousness with details, we ask that they follow something as innocuous as the novel's apple or dog imagery. We discuss the novel's indebtedness to both the Russian and American cultures and draw on the Russian masters and Nabokov's Russian works to locate the foreign antecedents of this "great American novel." While these pedagogical moves have various degrees of sophistication, most often they match the various degrees of readiness of our students.

Within the limits imposed by the size of this volume, we tried to be as comprehensive and diverse as possible. The articles before you illuminate the novel's multiple textual and contextual features and offer reflections and assessments of the ways *Lolita* comes to serve as a part of the cultural capital passed on in classrooms from Amherst to Teheran. They are written by seasoned Nabokovians and relative newcomers to the field; by those who teach *Lolita* in the United States and Canada and those who teach it in Israel, New Zealand, and Singapore. Our contributors represent small colleges, big research universities, and everything in between. They come from English departments, Russian or Slavic departments, and departments of comparative literature. Some, like Nabokov, were born and raised in Russia or the former Soviet Union and perceive a great continuity in the two cultural halves that shaped Nabokov as a writer; others first encountered *Lolita* as American undergraduates and are now eager to bestow their appreciation of the novel on a new generation.

We start our volume with articles devoted to teaching Nabokov's novel in specific courses. In his class, Samuel Schuman lets the students discover irony through the examination of the fictional and real worlds that bind and separate *Lolita*'s author and narrator to arrive at the meaning and value of style. Eric Naiman uses the novel to encourage students in his senior seminar to become aggressive, suspicious, and playful readers of both Nabokov and the scholarship that has developed around him. Marilyn Edelstein describes some profitable ways for senior English majors to explore the seeming and real discrepancies between the book's depiction of pedophilia and the extratextual traps Nabokov has put in the path of anyone seeking an untroubled way to link his ethics and aesthetics.

The section continues with Corinne Scheiner, who takes Nabokov's art on the road, allowing her students to trace and discover Nabokov's twin passions, writing and butterflies, through a series of fascinating field trips around Colorado, where Nabokov himself spent many happy hours hunting and creating. Jason Merrill devotes a full semester to an interdisciplinary look at *Lolita* as a cultural archetype. By examining *Lolita*'s precursors and descendants, Merrill's course ranges over Russian and Western European literature, film, theater, politics, sociology, American studies, legal studies, and gender studies. In the last article in this section, Tania Roy and John Whalen-Bridge use a cultural studies approach to literature, literary history, legal documents, and advertising to examine the peculiarly American challenge the publication of *Lolita* presented to unexamined notions of consumption and obscenity.

In the next section, which focuses on teaching the literary, generic, and cultural contexts of *Lolita,* our contributors question Nabokov's roots. Dale E. Peterson presents Humbert Humbert's confessional memoir as a "double-voiced" narrative in the tradition of the extended "mad monologues" penned by Poe and Dostoevsky. Claudia Moscovici explains how Nabokov's playful modernist reinscription of Romantic tropes and themes revitalizes Romantic passion while reenergizing contemporary readers to examine the role of passion and emotion in literature. Ellen Pifer shares her experience of teaching her students how, by undermining the assumptions of a technologically saturated culture that finds art a poor cousin to science (whereas Nabokov believed in the equal fascination, precision, and, ultimately, value of both), *Lolita* testifies to the central role that art plays in life.

The possible Russian roots of *Lolita* and pedagogical modes of presenting them to students are discussed by three longtime Nabokov scholars, well versed in both the Russian and American cultural underpinnings of Nabokov's art. They analyze Nabokov's use of and indebtedness to Russian literature and culture—especially the nineteenth-century works created by Pushkin, Gogol, and even Dostoevsky (whom Nabokov publicly berated as a "third rate writer" [*Dear Bunny* 172]). Julian W. Connolly believes that once his students become familiar with the Russian subtexts incorporated into *Lolita*, they gain an enhanced understanding of both the character of Humbert Humbert and

Nabokov's creative methods. Priscilla Meyer chooses to highlight the text from the nineteenth-century canon that Nabokov himself had singled out for many years of his professional attention and involvement, Aleksandr Pushkin's *Eugene Onegin*. Galya Diment reaches out to early Russian film, particularly works by Evgenii Bauer, to reveal a powerful factor in shaping the young Nabokov's artistic sensibilities.

Equally important, of course, is Nabokov's engagement with the American culture and our desire, as instructors, to teach *Lolita* from an American perspective. Brian Boyd, the author of the much acclaimed biography of Nabokov, discusses his technique of teaching *Lolita* through scenes—some of them unmistakably American—as they appear in the novel, the screenplay, and the two Hollywood films. Another eminent Nabokovian, Michael Wood, distinguishes no fewer than three Americas in *Lolita*: Humbert's, Lolita's, and Nabokov's. Dana Dragunoiu examines the ways Nabokov's knowledge of his father's legal work in Russia shaped his own American legal argument in *Lolita*. David Clippinger focuses on the reflection in *Lolita* of the "five Ds" of 1950s American culture: dramatics, dance, debating, dating, and democracy.

Finally we move to larger philosophical, ethical, and ideological issues in *Lolita*. Sarah Herbold locates the female reader's hidden role as the crux of the novel and explores the pedagogical potential of the double bind into which Humbert Humbert's direct addresses place women readers at key points of the book. Lisa Ryoko Wakamiya asks her students to consider Humbert's address to such American institutions as the "jury of his peers" and pay special attention to how intricately gendered his approach is to "the gentlemen and gentlewomen of the jury." Marianne Cotugno explores the ways in which teaching *Lolita* alongside Azar Nafisi's *Reading* Lolita *in Tehran* helped her shape the classroom discussions of what constitutes family, home, and freedom. Leona Toker describes the curricular gains to be had in moments when *Lolita's* readers catch themselves reflecting on their role as readers while accommodating other readerly habits and passions. Lisa Sternlieb invites her students to consider the particular resonances of the anagrammatic name Vivian Darkbloom, an exercise that demonstrates over and over to students the near inexhaustibility of *Lolita's* textual and intertextual riches. We end the volume on a lighter note, with Paul Benedict Grant's discussion of *Lolita* and humor. The message is quite serious, though, inasmuch as it points us to ways *Lolita's* humor teaches students how Humbert's rhetorical strategies "create a collective empathy, and, at times, cause moral myopia."

While all essays in this volume are equally rooted in their authors' experience in teaching *Lolita*, they fall into two distinct categories: some (most) feature concrete pedagogical approaches; others offer broader and more general ideas for discussion and analysis. We feel that in their sum and diversity the essays provide proper balance for a volume designed to help get the most out of this delightfully multiangled and enduring masterpiece of world literature.

Only Words to Play With: Teaching *Lolita* in Introductory Reading and Writing Courses

Samuel Schuman

Some years ago, I decided to try to teach *Lolita* in a required introductory freshman English course. By and large, the students were not prospective English or literature majors, nor were they honors students. I expected, accurately, that hardly any would be acquainted with Nabokov's work. They had been randomly assigned to sections of the course, which was intended as an introduction to college-level reading and writing—it was neither a pure composition course nor the first literature offering in the major sequence. At the time, I was teaching at a small, private, church-affiliated liberal arts college in central Iowa, with a solid, but not prestigious, academic program. A short autobiographical digression is required to explain what must seem a bizarre and pedagogically risky decision.

I was born in 1942, which means I was a rampantly adolescent mid-twentieth-century, mid-American male when hurricane *Lolita* came ashore in the late 1950s. In the unrealistic hope that the novel would live up to its lurid reputation, I acquired a copy at that time. It was my aspiration that, if caught with the goods, I might have a slight chance of persuading my parents that I was reading Nabokov for literary rather than pornographic purposes. As it worked out, I, like many other teenaged boys, found *Lolita* far too fancy to be satisfactory for my purposes. My parents never did find the soon-discarded book, and the literary card never needed to be played.

Flash-forward to the early 1970s, when a small Ford Foundation grant sent me to England, where I lived with my spouse and kids for a few transformative weeks in the house of a colleague from Northwestern University. After completing my doctoral work at Northwestern, I had briefly worked there as a teacher of composition, under the direction of Alfred Appel. The colleague (Richard Wilson) whose wonderful home in Beverley, Yorkshire, we borrowed had just acquired Appel's *The Annotated* Lolita. One rainy Yorkshire day, casting about for something to read, I idly started *Lolita* again. The enchanted isle mesmerized and captured me; I read the book from cover to cover, read it again, then staggered out to Beverley's best book shop and bought everything else they happened to have by Nabokov (*Pale Fire*; *Speak, Memory*; and *Invitation to a Beheading*), read them, and never turned back.

My initial exposure to Nabokov was as an unwitting adolescent, not much younger than the college students to whom I intended to teach the book. My more lasting beguilement with Nabokov came wholly without academic baggage. I never studied his works in any course; he did not really fit into any prescribed literary niche I had visited. On both occasions, then, I was as naive a reader as my first-year students were.

Not surprisingly, teaching Nabokov and *Lolita* to nonliterary first-year students at a not very sophisticated midwestern college generated fairly naive questions and classroom conversation, yet these queries proved to be springboards to productive discussions of important literary issues—indeed, just the sort of core issues introductory college literature courses should raise. Among those questions are the following:

Is Lolita *a dirty book?*

Enough of my students had vaguely heard of Nabokov and *Lolita* (book or movie or allusion) that this issue surfaced early on. The query proved to be a godsend, because I suspect that my preliminary response—"Maybe; read it and see what you think"—generated a quicker and a more universal reading of the text than is common in freshman English courses. Once students had made progress in the book itself, and realized (as I had when I first read it) that it was not going to present action "limited to the copulation of clichés" (V. Nabokov, "On a Book" 313), the "dirty book" issue led to some deeper classroom discussions. We were able to ask, for example, about the difference between a book in which sex is an important motif and a work of pornography. This difference is not immediately clear to many first-semester college students.

Is Vladimir Nabokov *a pervert, a pedophile, a sex maniac, or what?*

This is my personal favorite, a simple question that opens the door to an important set of issues for introductory literary work. It is easy to forget that young readers habitually confuse the narrative voice with the authorial perspective. (Perhaps that is one reason such readers tend to refer to the author, and often the characters, of works of literature as "they," as in "What do they mean at the end of *Hamlet* by calling him a 'sweet prince'?") The difference between the narrative persona and the author seems so obvious to more experienced readers that we often forget how crucial the discovery of that gap is to literary understanding. *Lolita* is an ideal book for helping students learn this lesson. Initially the novel's narrative voice is beguiling and seems to be presenting a strong, legalistic case: "Sensitive gentlewomen of the jury, I was not even her first lover" (135). Because Humbert is trying so hard to justify himself, it is easy to imagine that his creator is making that case. But because the underlying ethical soundness of the work is increasingly hard to ignore and moves increasingly away from the narrator's pathetic efforts at moral justification, attentive readers, even if inexperienced, come to realize that Nabokov and Humbert are very different entities. I believe that anyone who reads *Lolita* carefully cover to cover is going to learn that the author does not agree with, or much like, the narrator. If first-year readers can grasp this one lesson from *Lolita*, that alone justifies the entire course.

Well, then, is Humbert Humbert a pervert?

Another great question. And one that lets me recite a favorite passage from *Midsummer Night's Dream*, "The lunatic, the lover, and the poet / Are of imagination all compact" (5.1.7–8). This question is much less naive than the first, and it does not admit a glib answer. Humbert claims he is a poet-lover and, perhaps, a madman. Is he one or the other, neither or both? Some students argue he is pathetic, some that he is a dangerous criminal. Some say they find him likable, in a repellent sort of way; others find him disgusting. These are all interesting and legitimate reactions, and they make for animated and valuable discussion. They invite me to ask more questions, such as, What is the difference between a criminal imagination and an artistic one? What do we mean by "madman"? Can you like someone and still find him disgusting? And, perhaps most interesting, Can a book dominated by a powerful and perverse and dark voice be an attractive and even uplifting work of fiction?

Isn't this book degrading to women, treating them as objects of male fantasy?

Here's another query that is almost guaranteed to spark a lively class conversation. The pedagogical challenge is to keep students focused on the book itself and not on the merits of feminism versus traditional family values. Are women in *Lolita* full characters, or are they animated stereotypes? If the latter, is this actually the final stance of the novel, or is it a manifestation of Humbert's deformed vision? Should modern students view Charlotte Haze as a degrading representation of women? What about headmistress Pratt? And, of course, what about Dolores herself? After a spirited, but probably inconclusive, discussion, the questions invite the instructor to suggest that students might want to investigate what other readers have said about women in *Lolita*. Since there is no dearth of secondary commentary on both sides of the issue, students have a chance to discover that scholarly authorities can disagree and that reference sources do not always solve knotty questions but instead illuminate their complexity—another valuable lesson for an introductory literary study.

Of course, most of the time that we studied *Lolita* together, we were asking a different kind of question: Who are these characters? What exactly is happening here? What does this sentence mean?

After our first reading of the book, I do not imagine that any of the students gained a complete understanding of it. Indeed, I am not convinced after at least a dozen readings over the years that I have. It did seem to me, however, that there were at least two positive effects of teaching the novel: the students enjoyed Nabokov and *Lolita* (several reread the novel immediately), and what they did grasp about the work was well grounded and sensible. *Lolita* is a difficult book, but (to my surprise) it is not an easy book to misread if it is read carefully, and one of the points I have tried to make in teaching Nabokov to inexperienced readers is that anyone who is willing to take the time and do the heavy lifting can become a conscientious reader.

I offer several discoveries and tentative conclusions that suggest teaching *Lolita* to beginning college students is a productive, valuable enterprise. I maintain that T. S. Eliot had a point about the importance of literary tradition. Nabokov's works are saturated with references to a diverse cluster of artistic predecessors. Freshman readers of *Lolita* are not going to catch all those references; perhaps they are going to miss most of them. (I do not use Appel's *Annotated* Lolita in this exercise: it is better for students to try to puzzle the work out for themselves, albeit haltingly.) But reading such a densely allusive novel helps them begin to understand the way a modern work of art builds on its precursors. I concentrate on references to Poe and Shakespeare in *Lolita*, in part because they seem close to the surface of the work and in part because my introductory students have at least a slight familiarity with those two authors.

Nabokov in general and *Lolita* in particular offer a rich opportunity to ask core questions regarding the relation of reality and fiction. Many of the details of everyday American life in the novel are strikingly exact, even today, yet the work is a spectacular example of art and artifice. It is this issue, more than any other, that people who are starting to read fiction as adults need to consider. At the same time, *Lolita* encourages students to leave behind some bad reading habits picked up in high school. Students are often taught to see literature as a repository of ethical aphorisms (e.g., the moral of *Othello* is "don't be jealous"). *Lolita* will lead students away from such readings all by itself. I have sometimes asked students questions like "what is the theme or moral of *Lolita*?" just to begin a discussion that will conclude that the query is wrong. Nabokov does not give his readers a choice. Nobody can read *Lolita* seriously and decide that the point of the book is "don't sleep with people a quarter your age" or "don't murder cartoon perverts" or "don't marry your girlfriend's mother."

Finally, of course, the best reason to teach this novel in a freshman English course is its magical prose. I do not expect freshmen to emerge from first readings of *Lolita* writing like Nabokov, although I do not mind that some try. But one learns about fine writing by reading it. To read *Lolita*—or to reread it—is to heighten one's sense of the power of words, to see them dance and hear them sing. It is certainly not impossible to have read *Lolita* carefully and still write sloppy prose, but it is impossible to read *Lolita* carefully and not recognize when one writes poorly. Teaching first-year introductory English courses that focus on reading and writing we have only words to play with. We might as well play with the best.

Lolita in the Senior Seminar

Eric Naiman

> Up a trackless slope climbs the master artist, and at the
> top, on a windy ridge, whom do you think he meets? The
> panting and happy reader, and there they spontaneously
> embrace and are linked forever if the book lasts forever.
>
> —Vladimir Nabokov, *Lectures on Literature*

This image of aesthetic consummation between author and reader, sketched by
Vladimir Nabokov as part of his essay "Good Readers and Good Writers," poses
several problems for the leader of a senior, capstone seminar in a department
of English or comparative literature. The purpose of such a course, as I see it,
is to encourage students as they begin the transition from readers to scholars.
Even when they near the end of a major in literature, many students remain
passive when confronted with the demands of an intricate work of literature or a
forcefully written piece of criticism. A principal goal of a senior seminar should
be to motivate the students to adopt an independent, even aggressive point of
view toward a particular text. Good students in a seminar might not welcome
the clammy hug of an author; they might prefer to climb that peak and, goal
attained, look out across the low-lying clouds and, panting and happy, spy the
author on a different summit. They need not thumb their nose at the author;
perhaps a wave might be enough?

Part of the essential experience of reading Nabokov, however, is to pay such
close attention to his writing, to spend so much time "fondl[ing] details" that
we come to sense the author breathing down our necks. Nabokov encouraged
"kindness to authors," and that kindness—at least when Nabokov approved of
the author—entailed submission to the creator's fictional and hermeneutic universe (*Lectures on Literature* 1). Nabokov's reading of *Bleak House*, an essential
item in the syllabus for my course, begins with several paragraphs that present
this submission in a gendered and eroticized context:

> We are now ready to tackle Dickens. We are now ready to embrace Dickens.
> We are now ready to bask in Dickens. In our dealings with Jane Austen
> we had to make a certain effort in order to join the ladies in the drawing
> room. . . . We had to find an approach to Jane Austen and her *Mansfield
> Park*. I think we did find it and did have some degree of fun with her
> delicate patterns, with her collection of eggshells in cotton wool. But the
> fun was forced. . . .
>
> With Dickens we expand. . . . Here there is no problem of approach
> as with Jane Austen, no courtship, no dillydallying. We just surrender
> ourselves to Dickens's voice. . . . All we have to do when reading *Bleak*

> *House* is to relax and let our spines take over. Although we read with our minds, the seat of artistic delight is between the shoulder blades. That little shiver behind is quite certainly the highest form of emotion that humanity has attained when evolving pure art and pure science. . . . I repeat again and again it is no use reading a book at all if you do not read it with your back.   (*Lectures on Literature* 63–64)

This passage portrays the world of good authors and good readers as a community of men, and it depicts the good reader as one who at least begins to demonstrate his skills by assuming a receptive position. Rich discussions should be provoked by analyzing the pleasures and discomfort that ensue from reading Nabokov as he wants to be read, yet the power and profundity of Nabokov's writing will be missed by readers who refuse to engage closely with his world. A seminar on *Lolita* should produce frequent oscillation between receptivity and resistance, and I try to make the students conscious of this dynamic from the very start.

Dostoevsky and Tolstoy seek to teach their readers how to live. They pose and often answer fundamental questions about the meaning of life, the existence of God, the responsibilities of men and women in society. Nabokov teaches his readers how to read, and in many respects someone teaching Nabokov has an easy road to follow: cultivate particular aspects of reading and your students will become better readers. Four months of proper readerly practice will develop skills that last long into graduate school or other, equally demanding forms of intellectual life.

Spending four months with a single novel is something of a luxury. Fondling details is often not possible in a syllabus structured like a tourist's itinerary of European capitals. On the first day of class, I pass out index cards and ask the students to write on one side what they think *Lolita* is about. On the other side they are to say why they have signed up for the course. The purpose of this exercise is to focus attention immediately on the connection between the novel's subject and the subject reading it. The reader's desire and its (non)satisfaction is a particularly fraught issue in *Lolita* scholarship. Especially striking about the students' responses, however, is the anticipatory pleasure with which students contemplate devoting this much time to any text. They are already inclined toward enjoyment; at some point in the semester it is useful to focus on the rapport between this structured pleasure and the problematic issue of the reader's enjoyment of Humbert's and Nabokov's prose.

At the start of the semester I ask my students to begin turning in close readings of short chapters in the novel. The students are all expected to have read the novel at least once by the second week of class. The passages analyzed are thus part of a continual process of rereading. Initially, I ask the students to concentrate on the passage as a nearly independent piece of writing. How does the passage work internally, what are its poetic devices and points of reference?

As an example, I often start with a passage toward the end of the book:

> Gently I rolled back to town, in that old faithful car of mine which was serenely, almost cheerfully working for me. My Lolita! There was still a three-year-old bobby pin of hers in the depths of the glove compartment. There was still that stream of pale moths siphoned out of the night by my headlights. Dark barns still propped themselves up here and there by the roadside. People were still going to the movies. While searching for night lodgings, I passed a drive-in. In a selenian glow, truly mystical in its contrast with the moonless and massive night, on a gigantic screen slanting away among dark drowsy fields, a thin phantom raised a gun, both he and his arm reduced to tremulous dishwater by the oblique angle of that receding world,—and the next moment a row of trees shut off the gesticulation.   (293)

Michael Wood provides a wonderful reading of these lines, which I share with the students after they have provided their comments. He sees this passage as an exceptional moment where Nabokov's strong "signature," the bag of tricks that serve as his "visible shorthand," yields to "style," a term defined as "something more secretive, more thoroughly dispersed among the words, a reflection of luck or grace, or of a moment when signature overcomes or forgets itself" (23). Wood, however, misses the trick in this paragraph: the wonderful juxtaposition in "people were still going to the movies," where "still" suddenly balances between adverbial and adjectival meanings. I ask the students to consider how the perception of this verbal play affects their appreciation of the passage. Is the rest of the passage "ruined" once one has found the treasure buried in its middle? Would it matter if we knew that the passage had been born out of a desire to use this one, perhaps previously written sentence? (This same word play— "he was still young, still brash, still shifty, still married to the gentle, exquisitely pretty woman"—is also used in "The Vane Sisters," where it and other moments like it function as miniature versions of the verbal gimmick central to the entire story [620].) Finally, I ask the students to consider the significance of my use of Wood's reading. This question of readerly competition and performance anxiety is one to which we return later in the course, but a problem posed by a seminar on *Lolita* is the extent to which an instructor should work with or against the spirit of competition and one-upmanship that characterizes both Nabokov's relationship with his readers and Nabokov studies as a whole.

I ask the students to turn in five of these chapter analyses over the course of the semester. There are two longer papers, too, but in several respects these chapter analyses are the heart of the course. They encourage a continued active engagement with the text, and they foster a sense of collective discovery, particularly when I distribute to the students anthological bouquets of the most intriguing moments from the papers. I have found that it is especially important that students write frequently in a Nabokov seminar. Nabokov's writing can be so intimidating that it can have a paralyzing effect on potential paper writers who may be inclined to want to turn in impossibly perfect work. Having already written several short papers about *Lolita*, the students are used to proposing their own readings in writing before they begin their more substantial written assignments. (The short papers also afford the teacher a chance to identify stylistic and grammatical problems—and the students an opportunity to work on rectifying them—before the graded work is due.)

Both "The Vane Sisters" and "A Guide to Berlin" can serve as useful preparation for a prolonged engagement with *Lolita,* but I find it equally compelling to devote some time early in the semester to close readings of several of Shakespeare's sonnets, in Stephen Booth's edition. Nearly any of the sonnets will provide enough interpretive practice, though at least one sonnet analyzed should deal with the notion of loving, artistic reproduction (e.g., sonnet 15), and another should provide examples of the bawdy wordplay of which Nabokov is so fond (e.g., sonnet 151). It works well to assign a couple of sonnets with Booth's accompanying commentary and a couple without. A goal (albeit an impossible one) for the course should be to read every sentence of *Lolita* with the interpretive care devoted to an analysis of a Shakespearean sonnet. It is worth discussing with the students the feelings of excitement and inadequacy that such an attempt can provoke.

Good readers must always have dictionaries at hand, and they should pay attention to all seemingly arbitrary images, numbers, and names. I frequently "give" the students in the seminar unannounced quizzes. The value of quizzes—and of examinations in general—to an understanding of Nabokov cannot be overemphasized. Nabokov loved to assign examination questions to which the answers were succinct and clearly right or clearly wrong. A salient feature of his essay "Good Readers and Good Writers" is its reliance on the genre of the quiz, and the testing of readers is a fundamental aspect of his authoritative authorial stance. I want my students to appreciate the importance of continual examination in Nabokov's poetics, but since the ultimate purpose of the seminar is to encourage students to use their imagination to climb mountains other than the one scaled by the author, I do not include the grades on these quizzes in the final course grade. Rather, I give prizes—a secondhand copy of *Speak, Memory*; a volume of Brian Boyd's biography; or the Nabokov-Wilson correspondence acquired cheaply through Dover or Daedalus—to the students with the highest cumulative scores. Although I do not give points for imaginative wrong answers, I value them and share them with the class, because the writing of playful, incorrect responses enables readers to enjoy the process of testing even as they register inadequacies. (The danger for the teacher is that some of these answers are so good that they color all his subsequent returns to the text, and thus the name of the nutritionist—Dr. Johnson—with whom Humbert connects in Canada will always be haunted by "Margaret Atwood" or "Special K.")

Part of the process of becoming a good Nabokovian reader involves resisting apparent and habitual hierarchies of significance or temporality. Thus parentheses are never afterthoughts; often parenthetically or casually added remarks contain the central point of a Nabokov sentence. Causal and temporal connections are also to be challenged, as is commonsense interpretation of a sentence. Readers should be attuned to flickers of semantic suggestion that are immediately (not!) dispelled by the second half of a phrase. If the students are so inclined, they can work at overcoming the logic of narrative temporality by practicing "the Dunne experiment," an activity that fascinated Nabokov. The experimenter records his or her dreams in detail, then scans the subsequent day for images, words, and events that—had they occurred the day before— would have been seen as prompting aspects of the dream itself. This exercise helps the students overcome linear reading and see the text as a whole or, at the very least, understand the tension between moving through and hovering above a text, between a virtually inescapable identification with a character's perspective and the understanding—from the reader's point of view—of the character's limited field of vision.

The reading practices that I seek to cultivate in my students are in many respects literally preposterous and perverse. Parodic models of good readers pervade Nabokov's fiction; one of the most striking is provided by Luzhin, the hero of *The Defense*. Luzhin reads "with a funny stammer, pronouncing some of the words oddly and at times going past a period, or else not reaching it, and raising or lowering the tone of his voice for no logical reason" (226). Such reading is not so foreign to today's students as it must have been to students in Nabokov's day. Many senior literature students have had some experience with psychoanalytic or deconstructive approaches to reading. Although Nabokov certainly did not share the conviction that writing is ruled by developmental, psychobiographical influences and although his artistic achievement is proof that language does not always fail, the practice of reading against the grain is central to the successful interpretation of his texts. For a programmatic image of author-reader communication, I suggest that my students return to the first moment of physical contact between Humbert and Lolita, when he licks a speck out of her left eye and then repeats the contact with her untroubled right one (43–44). From his mouth to our eye, we just have to know how to dilate. (Although we now have statistical evidence that reading Nabokov can help high school kids get into college [M. Schiff], it is worth noting here Nabokov's insistence on the essentially nonutilitarian contact between author and reader. Contact is even more delicious when there is no speck to remove.)

But what if we are dilating incorrectly? The notion of authorized perversion is a complex and paradoxical one. How can perversion ever be authorized? Once it is authorized does not it cease to be perverse? What is the rapport between perverse interpretation and perverse sexual desire? And when does close reading become unauthorized perversion? While Nabokov was alive, this was a particularly fraught issue, as the close reader William Woodin Rowe, a professor at George Washington University, discovered when he wrote in detail about sexual symbols in Nabokov's work and Nabokov replied with a savage rejoinder in the

New York Review of Books ("Rowe's Symbols"). I use Nabokov's response to Rowe; other critics' nearly ritualistic use of it as a defense against the possibility of their own misreadings; and a wonderful rich letter posted on Nabokv-L by Andrew Fippinger, then a senior at Wesleyan, to explore the way in which bad reading subtends the concept of good reading and the very notion of genius in Nabokov's world. Nabokov's fiction and scholarship are full of bad readers; let us recall that his good reading quiz includes more traits of bad readers than of good ones. (Emma Bovary is a bad reader, Anna Karenin is another, and in Nabokov's lectures that is probably a worse sin than adultery [*Lectures on Russian Literature* 157].) The identity of his good reader is formed in large measure by not being a bad one: readerly anxiety comes from the difficulty of reconciling the desire to perform brilliantly—to make the text get up and dance to the astonishment of hitherto unenlightened readers—with the fear of appearing stupid. Complicating the stakes is the penchant of Nabokov's texts to pair hermeneutic and sexual proclivities and deviations. With this dynamic in mind, I explore with the students the extent to which Humbert's struggle with Quilty is a hermeneutic battle that reflects and sexualizes the reader's process of interpretation.

As a counterpoint to Nabokov's response to Rowe, we read Alfred Appel's introduction to and notes for *The Annotated* Lolita. Appel has a fine understanding of Nabokov's metafiction, but his approach to *Lolita* reveals several symptomatic moments of readerly anxiety. I ask the students to characterize Appel's approach to the text. They often focus on his desire for the author's approbation, the category of "anti-annotations" (a variation on New York City's "Don't Even Think about Parking Here") and the Stockade Clyde episode, the *locus classicus* of the assertion that Lolita is not an erotic book (Appel, Introduction xxxiv). They begin to think of commentary and annotation as part of readerly response, not simply as factual information or as part of the novel itself.

From Appel we move on to a variety of critical work, including Linda S. Kauffman, Boyd (the *Lolita* chapter from *American Years* and "'Even Homais Nods'"), Diana Butler, Elizabeth Patnoe, Elizabeth Freeman, Brandon S. Centerwall, Norman Podhoretz, Alexander Dolinin, Sarah Herbold ("'(I Have Camouflaged)'"), and Julian W. Connolly ("'Nature's Reality'"). Everyone in the class reads all the articles, but two students are assigned primary responsibility for each piece of criticism: one to present a summary and analysis, the other to critique or add to the first presentation. I ask the students to record their points of agreement with and resistance to the articles, to attempt to summarize the methodology used in each article, and to concentrate on rhetorical devices and strategies. I ask them to pay special attention to passages that are repeatedly cited in the scholarly literature. What do the authors omit? How do critics of Nabokov interact? When do they attack each other and why? How do the strongly opinionated responses of Nabokov to critics during his lifetime continue to influence, police, or normalize the field from beyond the grave? A readiness to critique the work of others may generate a reluctance to propose readings of one's own. To encourage students to overcome their fears of getting something wrong, I speak about the commonality—indeed, in the case of Nabokov's reader, the textually induced commonality—of such inhibitions and the necessity of dealing with hermeneutic hesitations in a productive way. As part of this discussion, I have shared with students moments when my own work missed something or has been the object of scholarly attack or derision. (Nabokv-L, a forum for relatively unguarded exchange, is an extremely useful resource for exploring the communal dynamics and even the symptomotology of the field.)

Each time I have taught this seminar, there have been about twice as many women as men in the class. Several of the best discussions have centered on the status of women within the text and as the text's readers. Laura Mulvey's work, with its discussion of the female viewer of Hollywood cinema "shifting restlessly in her transvestite clothes" (33), is useful, as is consideration of the novel's rapport to female sexual and readerly pleasure. Several students have criticized Humbert—and Nabokov—for being unable to envision or represent Lolita's experience of physical pleasure in her sexual encounters with Humbert: the reality, they argue, would be more complex. This argument inevitably leads to a discussion of whether the reality of sexual abuse or statutory rape should matter for a good reading of *Lolita*, as well as to a consideration of the habitual uses of representations of female pleasure in pornographic, usually male-oriented, verbal and cinematic texts.

The seminar participants use their insights into the strengths and weaknesses of other, professional readers as they prepare their own seminar papers. These papers must deal with some aspect of *Lolita*, but the topic and approach are left entirely to the student. In the final month of the course, we consider several adaptations of *Lolita*, ranging from Nabokov's screenplay to the two *Lolita* films to Pia Pera's *Lo's Diary* to Todd Solondz's film *Happiness*. If the members of the seminar can read another language, I ask them to consider a translation of the novel. (Nabokov cherished bad translations as much as he did bad readers.) Each adaptation is seen as a kind of critical reading, an interpretation of what the novel is (and is not) about.

Nabokov wrote that after reading Nikolay Gogol, "one's eyes tend to become gogolized, and one is apt to see bits of his world in the most unexpected places" (*Nikolai Gogol* 144). The same can be true of reading Nabokov. In the final classes, I ask the students to consider what aspects of good reading mastered in this class might be productive or counterproductive in other classes or in life. When is noticing things bad? What sorts of readings and types of activities does perverse interpretation impair? On the last day, I ask the students to talk for a few minutes about how they would reinterpret another author's work or even their experience of the preceding day if they thought it had been written by Nabokov.

Student reactions to the class have been enthusiastic, not surprising given the self-selecting nature of any group choosing to study *Lolita* for an entire semester. Nearly all the students are empowered as readers. (This has not always been the case when I have taught *Lolita* to a larger audience as part of a lecture course on Nabokov. There, some students give up and, distressingly, accept the notion that they are bad readers.) When I first envisioned this senior seminar, I expected some students would object to such a strong focus on reader reception and authorial intention. In fact, I have never received an evaluation that expressed distaste with Nabokov as a pedagogic character. The students enjoy at least the mediated contact with his authorial presence. A few seminar participants have found the classroom relations and the process of examination too tempered; since traveling back to Ithaca in the 1950s is impossible, they wish that the quizzes were graded, that the anxiety of readerly apprenticeship were more authentic. A more rigorous channeling of Nabokov's ghost would, I fear, discourage some of the less confident but still imaginative students and shut off some original, productive readings. I am tempted, however, by this possibility of a more complete identification of teacher and subject, and in some future seminar I may risk that experiment.

Teaching *Lolita*
in a Course on Ethics and Literature
Marilyn Edelstein

The late 1980s saw a resurgence of interest in ethics and literature, with the publication of new books on the subject by major scholars like J. Hillis Miller and Wayne Booth. In recent years, many critics and theorists (including some Nabokov scholars) have (re)turned to ethical questions about literature: Does literature imitate life, and will readers, in turn, imitate the actions (whether virtuous or ignoble) of characters in literary texts? How and why can literary works be ethically beneficial or harmful for their readers? Are authors responsible for any ethical effects—positive or negative—their works may produce in readers? What are the relations between aesthetics and ethics?

Vladimir Nabokov's brilliant, funny, and poignant novel *Lolita* foregrounds such questions. After years of teaching *Lolita* occasionally in courses on contemporary American literature, I decided a few years ago to make it the centerpiece of a new course I was designing as a senior seminar for English majors, Ethics and Literature. The novel might have seemed a strange choice to students and even colleagues who had heard about but not read *Lolita*, whose reputation always precedes it. After all, the novel is about and narrated by a grown man who repeatedly proclaims his lust and, finally, love for a barely pubescent girl who becomes his legal stepdaughter and with whom he has frequent and often nonconsensual sex. To put it more bluntly, this is a novel "about" pedophilia and (pseudo) incest. Yet *Lolita* may also be, in John Hollander's formulation, the "record" of its author's "love affair with the romantic novel" (559), or, as Nabokov prefers, with the English language ("On a Book" 316). Or is *Lolita* "both a love story and a parody of love stories" (Appel, Notes 395) or both a romance and a parody of romance (Frosch)? Is it a novel about the (im)possibility of love or the wages of solipsism (and sexism) or "aesthetic bliss," as Nabokov himself suggests in the afterword to *Lolita* ("On a Book" 314), or the quest for immortality through art (if not eternal youth through sex with nymphets)?

Assigning *Lolita* in a course on ethics and literature might also have seemed strange to Nabokov scholars familiar with Nabokov's many statements railing against Freudian, Marxist, and ethical analyses and advocating instead more aesthetic readings of his work. Although the fictional editor of *Lolita*, John Ray, Jr., asserts in the foreword "the ethical impact the book should have on the serious reader" (5), Nabokov claims in *Lolita*'s afterword that he is "neither a reader nor a writer of didactic fiction" and that "*Lolita* has no moral in tow" ("On a Book" 314). Proving, however, that there are not only unreliable narrators (like Humbert Humbert) but also unreliable authors, Nabokov argues, in his essay "Good Readers and Good Writers," that "a major writer combines these three—storyteller, teacher, enchanter" and that readers "may go to the teacher for moral education" (*Lectures on Literature* 5).

Much early Nabokov criticism did focus on Nabokov as enchanter—as a writer in love with language, games, and artifice (see, e.g., Bader; Appel, Introduction)—rather than as storyteller, let alone as moral educator. Yet, in her 1980 book *Nabokov and the Novel*, Ellen Pifer argued persuasively for an ethical reading of *Lolita* and other works in Nabokov's oeuvre (see also Green). Pifer argues that Nabokov is a "rigorous moralist" whose texts challenge and unsettle the reader, thus expanding perception (169, 129–30). Some later critics have followed Pifer's lead; for example, Stephen Jan Parker states that "a strong moral vision underlies [Nabokov's] art" (*Understanding* 5).

Since *Lolita* foregrounds and complicates ethical questions, I chose it as the central literary work for the ethics and literature course. Although all undergraduates at Santa Clara University—a Jesuit institution emphasizing values and social justice—are required to take a course in ethics (as part of our extensive core curriculum), the English department had never offered a course on ethics and literature. I designed one that linked my longstanding interest in Nabokov with my other teaching and research interests: literary theory and the history of criticism, feminist theory, contemporary American literature, as well as ethical approaches to literature.

I knew most students taking this course would have little if any background in contemporary literary and critical theory—since our department only recently added a major requirement in theory—or in the history of literary criticism. My primary goals were to enable students to understand and join a lively two-millennia-old conversation about ethics and literature and to apply the theoretical work we were reading—from Plato to the present—to their analyses of *Lolita* and other literary texts (without reducing the literary texts to mere test cases for the theories). In the seminar, I foregrounded three central issues: whether and how literature is mimetic; the potential ethical effects of literary texts, even those—like *Lolita*—that do not seem to have any explicit moral messages; and the role of affect and emotion in both ethics and the reading of literature.

We began the seminar where Western philosophy and literary theory began, with Plato and Aristotle. In book 10 of the *Republic*, Plato claims that poetry is "thrice-removed from the truth" (that is, the Ideas or Forms) and thus incapable of being morally improving (25). Plato also argues that poetry is morally harmful because it "feeds and waters the passions instead of drying them up" (28) and thus inhibits rather than encourages reason (and therefore philosophy). Aristotle shares his teacher Plato's view that literature is essentially mimetic but, contra Plato, argues that poets (unlike historians) can imitate not only things "that are" but also "things that ought to be" (62) or that "might possibly occur" (48). The poet is thus freed from bondage to "reality" (a term Nabokov, unlike Aristotle, always uses in quotation marks).

Exploring later challenges to Plato's narrowly mimetic view of literature, we discussed Sir Philip Sidney's *An Apology for Poetry* (1595), in which Sidney asserts that the poet is not limited to the mere imitation of nature but "doth grow in effect another nature, in making things either better than nature bringeth forth, or, quite anew, . . . freely ranging only within the zodiac of his own wit" (137). Nabokov, as I told students, has a similar view: "the work of art is invariably the creation of a new world . . . having no obvious connection with the worlds we already know"—even though readers can draw this connection once they have carefully studied the writer's newly created world (*Lectures on Literature* 1). Sidney argues that, contra Plato, poets should not be accused of telling lies since they do not claim to be telling the truth (149). Yet, as I asked students in the seminar, can a fictional world, "another nature," not be mistaken for or equated with "reality" or "truth" but still have some ethical relevance for real readers in their real lives?

Most readers—and especially student readers—of fictional works assume that the characters are, if not real, then relatively transparent representations of real people. I often find students speculating about what happens after the novel ends or what would have happened if the characters had made different choices. In the seminar we discussed Nabokov's claims, echoing Sidney's, that literary texts are independent fictional worlds and that only bad readers identify with characters in books (*Lectures on Literature* 4). I wanted to subvert students' common and often unexamined assumption that characters are real yet also encourage students to examine their own human—including affective and intellectual—responses to and judgments of these characters, who seem, when we read, as if they were real.

Continuing our exploration of the relations between aesthetics and ethics (or words and world), we next read Immanuel Kant's "First Book: Analytic of the Beautiful" from *Critique of Judgment,* in which Kant distinguishes the beautiful from both the good and the pleasant. He argues that the judgment of the beautiful must be completely disinterested (and, in principle, universal). Although most students—like many before them—found Kant's aesthetic theory rather baffling, they understood at least some of his ethical theory, such as the "categorical imperative": "act only in accordance with that maxim through which you can at the same time will that it become a universal law" (*Groundwork* 31). Students readily discerned the similarity between this principle and one they were more familiar with—"the golden rule." Thus, following Kant, one should not choose to abuse a child or to murder unless one were willing to have all people on earth do such things—including to oneself.

Particularly helpful in our later discussion of Humbert's treatment of Lolita was Kant's idea that one should treat other people as "ends-in-themselves," not as means (*Groundwork* 37)—for instance, not as a means to achieve one's own pleasure or even to create immortal art, as Humbert variously admits to doing through Lolita. I reminded students that Humbert and Lolita are not "people" but rather, as Nabokov punningly calls his characters, "galley slaves" (*Strong Opinions* 95); so it is not the characters but the author who chooses actions for the characters within the fictional world for specific literary (and perhaps ethical) reasons.

The next two writer-critics we read, Percy Shelley and Leo Tolstoy, helped us think about whether and how a literary work might have ethical effects even if, like *Lolita*, it does not have any obviously ethical characters to emulate. In "A Defence of Poetry," Shelley suggests that poetry can have a moral *effect* even (or especially) if it does not convey a moral *message*. He writes that "poetry awakens and enlarges the mind itself" and better allows us to imagine how others feel, thereby increasing our capacities for empathy, sympathy, and compassion. For Shelley, "the great secret of morals is love, or a going out of our own nature," and therefore "a man, to be greatly good, must imagine intensely and . . . must put himself in the place of another" (344). As my students discovered, Humbert (although an imagined character rather than a man) is supremely capable of the former but not the latter. My students further developed the links I suggested between Shelley's Romantic views of literary ethics and Nabokov's, especially regarding the transformative (and ethical) potential of both imagination and feeling.

Selections from Tolstoy's polemical treatise *What Is Art?*, written after his late-life religious conversion to his own version of Christianity, provided another approach to our ethical analyses of *Lolita*. Tolstoy repudiates any aesthetic definitions of art or criteria for judging art, replacing them with religious and ethical criteria. He argues that true art must unite all people by reflecting the best religious thought of its age and by sharing simple, honest human feelings and that art should be judged by how well it does these things. For Tolstoy, there are two kinds of "religious art": the higher one, conveying "positive feelings of love of God and one's neighbor," and the lower one, conveying "negative feelings of indignation and horror at the violation of love" (152). Granting a provisional reality to the characters and events in *Lolita*, we discussed in class whether readers can find in Humbert a "negative" ethical example, an example of how *not* to act: solipsistically or selfishly, using others as a means to one's own ends.

After surveying centuries of Western thought about ethics and literature, we began our extended discussion of *Lolita* (and then of both the Stanley Kubrick and Adrian Lyne films of the novel) about midquarter. We also read several essays by Nabokov, John Gardner's *On Moral Fiction*, and substantial sections of Booth's *The Company We Keep: An Ethics of Fiction*. After *Lolita*, we read several short stories that foreground ethical issues, including Ursula Le Guin's "The Ones Who Walk away from Omelas." This self-reflexive, quasi–science fiction story was, as Le Guin tells us, inspired by a philosophical question posed by Fyodor Dostoevsky and William James: Would we be content to live in an idyllic society whose citizens' complete happiness was assured by the absolute suffering of one—and only one—small child? The story provoked lively classroom debate; the story's explicit focus on a central ethical question—and the nature of this question—also provided some interesting comparisons with *Lolita*.

I began our discussion of *Lolita* with an approach I often use—one that draws on reader-response theory as well as an ethics and literature perspective—asking students to share their initial intellectual and emotional responses to the text. The most problematic aspect of *Lolita* for many students—especially women students—was their enthrallment with Humbert's language and literariness and their identification through much of the novel with his point of view. Many students thought the novel's subject matter—pedophilia—was shocking but were surprised that they were not shocked by Humbert's confessions; some found their own lack of shock rather shocking.

Of course, as Nomi Tamir-Ghez has ably shown, Humbert's skilled rhetoric as narrator persuades most readers to share his way of seeing Lolita and everything else. Yet my students engaged in a great deal of self-questioning when they found themselves liking Humbert despite their varying degrees of repulsion for his use and objectification of Lolita. In fact, as I told students, many Nabokov scholars have also been persuaded by Humbert's (and Nabokov's) brilliant rhetoric to see Humbert as the only relevant subject or "person" in the text, disregarding or denigrating Lolita (cf. Linda Kauffman's and Gladys Clifton's feminist analyses of these trends in *Lolita* criticism). An important added complexity in *Lolita* is that even the facts of the novel (e.g., that Lolita first seduced Humbert) are given to us by a narrator who admits to being hospitalized more than once for mental illness and to reconstructing events from a not always infallible memory; clearly Humbert qualifies as an unreliable narrator as well as a pedophile.

Many of my students, like other readers of *Lolita*, eventually agreed with Nabokov that "Humbert is a vain and cruel wretch who manages to appear 'touching'" and that only Lolita herself, Nabokov's "poor little girl," is truly touching, even though Nabokov also believes that each character is merely an "eidolon" (*Strong Opinions* 94). We discussed whether, by the end of his narrative, Humbert was sincerely penitent for his treatment of Lolita and whether he really loved her (long after her nymphethood had faded), as he states. Even students who believed one or both of these claims also felt that Humbert had destroyed Lolita's youth, if not her life. Yet most students wound up feeling at least some pity or compassion for Humbert, even if they felt much more for Lolita.

The difficulty my students had in arriving at moral judgments of Humbert and of their own sympathy for him may itself serve a larger ethical purpose. In addition to expanding our awareness of the possibilities of language and of art and enlarging our imaginations and thus our capacities for compassion, *Lolita* encourages its readers to examine their own ethical responses to the text and its relation to our world.

Can a literary text be ethical if it is not explicitly didactic and does not have a clear moral lesson (since "thou shalt not commit pedophilia" is hardly a lesson worth writing a complex, sad, and funny novel about or that needs to be taught to most readers)? Even Gardner, an outspoken advocate of "moral fiction," argues that "didacticism and true art are immiscible" (19) and defines morality as "nothing more than doing what is unselfish, helpful, kind, and noble-hearted" (23). This definition is not so different from Nabokov's "aesthetic bliss" (a term often taken out of context from *Lolita*'s afterword), "a sense of being somehow, somewhere, connected with other states of being where art (curiosity, tenderness, kindness, ecstasy) is the norm" ("On a Book" 314–15).

In a 1945 letter I shared with students, Nabokov explains his position on the relations between ethics and aesthetics:

> I never meant to deny the moral impact of art which is certainly inherent in every genuine work of art. What I do deny and am prepared to fight to the last drop of my ink is the deliberate moralizing which to me kills every vestige of art in a work however skillfully written.   (*Vladimir Nabokov* 56)

We also considered Nabokov's statement, in a 1956 letter, that *Lolita* "is a highly moral affair" (*Dear Bunny* 331). Such statements provoked fruitful class discussions—drawing together much of what we had read during the quarter—about the diverse ways in which literary texts can be ethical or have ethical effects (and about authors' relations to their texts).

My students seemed to agree that *Lolita* raises important ethical questions even if it does not provide any clear ethical messages or answers. I teach *Lolita* in part because I think education is more about asking good questions than arriving at clear answers, although I know that many students prefer the latter. I also teach *Lolita* because I think it is one of the greatest novels of the twentieth century. Perhaps we do our best work as teachers of literature when we help students develop the skills to analyze not only literature but also themselves—including their own ethical and aesthetic responses to literary texts like *Lolita*.

Teaching *Lolita* with Lepidoptera

Corinne Scheiner

In *Speak, Memory*, Vladimir Nabokov writes, "It is astounding how little the ordinary person notices butterflies" (129). He then recounts the following story:

> "None," calmly replied that sturdy Swiss hiker with Camus in his rucksack when purposely asked by me for the benefit of my incredulous companion if he had seen any butterflies while descending the trail where, a moment before, you and I had been delighting in swarms of them.   (129)

In contrast to "the sturdy Swiss hiker" or "the ordinary person," Nabokov is always deeply aware not only of the butterflies around him but also of the flora, the fauna, and the man-made structures among which he finds himself and which serve as the backdrops for his novels and other writings. It is Nabokov's knowledge of Lepidoptera that leads to an awareness of their presence and thus to a new way of seeing. Nabokov himself links the acts of seeing and knowing to each other, commenting in a 1957 interview with Robert H. Boyle, "I cannot separate the aesthetic pleasure of seeing a butterfly and the scientific pleasure of knowing what it is" (qtd. in Boyd and Pyle 529). As I demonstrate in this essay, teaching *Lolita* with Lepidoptera provides students with knowledge that enables them to see in a new way and, therefore, to read the text in a new way—that is, with an eye to both the aesthetic and scientific pleasures to be found in Nabokov's attention to detail, particularly in his depiction of the landscape of *Lolita*.

Robert Michael Pyle remarks that "[i]n any discussion of Nabokov and butterflies, *Lolita* inevitably comes up. This is partly because *Lolita* is the only thing many people know about Nabokov" (71–72). Yet, in many respects, *Lolita* is not the obvious choice to examine the link between Nabokov's fiction and Lepidoptera. Other of Nabokov's writings contain far more references to Lepidoptera—for example, *Speak, Memory*; *The Gift*; and *Ada*. Moreover, other of his fictional texts more pointedly address butterflies either through characters who are lepidopterists, such as Pilgram in "The Aurelian," Fyodor's father in *The Gift*, and Ada; through the central role of Lepidoptera, such as *Attacus atlas* (the Atlas moth) in "Christmas"; or through lepidopterological concepts, such as the holotype in *The Eye* and metamorphosis in "Christmas." In *Speak, Memory* (in particular, chapter 6); in numerous interviews, lectures, and letters; and in certain poems (most notably, "A Discovery"), Nabokov directly describes the various activities in which he engages as a lepidopterist: hunting, catching, pinning, spreading, identifying, and occasionally naming a new species.

This is not to say that *Lolita* is wholly without lepidopterological elements. Indeed, the novel contains references to actual butterflies and moths (see, e.g., pages 110, 126, 156, 157, 234, and 258), to insects, and to a lepidopterist: John Ray, Jr., PhD, who ostensibly pens the foreword to Humbert's narrative, "a descendant, no doubt, of the well-known English systematist of the seventeenth century, a predecessor to Linnaeus" (Johnson and Coates 305 [McGraw]). In his notes to *The Annotated* Lolita, Alfred Appel, Jr., identifies many of the novel's more subtle allusions to Lepidoptera in the names of characters such as Vanessa van Ness, which references the Red Admirable or Admiral (*Vanessa atalanta*; 336); Miss Phalen, "from the French *phalène*: moth" (363); Avis Chapman, *Callophrys avis* Chapman (393); Edusa Gold, the Clouded Yellow (*Colias edusa*; 400); Electra, "a close ally of the Clouded Yellow" (400); Schmetterling, the German word for butterfly; and above all Dolores, the given name of Lolita, referring to the town in Colorado where Nabokov "caught the first known female of *Lycaeides sublivens* Nabokov" (V. Nabokov, "On a Book" 316). The novel also includes allusions in the names of places: some refer directly to Lepidoptera, such as Pisky, which means "moth" (Appel, Notes 358); Snow, which relates to *Lycaena cupreus snowi* (Snow's Copper; Pyle 75); and Elphinstone, which relates to *Elphinstonia charlonia* (the Greenish Black-tip; Pyle 75); others refer to the act of "lepping" (butterfly hunting), such as Lepingville.

Despite these references, Nabokov seems to discourage the reading of *Lolita* in conjunction with Lepidoptera, saying that "H. H. knows nothing about Lepidoptera. In fact, I went out of my way to indicate . . . that he confuses the hawk-moths visiting flowers at dusk with 'gray hummingbirds'" (qtd. in Appel, Notes 328–29). I assert, however, that no inherent problem exists in exploring the connection between *Lolita* and Lepidoptera; Nabokov's critique results from the way in which many critics have engaged in such exploration. Specifically, as Pyle notes, "[c]omparing Humbert's pursuit of Dolores and Quilty to a butterfly hunt is a cliché that few commentators or magazine writers have managed to avoid" (72). Perhaps the most well-known example of this approach is Diana Butler's essay "Lolita Lepidoptera," in which the author claims that "in *Lolita*, Nabokov has transposed his own passion for butterflies into his hero's passion for nymphets" (60). Nabokov dismisses Butler's assertion as "pretentious nonsense," and Véra Nabokov, on her husband's behalf, states that "there is no connection whatsoever either in his work or in his mind, between entomology and humbertology" (V. Nabokov, *Selected Letters* 393, 394). Although Joann Karges also rejects Butler's reading of Lolita as "a personification of a butterfly" (45), she still maintains that there is a connection between *Lolita* and Lepidoptera: "the underlying theme is Lepidoptera activity from schematic classification and the description of a new species to the finding of the female *Lycaeides a. sublivens* Nabokov near Dolores, Colo." (46).

I contend, however, that the connection between *Lolita* and Lepidoptera is not in the novel's plot or themes, nor does it occur primarily in the form of lepidopterological references. Rather, the connection lies in the text's production and its style, both of which express the link between seeing and knowing— between aesthetic and scientific pleasure—discussed at the start of this essay.

Nabokov's writing of *Lolita* parallels (and coincides with) his butterfly-hunting activities in the southwestern United States in the summers of the early 1950s. Hunting butterflies depends on an ability to know and to see the connection between a species and its habitat(s), as does the examining of Nabokov's text in context. The style or formal features of the text derive from the aesthetic—itself an expression of the capacity to see and to know—that informs Nabokov's work both as a lepidopterist and as a writer.

Stephen Jay Gould claims that "because Nabokov was no dilettante spending a few harmless Sunday hours in the woods with his butterfly net, but a serious scientist with a long list of publications and a substantial career in entomology . . . we crave some linkage between his two lives" (30). He suggests that "[p]erhaps the major linkage lies in some distinctive, *underlying* approach that Nabokov applied *equally* to both domains—a procedure that conferred the same special features upon *all* his efforts" (43). This underlying approach is what I have termed above Nabokov's "aesthetic," an attention to detail and accuracy in description and a penchant for patterns. As Nabokov himself puts it, "As an artist and a scholar I prefer the specific detail to the generalization, images to ideas, obscure facts to clear symbols, and the discovered wild fruit to synthetic jam" (*Strong Opinions* 7). It is Nabokov's aesthetic, his way of seeing—that is, his focus on detail in nature and literature and, in particular, on observation and patterning—that one can access in teaching *Lolita* with Lepidoptera.

Nabokov aptly links his knowledge of Lepidoptera to the act of seeing since his lepidopterological pursuits depend on and reveal what taxonomists call a good eye, an ability to see distinguishing traits, to recognize "the (often subtle) distinctions that mark species and other natural groups of organisms" (Gould 32). Nabokov's good eye allows him to identify the flora on which certain butterflies and moths feed, informing him of where he can find particular species. It enables him to spot the Lepidoptera as they fly or to note where they land and then to deftly catch them in his net. Finally, it is responsible for his skill in classifying specimens, and in turn species, through their morphology (specifically, the counting of the scales on their wings) and their genitilic structures. In *Lolita*, Nabokov employs his ability to see both in the amassing of the details that form the landscape of the novel and in the rendering of the text itself.

In his famous afterword to the novel, Nabokov writes:

> Every summer my wife and I go butterfly hunting. The specimens are deposited at scientific institutions, such as the Museum of Comparative Zoology at Harvard or the Cornell University collection. The locality labels pinned under these butterflies will be a boon to some twenty-first-century scholar with a taste for recondite biography. It was at such of our headquarters as Telluride, Colorado; Afton, Wyoming; Portal, Arizona; and Ashland, Oregon, that *Lolita* was energetically resumed in the evenings or on cloudy days. ("On a Book" 312–13)

In a 1951 letter to Edmund Wilson, Nabokov offers the following reason for one of these summer expeditions: "I want to study in the field a butterfly I described from preserved specimens" (*Dear Bunny* 293). Similarly, unlike teaching *Lolita* as a "preserved specimen," that is, divorced from its habitat—both the landscape of the novel and the landscape in which Nabokov wrote it—teaching *Lolita* with Lepidoptera affords students the opportunity to examine the novel "in the field," set against these backdrops. I am fortunate to live in southwestern Colorado and to teach on an unusual schedule; unlike most colleges, Colorado College employs the block plan wherein students take only one class at a time for a three-and-a-half-week block. The course in which I teach *Lolita*—Nabokov's Butterflies—culminates in a week-long field trip designed to mimic one of Nabokov's butterfly-hunting expeditions in the Southwest. As it is too cold in May to catch butterflies in southwestern Colorado, we head further south to Walsenberg, Colorado; Socorro, New Mexico; and Abiquiu Lake, New Mexico.

Throughout the course, students keep journals, which are essential to both field biologists and writers. On the field trip, the journal assignments ask students to observe and record details about the different environments in which we find ourselves. Nabokov describes the process of depicting the landscape of 1950s America as "the task of inventing America":

> The obtaining of such local ingredients as would allow me to inject a modicum of average "reality" (one of the few words which mean nothing without quotes) into the brew of individual fancy, proved at fifty a much more difficult process than it had been in the Europe of my youth.
>
> ("On a Book" 312)

As we drive along the smaller, less-traveled roads in Colorado and New Mexico, we are able to observe many of the "local ingredients" of Nabokov's day still intact: the small, family-run motels and the roadside attractions. Most of our students, like Nabokov, find it difficult to invent (or reinvent) the America of the 1950s that *Lolita* depicts. Observing these local ingredients firsthand helps students contextualize the novel: having learned to see, they can begin to know. Similarly, one can address the novel's context in the classroom by showing images of 1950s America, both of the man-made structures and of the natural phenomena, the flora and fauna.

Recall Nabokov's remark in the afterword to *Lolita* that "the locality labels pinned under [the] butterflies" that he caught on his expeditions in the Southwest "will be a boon to some twenty-first-century scholar with a taste for recondite biography" (312). Perhaps. Yet these locality labels do not merely provide the type of information that a biographer seeks (date, place, activity). Rather, as Pyle notes,

> [t]hey also imply something of the plants, the soils, the elevations, the cohort of other living things, and the skies, horizons, and topography of their

habitats—something, in fact, of where and how [Nabokov] passed his days
between writing the books for which he is mostly known.   (54)

Moreover, the local ingredients of *Lolita* function as locality labels for the
images and scenes of the novel, clearly identifying them and pinning them
down, grounding them in a specific time and place. These labels also reveal
Nabokov's meticulous attention to detail and accuracy, the aesthetic or way of
seeing that unites his work as a lepidopterist and as a writer. As Brian Boyd
notes, Nabokov's "love of Lepidoptera drew upon and further sharpened his
love of the particular and the habits of detailed observation that gave him such
fictional command over the physical world" ("Nabokov" 18–19).

By studying *Lolita* on the road and, more generally, in conjunction with lepidoptery, students gain an increased awareness of Nabokov's attention to detail,
his accuracy of description, and his fondness for patterning. Yet, bearing in
mind Nabokov's claim that "in a work of art there is a kind of merging between . . .
the precision of poetry and the excitement of science" (*Strong Opinions* 10), in
reading *Lolita* with Lepidoptera, students do not merely observe the beauty of
Nabokov's writing. Throughout the course, and on the field trip in particular,
they actively experience "the excitement of science" as they engage in hands-
on lepidopterological activities. Like Nabokov, we spend our "evenings" and
"cloudy days" with *Lolita*: when camping, we discuss *Lolita* by the fire or in the
shelter of a canyon; when staying at our run-down, roadside motel, we watch
and discuss the two film adaptations. And we spend our sunny days lepping.
The students learn how to catch butterflies, moths, and other insects; how to kill
them (using both Nabokov's preferred method of pinching the thorax and the
less intimate method of placing the catch in a kill jar); how to spread the insects
they catch; and how to identify their specimens.

In his 1957 interview with Boyle, Nabokov remarks, "Butterflies help me
in my writing. Very often when I go [hunting] and there are no butterflies, I
am thinking. I wrote most of *Lolita* this way. I wrote it in motels or parked
cars" (Boyd and Pyle 536). Similarly, engaging in lepidopterological activities
and possessing the heightened awareness of detail that such activities demand
directly affect students' readings and understandings of *Lolita*; in particular,
they allow students to move beyond a purely moral reading of the text and
to consider its aesthetic qualities. As we know, students are often unwilling or
unable to examine *Lolita* apart from its subject matter and are likely to focus on
moral questions derived from the plot. Students who read the text in this manner may be said to resemble the readers Nabokov describes in the afterword
who believe the novel to be "a lewd book" and who, therefore, do not appreciate its stylistic elements: "in pornographic novels, action has to be limited to the
copulation of clichés. Style, structure, imagery should never distract the reader
from his tepid lust" (313).

Style, structure, and imagery—those elements of the text that produce what
Nabokov calls "aesthetic bliss" (314)—do, and indeed should, distract the reader

of any Nabokov text, and *Lolita* is no exception. Nabokov enumerates ten images in the novel that he seems "always to pick out for special delectation" (316); these images are "the nerves of the novel. These are the secret points, the subliminal co-ordinates by means of which the book is plotted" (316). The images Nabokov cites do not move the plot along nor do they concern moral issues; they are not utilitarian. Rather, they are beautiful in their own right and are to be appreciated for the detail and precision with which Nabokov renders them.

One student vividly describes how a knowledge of Lepidoptera can facilitate such a reading of *Lolita*:

> Before this class, I was not aware of the fact that butterflies even had scales, much less that someone would sit down with the intention to count them. I perceived an image, a butterfly, without the awareness that there was a smaller world within that image, a world of scales refracting the light. I really think knowledge of this specific practice drove my reading of *Lolita*. Humbert presented me with this revolting, perverted image of desire. When I look at that image, all I want to do is turn away, but when I look into the smaller parts of that image, I find a world of scales—both metaphorical and judicial. . . . The details, the scales, break up the light cast by the glow of Humbert's desire, and I am left in the refraction, the iridescence of art.

Similarly, when reading *Lolita* while lepping, students must confront, in their own actions, the relation of the moral to the aesthetic that pervades the action of the novel. They desire the butterflies they see—they wish to capture them, to own them, and to preserve them in all their beauty—yet to preserve them, they must kill them. Negotiating this problematic situation enables students, these novice butterfly hunters, to perhaps see Humbert—who, although no lepidopterist, wishes to possess Lolita and to keep her forever in her nymphet state, yet who destroys her childhood—in a different, perhaps more knowing, light.

Lolita as Cultural Archetype:
Teaching a Semester-Long Course on Nabokov's Dolores Haze and Her Descendants

Jason Merrill

The name of Vladimir Nabokov's best-known character has many associations; even a cursory Internet search will reveal how Lolita is commonly understood today (and also raise eyebrows among your network administrators). The media are quick to mention Nabokov's novel in any case involving an older man and an underage girl, and they seem in a rush to crown new Lolitas (e.g., Amy Fisher, the "Long Island Lolita," and Anna Kournikova, the "Lobbing Lolita"). New fashion trends with erotic overtones are named after her (see "Gothic Lolita"; Preissler), as is the Japanese "Lolikon" (Lolita complex; for many more references to Lolita in popular culture, see Stringer-Hye).

Works of literature proclaim connections with Nabokov's famous character on their covers: the 2004 edition of Patricia Highsmith's *The Price of Salt* declares it "[t]he novel that inspired Nabokov's *Lolita*," and Pia Pera's *Lo's Diary* claims to be "[t]he last word on Humbert Humbert and Lolita—from Lolita herself."

It is clear that the name Lolita is today used in contexts far removed from the novel; in fifty years it has assumed a life of its own and grown distant from its source. I outline here a seminar devoted to Dolores Haze, her remakes, and echoes that follow her transformation from the heroine of one of the twentieth century's greatest novels to a worldwide cultural archetype.

In my experience, the course I describe is best taught as a weekly seminar; longer class periods lend themselves well to film screenings, student oral reports, and the intensive discussion often generated by the course topics. If necessary, however, film screenings could be done outside class. I taught the course in a fourteen-week semester, but the Lolita seminar's length could be easily adjusted by adding or removing certain works or by devoting more or less discussion time to them. My suggested readings are not an exhaustive list of Lolita texts but a representative sample with indications of the wide range of questions they raise.

Weeks 1–2: Preparing for Lolita

The first day of class begins with a discussion of students' initial impressions. I ask students to freewrite for five minutes on the following questions: What is a Lolita? Can you think of any examples? Who is Lolita? What is your impression of Nabokov's novel and its content? After going over responses in detail, I ask students to keep them in a safe place so we can revisit them after discussing the novel and again at the end of the course. I have found that students are amazed at how their thoughts on this topic change over the semester.

I ask students to bring to class any references to Lolita they encounter during the semester and also to keep the first day's discussion fresh in their minds, because an important aspect of the seminar is comparing popular perception with the reality of Nabokov's novel.

Next I present students with examples from other fields of the use of the term "Lolita." Russell Trainer and Marianne Sinclair argue that *Lolita* supplies terminology for problems that their fields (psychology and cinema) experienced well before the publication of Nabokov's novel. Much like any Internet search, these books reveal how Dolores Haze has developed from a literary character to a type with a much wider definition.

In the second week students begin their exploration of Nabokov's texts, supplemented by lectures on the author's biography and important themes in his oeuvre. The first book they read is *The Enchanter*, a good starting point because it contains thematic previews of *Lolita* and serves as an excellent introduction to reading Nabokov. Emphasizing Nabokov's insistence on the primacy of details in reading (Boyd, *American Years* 110–11, 264–65, 308–09), I encourage students to scrutinize the text, searching for connections and looking up unfamiliar words.

Instructors who want to include additional instances of the Lolita theme could place Nabokov's *Laughter in the Dark* (1933) on the reading list before *The Enchanter*. Over the course of the semester I assign excerpts from *Strong Opinions*; students greatly enjoy Nabokov's witty nonfiction voice, and many of its pages (5–6, 15–16, 20–26, 47, 49, 52–54, 73, 74, 93–94, 106–07, 123, 159, 165–66, 167, 180, 198, 211–12, 216, 217, 268–79, 285, 294, 304–06) are relevant to *Lolita* and the subsequent controversy it engendered.

Weeks 3–7: Lolita

The seminar strives to strike a balance between treating *Lolita* as a major work of literature and as the source of the Lolita archetype. There are many fruitful ways of approaching it as a work of literature, as discussed elsewhere in this volume. While examining the novel's literary aspects, students should also be looking back to the discussion of the first day of class and thinking about the relations between the novel and the cultural stereotypes. How do Dolores Haze and Humbert Humbert compare with common perceptions of them? *The Enchanter* should also be included in the dialogue, now that similarities and differences can be discussed; is *Lolita* simply a longer, more detailed version of the same basic plot? What is the connection between these two texts?

Another activity relevant to this seminar is the introduction of texts not included in the course reading list that critics have connected with *Lolita*. I take a few minutes of class time to introduce works such as *The Confessions of Victor X* (1912), whose first-person narration and sexual themes supposedly influenced *Lolita*, and Raymond Queneau's *Zazie in the Metro* (1959), in whose precocious, streetwise young heroine many have seen echoes of Dolores Haze. Students enjoy these minilectures and feel they are relevant, because they provide a sense of the wide range of texts that have been associated with *Lolita* and can be used as a springboard to discussion of the themes that connect the texts as well as of Nabokov's use of other texts and others' use of his. Students also appreciate hearing about works to which they otherwise would not be exposed. Although I present these works to the students, instructors could instead ask students to report to their peers about a selected work.

One important aspect of *Lolita* is the controversy that swirled around it at the time of its publication, both among critics and between the author and publisher. The students read F. W. Dupee's surveys of *Lolita's* long road to publication ("'Lolita'"; "Preface") as well as Maurice Girodias's accounts of his "conflict" ("Pornologist"; "Lolita") with Nabokov over publication rights and royalties and also Nabokov's stinging reply ("*Lolita* and Mr. Girodias," republished in *Strong Opinions* 268–79). For a survey of contemporary opinions they also read the collection of reviews from Norman Page's *Nabokov: The Critical Heritage* (81–107). There is much in them that stimulates student reactions, such as Howard Nemerov's description of *Lolita* as a "moral work" (92); Lionel Trilling's insistence that the novel is "not about sex but about love" (95); and claims that the reader comes "virtually . . . to condone the violation it presents" (93).

After examining *Lolita's* critical handling at the time of its publication, students consider a different type of reaction to the novel, the scholarly article. I try to select articles that are not too esoteric and would be of interest to an undergraduate audience. I also want students to gain a sense of the wide range of topics scholars discuss in their work, so I look for articles with varying approaches on diverse themes. Studies by Christina Tekiner (time discrepancies in the novel), Richard H. Bullock (Humbert as character in his own work), Brandon S. Centerwall (Nabokov as conscious pedophile), Gavriel Shapiro (detailed analysis of Dolores's class list) and Diana Butler (butterflies in *Lolita*) work well in this context. I ask students to prepare a two-part class presentation, a summary of the scholar's argument, followed by a critique of that argument (both positive and negative). After discussing their articles and receiving feedback from their classmates, students write a paper based on their presentation; this assignment asks them to think critically about another argument and base their reaction on textual evidence. Often students are reluctant to question anything that has appeared in print, but I remind them that they are quickly becoming *Lolita* experts and know enough to competently question others' opinions.

Weeks 8–10: From Page to Screen (and Back)

Many film versions of Nabokov's works have been made, with varying degrees of success (see Appel, *Nabokov's Dark Cinema*; Wyllie, "Nabokov" and *Nabokov*;

Zimmer, "Nabokov Filmography"). Two directors better known for other films have attempted to translate *Lolita* to film: Stanley Kubrick (1962) and Adrian Lyne (1997). Before viewing the films I ask the class to consider some general questions about the novel-to-film transition. Can a film successfully be made from a novel? How? Kubrick once said, "If it can be written or thought, it can be filmed" (Corliss 19)—do students agree? Why do we always seem to say the book is better than the film? Whom would students cast in the leading roles? What special problems does *Lolita* pose to filmmakers? Do Kubrick and Lyne address those problems, and if so, how?

Before students view the films, it is useful to supply them with information about the many versions of screenplays and other obstacles each director faced in the light of the controversial nature of the source (for Kubrick, see Boyd, *American Years* 387; Corliss; and Nelson; for Lyne, see Stephen Schiff x–xxix; Hudgins).

Class discussion can examine each film as a work of art and as an adaptation of *Lolita* and ask comparative questions: Which is a better film and why? Which is a better representation of *Lolita* and why? Does either of them capture the spirit of the novel? Who better plays Humbert Humbert, James Mason or Jeremy Irons? I like to ask open-ended questions and allow students to determine the criteria for terms such as "better." Many students agree with Tom Stoppard, who, speaking of the many failed attempts to bring Nabokov's novels to the screen, declared, "I don't think anybody's cracked Nabokov yet" (Kobel).

Students are able to compare what Nabokov wanted on the screen with what actually appears there by reading Nabokov's own screenplay, written for the Kubrick project but not used. Nabokov intended not to film pieces cut from the novel but to reinvent the novel for the screen, and differences between the screenplay and the novel abound. Students, who by now know the text of *Lolita* well, enjoy searching for such differences and discussing their potential success in a film version of *Lolita*.

Week 11: Lolita *on Stage*

Edward Albee is another familiar figure who adapted *Lolita*, perhaps with even less success than Kubrick and Lyne. Instead of producing a film version, he attempted to make a play from the novel. Despite the presence of well-known actors such as Donald Sutherland (as Humbert Humbert), Albee's dramatic version ran only twelve days (it premiered on 19 March 1981) and is not considered one of his better plays. It resorts to graphic discussions of sex and the use of obscenities and lacks almost everything that makes *Lolita* a great work of art. The play's weaknesses further convince students of the greatness of Nabokov's novel.

Another *Lolita* remake for the stage is Alan Jay Lerner's 1971 musical, *Lolita, My Love*, which is worth mentioning to the students, if only for asking them how (or why) one would make a musical of the novel (for background, see Proffer,

"Profit," and Nabokov's reply, *Strong Opinions* 217). The musical had a shorter run than Albee's play, and while Lerner's script has not been published, songs such as "Tell Me, Tell Me" and "In the Broken Promise Land of Fifteen" were recorded and are available on albums of Lerner's songs. Students are amused by lyrics such as "A demi-Delilah / A guileless beguiler" and "Dante exploded / As Petrarch and Poe did / And this is the story / In all its nymphic glory" (Corliss 16). They also enjoy trying to picture the *Lolita* opera, written by Rodion Shchedrin, which premiered in 1994 and is occasionally performed today.

Week 12: Plagiarism or Artistic License?

Pera's *Lo's Diary* raises important issues concerning copyright laws, artistic license versus plagiarism, and the nature of literary characters (are they the property of the author, or do they live in the public domain?). I conduct an initial discussion on these topics before the students read *Lo's Diary*, because I suspect the poor quality of this book will affect their opinions. Somewhat permissive before reading the novel, afterward students often feel that borrowing authors have a responsibility to create a work with some literary value and wish that a committee could be established to grant or deny permission to use others' characters. Pera would not have received their approval. *Lo's Diary*, like Albee's play, students agree, is an important text to read because of the questions it raises, not because of any intrinsic literary value.

Pera's lawyers claimed that *Lo's Diary* was a parody of *Lolita* and therefore protected by laws allowing the use of similar characters and plots for such works. Should the authors of parodies be allowed the use of existing literary material that authors of other types of works cannot legally use? Do students see *Lo's Diary* as a parody? How is it different from a book like Emily Prager's *Roger Fishbite*, which the author herself has described as "a literary parody of *Lolita*" and which her publisher advertises as "the revenge of Lolita" (http://www.randomhouse.co.uk)? Why has Prager's work experienced none of the legal trouble Pera's did? At what point does a literary work become a parody of another, and what constitutes acceptable use of existing characters and situations?

Weeks 13–14: Echoes of Lolita

At the end of the semester we examine texts that contain echoes of and references to *Lolita*; students enjoy the detective work of discovering the connections and are also pleased that the texts are of higher quality than Albee's or Pera's. The name of the heroine of Sam Mendes's *American Beauty*, Angela Hayes, suggests that the film's many other parallels with Nabokov's novel are not coincidence: it is a murder mystery set in suburban America narrated by a man approaching middle age who is infatuated with a teenaged girl. Lester Burnham, the narrator, develops his story as a search for beauty, and photographs and memory play an important role. Students view and interpret *American Beauty* differently after their experience with *Lolita* and enjoy having inside knowledge of the film's subtext.

After watching *American Beauty*, students read Donald Harington's *Ekaterina*, which, the back cover claims, "is a wicked turn on Nabokov's most celebrated novel" and which does have several direct and numerous subtle references to Nabokov. Harington echoes *Lolita* on a large scale (Ekaterina Vladimirovna is also an émigré who plays chess, drinks, and travels across the country in the company of a young child of the opposite sex) and in many details (e.g., a comic struggle for a pistol [342] and a character's exclamation that "all we have are words" [83]). The allusions to *Lolita* are done in a playful manner somewhat reminiscent of Nabokov's style.

Harington's novel challenges and entertains students and leads well into a general summary discussion of the semester. The "process of vulgarization" of the name Lolita began almost immediately after the novel's publication; Brian Boyd recounts Nabokov's shock when in 1958 a "little girl of eight or nine came to his door for candy on Halloween, dressed up by her parents as Lolita," replete with a sign reading "L-O-L-I-T-A" (*American Years* 373). The vulgarization continues unabated today; students consider why this has happened and what, if anything, there is in Nabokov's novel to support such a development. What does it say about society and the place of art and literary characters within it?

Russian-Language Lolita

My course does not have a Russian-language component, but one could be easily added. As George L. Cummins's and Carl R. Proffer's articles titled "Nabokov's Russian *Lolita*" show, Nabokov did not translate *Lolita* into Russian word for word but rather reinvented entire parts in an attempt to retain the style and feel of the English original. Students with knowledge of both languages could complete projects on Nabokov's rendering of his "record of [his] love affair" with the "English language" into Russian (V. Nabokov, "On a Book" 316). Alexander D. Nakhimovsky and S. Paperno provide a good reference source for such research. Those wishing to read *Lolita*-spawned texts in Russian will not be disappointed; one example is Boris Nosik's *Pionerskaia Lolita* ("Pioneer Lolita"), in which a "humble bibliographer" ends up working as a counselor in a Pioneer camp, where "he falls in loves with a young Pioneer, but does not follow in the steps of Nabokov's Humbert" (back cover).

Why Teach a Lolita Seminar?

While the topic may seem controversial, there are strong arguments for including a seminar on *Lolita* in a university or college curriculum. It is far from a traditional literature course, and it will answer the demand at many institutions for interdisciplinary courses, because it touches on Russian and Western European literature, American studies, film, theater, politics, sociology, and popular culture; feminist and other approaches could be included, depending on what the individual instructor chooses to add to its flexible model. The seminar requires students to wrestle with many types of texts, such as novels, films, theater, popular literature, critical reviews, and scholarly articles. Current events also come into play, because inevitably every semester *Lolita* is mentioned in connection with cases of pornography or freedom of speech. Students are sometimes asked to examine these texts in great detail and other times must grapple with related larger questions such as censorship and an author's rights to a character. Students must react to these texts in a range of ways, not just in the traditional literature paper. I assign various papers and oral reports. The first paper is a standard five-page paper on *Lolita*; the second asks students to summarize and react to a scholar's argument about the novel; the third asks students to argue which of the film versions of *Lolita* is closer to the spirit of the novel or to compare Nabokov's screenplay and novel; in the fourth essay students consider the ethical issues surrounding *Lo's Diary*; and in the final paper they write about the role *Lolita* plays in Harington's *Ekaterina*. They are asked to make several oral presentations, including initial thoughts on the paper topics and others designed to facilitate class discussion. The flexibility of the course adds to its interdisciplinary value; it could be taught by faculty members from different departments, who could all add their emphases (e.g., in text selection) to the basic model. While at first glance it might seem unlikely that an entire semester could be spent studying *Lolita*, such a course can be a valuable, entertaining, intellectually challenging, and memorable offering in any curriculum.

Teaching *Lolita* in (a) Consuming Culture (a Seminar in Cultural Studies)

Tania Roy and John Whalen-Bridge

Consumption Models: Aesthetic Bliss, Freedom Banner, and Forbidden Fruit

Our students at the National University of Singapore understand their national identity as particularly marked by consumption; the "five Cs" of Singaporean identity refer to the status symbols cash, a credit card, a car, a condominium, and a country-club membership. The (only slightly) ironic embrace of consumer identity is a mark of national pride in having moved far beyond colonial origins, and in our course Consuming Culture attention to this detail begins our work of suggesting to our English majors that consumption is not merely something that business or law school students do. *Lolita* is an especially rewarding text for our approach, since the disgust Humbert Humbert often expresses about American consumerism may even—when the students go beyond their initial resistance to this kind of approach—turn inside out and consume itself.

A cultural studies approach, insofar as it adopts a critical stance toward conventional assumptions about reading and other modes of intellectual consumption, requires a bit of theoretical preparation before we begin to discuss the primary text, *Lolita*. When introducing students to consumption models, we mean to indicate the ways a given text can be put to use in a given culture. Through an overview of key theoretical perspectives in the study of consumption, we present cultural studies strategically, beginning with topics like shopping, advertising, and the cultural leveling of the distinction between high art and commodities through mass media.

Students bring to our class (a two-hour large lecture-discussion meeting and one hour of discussion in a smaller group each week) some familiarity with Theodor Adorno and Max Horkheimer's essay attacking "the culture industry." Just to test the waters, we begin with a loose discussion of the difference between culture and industry before we pass out a handout consisting of a few trenchant paragraphs from the essay. After students have read the handout, we introduce them to theorists such as Roland Barthes (on advertising and false choice [*Mythologies*]), Walter Benjamin (on shopping and on the arcade as a precursor to the mall), and Michel de Certeau (on everyday activities as a means for reclaiming autonomy from organized commerce and politics). We ask them to compare these theorists on consumption as a tactic for recuperating the organized spaces of contemporary urban life. Some students ask for accessible historical and critical overviews of these models, and we have found John Storey's *Cultural Consumption and Everyday Life* a useful supplementary text. Topically focused supplementary material can also be found in Pasi Falk and Colin Campbell's *The Shopping Experience*.

These various models guide students through a series of critical debates on the relation between consumption and the production of social meaning in everyday life. This initial review exposes students to the foundational concerns of cultural studies; we stress that these readings anticipate Nabokov's parodic description of postwar American consumerism, priming students to connect texts later in the course.

A lively debate on the politics of choice and exploitation in consumer societies usually concludes our theoretical section. Shopping with a credit card (lightly regarded as the national pastime of Singapore) and the experience of walking or traveling through urban spaces like the mall, the motel, or, indeed, the Singaporean food court are revealed as unrecognized forms of consumption. With a bit of prompting, students also learn to see ways in which consumption, not unlike the production and interpretation of art works, is creative.

Once students start to open up their notions of consumption, we are able to connect cultural studies approaches to *Lolita*. The novel itself can be at once a symbol of cavalier intellectual freedom in America and, in Singapore, a highly entertaining anthropological document about life in America. It testifies across contexts to the experience of an increasingly globalized middle class; to the material comforts and contradictions of safe suburban spaces; or to canny adolescent knowledge of markets, commodities, desire, and gratification. The novel is not exactly the same product in each of these contexts. To give our (non-American) students confidence in approaching a foreign text, we ask them to consider the fact that Nabokov, a transplanted Russian, creates his imaginary world through the recollections of a foreigner, Humbert Humbert. Humbert Humbert sexually consumes the nymphet Lolita, Humbert and Lolita consume the American landscape as they tour the country, and Charlotte Haze attempts to assimilate the immigrant Humbert. Consumption appears in metaphoric and literal guises. We are pleased if students pick up the idea that the book is at once a representation and an act of consumption, but if they do not, we nudge them toward the point through Socratic questioning.

Surprisingly, students often have more trouble consuming Nabokov than they do Adorno. *Lolita* is one of the most challenging texts many undergraduate students will read, and we ask our students to explain which parts of the narrative (and which of the theoretical texts) require more effort. The extreme erudition of Nabokov's allusions, whether drawn from high or low cultural strata, challenges students. Some students may complain about Nabokov's claim that only "aesthetic bliss" matters ("On a Book" 314); they wonder if Nabokov is an amoralist. We bring the problems of polymathic reference and ironized morality together by drawing attention to the material embodiment of the text—to the book itself. We assign the annotated text for our class but take the opportunity to point out that different embodiments of the text—the Olympia Press edition, the standard Vintage edition, and the Vintage annotated student edition—generate widely different meanings and associations, even though the printed words are roughly identical. Rather than rest with the realization that such a finely crafted and brilliantly allusive novel is an important dietary supplement for malnourished young minds (the Hirsch-Bloom model of cultural literacy), Consuming Culture examines the role of the text within a larger cultural food chain: moving from readerly consumption of the text to representations of consumption in the text, students practice understanding consumption as a thoroughly dialogic model of cultural exchanges.

Next, we point out that not everyone reads the story we are discussing. Different forms (e.g., films) presume possibly divergent, possibly overlapping audiences. Students are asked to consider some of the ways *Lolita* and Lolita are consumed. Initially students state that readers read the book (or see the movie). They are then asked to judge the book by its cover: after looking carefully at the packaging and labeling of the product for clues about the intended audience, they are asked whether the cover and various manifestations of "Lolitaness" (e.g., Internet references and filmic versions and allusions) match up with the ideal consumer supposed by Nabokov in "On a Book Entitled *Lolita.*"

We then shift into a close-reading activity to set up the class discussion that will follow, breaking a seminar of twenty or so students into about five groups. We ask each group to work out a view of how consumption exists in the novel and how, if at all, this consumption is analogous to our own activity as readers. After the whole class comes together to discuss their findings, we follow up with questions about who produces the cultural stereotype of a Lolita, a too-young girl who is cast as temptress. Did Nabokov invent this figure? Is he the messenger who reveals the predatory side of American literary liberalism? Does anyone who consumes a book or an idea have an inner Humbert, and are readers who experience "aesthetic bliss" permitting a kind of symbolic pedophilia? Such proleptic questions are put forward as teasers to arouse strong responses, which, after brief discussion, are put on the back burner: we wish to delay a full engagement with the ethical question until we have covered a few more aspects of the novel.

In small-group discussions, students note with interest that the Vintage edition has the photograph of a young girl on the cover, taken from the hips down. Some students will make the connection between the novel as a representation of consumption and the reader's own secondhand consumption of Lolita's beauty. We ask students to connect this point to Nabokov's afterword, "On a Book Entitled *Lolita,*" and the fictional foreword by the professorial pedant John Ray, Jr. If we see these texts as labels on or advertisements for the product, what do the texts cover, and what do they uncover? The danger of this exercise is that students will moralize too quickly in a way that shorts the circuit between consumption in the text and our own consumption of its images.

The *Vanity Fair* blurb on the cover of the Vintage edition, "The only convincing love story of our century," is of interest, especially in relation to the visual image: clearly there is a tension between motivations, at least as far as the marketing department is concerned. *The Annotated* Lolita has no photo-graph on the cover, and this absence is accompanied by comparisons of Nabo-kov, James Joyce, and Herman Melville, as well as "recondite materials" and "elaborate verbal textures." "So," we coyly ask, "is *Lolita* a sexy book?" Some students argue that you cannot judge a book by its cover, stating that the text is the same whatever the blurb rhetoric might indicate. Some students disagree, arguing that the allusive textures, witty Humbertian commentaries, and artful repetitions are simply ways to cover the tracks of desire: we are, through our reading, consuming illicit sexuality, even if we have the permit of elite culture in hand. This is an occasion to discuss briefly the publication history of the novel, including the first French edition, in 1955, and the publication of long excerpts in the *Anchor Review* in 1957. Nabokov's account of the French publication, "*Lolita* and Mr. Girodias," is recommended. We believe that a direct approach to arcane matters such as publication history will be much more successful if we motivate student interest by connecting ethereal text to marketing realities: the publication of *Lolita* was conditioned, at several steps, by concerns about the novel's sexual content.

Since students are generally unfamiliar with America's struggles over censor-ship in the 1950s and early 1960s, we include secondary readings such as Charles Rembar's *The End of Obscenity* (an account by an anticensorship lawyer of the trials over the publication of *Lady Chatterley's Lover*, *Tropic of Cancer*, and *Fanny Hill*), with the expectation that each student will read Nabokov carefully and review the secondary material and then make his or her findings available to the class. We ask students to post responses to at least one of these readings on our online forum. Other secondary texts for this exercise include Lynn Hunt's collection *The Invention of Pornography*, James Kincaid's *Child-Loving: The Erotic Child and Victorian Culture*, and Roger Shattuck's *Forbidden Knowl-edge: From Prometheus to Pornography*. Writings parodied by Nabokov, such as the Kinsey reports, and pulp fiction by authors such as Mickey Spillane are also helpful. Students can look at cinematic versions of *Lolita*, as well as other nymphocentric movies such as *Pretty Baby* or *American Beauty*, or search the term "Lolita" on the Internet and report on the embodiment of this signifier. The list of popular culture references on Zembla (e.g., the song "Don't Stand So Close to Me," by The Police) is another valuable secondary source, as is *Reading* Lolita *in Tehran*, by Azar Nafisi, in which the novel *Lolita* figures as a voice of freedom within a totalitarian culture. Students are asked to relate the signifier "Lolita" to each of these texts and their implied contexts. We close this section with the question, What meanings does the word "Lolita" generate in Singapore?

To bring this centripetal exercise back to a center, we assign students a three- to five-page essay, due the week after discussion of *Lolita* has been com-pleted. Their assignment is to read the conservative commentator Norman Podhoretz's review essay "'Lolita,' My Mother-in-Law, the Marquis de Sade, and Larry Flynt" in relation to Nabokov's afterword and other similar materials the students have read; examine the various ways concerns about obscenity and pornography impinge on the consumption of literature; and assess Nabokov's defense of "aesthetic bliss" in relation to communal issues. We also lecture a bit on *Lolita* as a revisionary text that returns to established literary frameworks such as the confessional memoir and the road novel and consider intertextual relations with authors such as Edgar Allan Poe, Marcel Proust, and the artist Aubrey Beardsley.

Escaping the "Art or Ethics" Dilemma through a Focus on Consumption

Class discussion of the text in relation to notions of obscenity turns on students' understanding of the ways in which this portion of the American cultural food pyramid has grown dramatically in the postwar years: large swaths of high and popular culture have become saturated with sexual imagery in ways that they were not in the first half of the century, and texts such as *Lolita* are often associated with this cultural change. *Lolita* anticipates and, to some degree, authorizes the infusion of sexual desire into various expressive forms, and so Consuming Culture structures approaches to this novel in ways that foreground the changing status of obscenity within culture. After considering Nabokov's novel in relation to terms such as *obscenity, pornography*, and *censorship*, class discussion shifts from sex as an object of cultural consumption to sex as symbol, perhaps symptom, of larger patterns of cultural consumption.

In our experience, the concern with obscenity in this novel remains both consistent and permeable, shifting through class discussion in terms such as *pornography, literature*, and *consumption* (of which the idealized adolescent body is both object and consuming subject). The linkage between sexual exploitation and the pleasures of consuming (and even of being consumed) should be acknowledged as both compelling and elusive for the student at any level of instruction. We choose to delay addressing the question of Lolita's violation until we have established consumption as a particularly effective, if oblique, entry into a discussion of Humbert's crime. An exposition of the text through a focus on the topic of consumption eventually returns students to the ethical elephant in the room, but from there we may return to the larger themes of the class, in particular to a critical consideration of perspectives that would link advertising and obscenity with the politics of sexual exploitation.

In our lectures, we call attention to the novel's deliberate and ironic emphasis on consumerism, presenting it as Nabokov's attempt to defamiliarize and make visible the everyday world of consumer culture. Lectures begin from initial contributions to class discussions of *Lolita*, which typically turn on the tension between the aesthetic and moral value of the text. We illustrate this point by asking groups to locate the most entertaining passages and then to discuss the ethical and aesthetic tensions of their selections. Are ethics and art at odds?

Most students detect a tension. Students at this point are invited to reflect on how the historical concern with obscenity continues to govern the terms of their own debate, where the putative pleasures of representing and consuming child abuse are iterated through various revealing assumptions about art, sexual freedom, and consumption. This preoccupation may be quickly identified in the reader's impulse to rescue the text or in a student's wish to charge the text with subtle crimes. Typically, defenses of *Lolita* are articulated through didactic arguments. These include variations inflected by feminist intuitions, in which the immorality of the novel's content is not redeemed just because it is revealed through art. Aesthetic defenses sometimes voice the idea that meaningful art involves a radical emancipation from taboo: the *jouissance* of reading *Lolita* depends on its fictional transgression of sexual and cultural norms.

Having discussed cultural studies theory, packaging, and the ethical pressures that bear on a reader's consumption of the text, we turn our attention to academic responses and focus in particular on feminist apprehensions of consumption. Introducing students to excerpts from literary criticism at this point in class raises the level of discussion substantially. Students are quick to discover how such commentary repeats the terms of their own debate, a situation that the fictional foreword anticipates and deflates through a defense that is simultaneously moral and artistic. When students begin to notice how John Ray, Jr., has beat them to the punch, they become somewhat self-conscious but also intriguingly critical of the motives of literary critics. In this way, students become alert to the predicament of reading. A nonideological reading of *Lolita* (and perhaps of literature generally) begins to seem impossible.

A focus on consumption in relation to plot provides a particularly effective escape from this bind. We have students consider passages from Rachel Bowlby's *Shopping with Freud*, a concise, accessible, and lively exploration that historicizes the text and situates the advertising clichés of *Lolita* within more obvious literary-erotic ground from Poe through Baudelaire and Proust. Bowlby treats the image of Lolita as the twentieth-century ideal of youthful, aestheticized perfection and helps us show how cultural studies and conventional literary history can work together.

In our view, the dichotomy between literature and its others (pornographic reprehensibility, advertising clichés, but also morality) is, effectively, a rehearsal of the question of consumerism: in Nabokov's imagination the pleasures of boundless consumption weave together the novel's treatment of eroticism, a particular cultural aesthetic of adolescent perfection, and even the politics of sexual exploitation. Indeed, the centrality of consumption within the novel is easily demonstrated on a first reading. Lolita, the quintessential consumer, can only be discovered within the trappings of suburban American vulgarity, and so she performs as a deliberate antithesis to the European narrator's (self-established) cultural superiority. Such an entry into the text is pedagogically useful, insofar as it both requires and clearly orients the task of close reading. In group discussion, students are asked to explore various iterations of this opposition through their own close reading. Our lectures help manifest the dichotomies that run through the text, those that divide elite literature from popular culture and Europe from America. The anthropology of limitless cultural debasement appears but is not necessarily antithetical to a parodic account of cultural estrangement and redemption. The aesthetic delay of literature as opposed to pornography arises from a rejection of the short circuit of immediate gratification in consumption, and yet the novel challenges taboos in ways that have, historically, expanded the possibilities of literary consumption. Each of these dichotomies is explored in small-group discussion; each group must select an appropriate passage and then account for Nabokov's development of ideological tension within its images and sentences.

Lolita's plot takes the reader through the theme park landscape of America, but this perspective is made available only through often hackneyed images of Europe. Students are asked to enumerate the topography of contrived life—America as represented through Humbert's account—to examine how deliberate clichés and stilted cultural frames (both literary and cinematic) are an indispensable bridge to whatever "aesthetic bliss" this novel has to offer. The class is now in a position to consider how *Lolita* unmakes the implied difference between the highbrow work of art and the "Komfy Kabins" package-tour rhetoric it often parodies. The derivative aspect of the landscape—its simulated life, reproduced through the seriality of its names—may at first strike students as applicable only to America. Our lectures and small-group assignments reveal how the text undermines the view it seems most clearly, on first reading, to undergird. America is discovered to be not a New World opposed to its European origins but rather a quilt made of a European's stereotypes of it. Humbert accepts the American landscape "with a shock of amused recognition because of those painted oilcloths which were imported from America in the old days to be hung above washstands in Central-European nurseries" (152).

The astute (or skeptical) student may object that, because of the defamiliarizing force of literary quotation, the distinction between kitsch and art is still implicit, even if art is now an occasion for comedy or nostalgia. If the rhetoric of advertising is ostensibly derided through Humbert's literary pretensions, in effect it hijacks his own version of events. There is poetry in *Lolita*'s rhetorical use of the dominant language of consumption—advertising—that resists and works against the direction of the narrator's view of things. We ask students to consider and debate a point that would have been unthinkable at the outset, namely that the ubiquity of advertising in *Lolita* provides an appropriate point of identification with Lolita's own desires and exigencies: "[t]he words 'novelties and souvenirs' simply entranced her by their trochaic lilt. . . . She it was to whom ads were dedicated: the ideal consumer, the subject and object of every foul poster" (148).

Some students resist this deconstructive turn; some embrace it. Their varied responses to the novel help them better understand what is at stake when questions of difficult language arise in debates about cultural studies. For some students, Lolita is the ideal consumer; she is also like us, like the reader of poetry or literature. She is unmoved by things as they really are and is entranced by words that present pictures of her particular desires, promissory images that are fulfilled every time in an act of consumption. Our lectures suggest that Lolita, in her adolescent perfection, is iconic of the literary love-object. Her world of glossy advertisements and one-liner logos are, according to this view, a culmination of a poetic tradition. The question arises, If Lolita levels the distinction between the world of advertising and the world of literature, does her presence promise the termination of literature altogether? Or does Nabokov's idea that all literature is a kind of fairy tale rescue his celebration of Lolita from cultural apocalypse? Students, more or less ironically, judge for themselves whether advertising contaminates the purity and originality of poetry in *Lolita* by intruding on Humbert's lyric perceptions, or whether poetry is rediscovered (as de Certeau or Benjamin would have us believe) as the everyday aestheticization of commodified cultural norms. Students later write essays, since a longer form of response allows for a more developed sense of the stakes involved.

Lolita *and Choice*

When our students have finished reading part 2, we ask them to consolidate the approaches considered so far before moving on to a discussion of cultural analysis that will prepare them for their own assignments. An important point to review at this juncture is that gender- and class-based presuppositions tend to condition views of apparently independent cultural objects, *Lolita* being a case in point. Approaching the novel as a dirty book rather than a literary masterpiece formats subsequent evaluations, but this view can lead to a rather dull determinism. Communities of interpreters consciously frame texts according to their interests, and *Lolita* has been used as an important symbol in various cultural struggles. In relation to this point, students are invited to consider Pamela Steinle's *In Cold Fear*, a study of the cold war censorship battles over *The Catcher in the Rye*. This secondary reading helps Singaporean students understand why seemingly innocuous books like J. D. Salinger's *Catcher* or Mark Twain's *Huckleberry Finn* have been censored as much as *Lolita*: culturally cavalier attitudes may have as much or more to do with attacks on the novel as any sexual representation does.

Here we pause to have students take stock and regroup. We ask them to reflect on cultural studies as a discipline in relation to both high and low cultural objects. Lolita—poster child for what Adorno once decried as advertising for advertising's sake (163)—is the contemporary ideal for the poetic pursuit of youthful feminine perfection. Does the market ideal of freedom as a vibrant commodity mean that no crime is committed against Lolita? There are always students who argue that *Lolita* is a story of volition rather than violence, that Lolita gets what she wants in the play of mutual manipulation and seduction.

Students are asked to reflect not just on the ethical dimensions of Humbert Humbert's machinations, which require less analysis, but also on what conditions underwrite Lolita's own situation. Is Lolita's personal tragedy intrinsic to the logic of consumer society at large, so that the construction and management of feminine pleasure in consumer society are linked, necessarily, to exploitation?

Final essay topics return students to their pretheoretical intuitions about Lolita's exploitation. Students are given a choice of topics, are expected to comment critically on their particular interpretations of the text, and are asked to situate close readings within the broader topic of the seminar. Accordingly, we ask students to engage *Lolita* with classic statements on the culture industry (where compulsions of the market are internalized in bodily desire, so that the exercise of choice in consumer cultures, from this standpoint, is empty). Alternatively selections from Betty Friedan's *Feminine Mystique* and feminist commentaries on *Lolita* such as Linda Kauffman's "Framing *Lolita*: Is There a Woman in the Text?" are set together, and students are invited to assess the drama of *Lolita* in the light of these analyses of bodily desire, the market, and the rhetoric of advertising. Critical assumptions explored during the course may be rejected or revised through close(r) readings.

By reading *Lolita* in relation to philosophical links between consumerism and the production of cultural meaning, students are able to gain insight into the potentials of these models and their contradictions. Such a contrapuntal approach helps students appreciate the intricate relations among identity, sexuality, pleasure, and power in the novel. By parodying the theater of everyday life through representations of its mise-en-scène, consumption, *Lolita* textualizes and estranges us from this otherwise familiar realm, as do essays by Barthes, Benjamin, or de Certeau. As students begin to see parallels between the ways in which the two kinds of text defamiliarize in order to renew, estrangement in both literature and cultural criticism takes on new meanings. By taking students on a tour of commodified banality, *Lolita* historicizes but also reenchants everyday life, revealing it as both tragic and magical.

Teaching *Lolita* with Dostoevsky and Poe in Mind

Dale E. Peterson

Whatever else it is, the elegant memoir written in fifty-six days of legal captivity under the "bizarre cognomen" Humbert Humbert must be seen as a highly self-conscious performance in the tradition of the literary confession (3). Like its author's pseudonym, H. H.'s pretrial testimonial is a cunningly masked exercise in the doublespeak of confessional discourse. In its performed rehearsal of guilt, Peter Brooks writes, the speech act of confession simultaneously exonerates and inculpates the defendant (22). Since elaborate self-explanation only further incriminates the speaker, Humbert's own rhetoric, in its plethora of evasions, becomes his "tangle of thorns" (9). Moreover, when Humbert addresses his readers as ladies and gentlemen of the jury, every word he writes is pitched in anticipation of a judgmental response. Humbert Humbert would thus seem to be caught in a discursive dilemma very familiar to readers of Fyodor Dostoevsky. As Mikhail Bakhtin reminds us, the uneasy defendant's posture of "confessional self-definition with a loophole" is everywhere in evidence among Dostoevsky's unattractive and slippery narrators (233). Presumably Humbert, the suave and literate European, would prefer to place himself in better company. In America, Humbert chooses an appropriately native bard to decorate his dolorous tale.

Readers of *Lolita* cannot help recognizing Edgar Allan Poe as the most conspicuous source of allusions in Humbert's polished account of his fatal attraction for the living facsimile of his Riviera love, Annabel Leigh (see Appel, Notes 330–33; Maddox 72–76; Proffer, *Keys* 34–45). As the recuperated image of an initial girl-child found and fondled in "a princedom by the sea," Humbert's Lolita is consciously evoked as a found poem, a warm-blooded incarnation of a haunting poetic echo (9). Humbert's trial notes consistently put a "Poe-etic" gloss on prosaic crimes like pedophilia and the murder of a hated "double." Wielding his pen to save his soul rather than his head, Humbert performs an act of lyrical conjury that transforms the prepubescent Dolores Haze into the imaginary Lolita who can forever be immortalized in durable pigments. Seeking security in the refuge of art, Humbert offers his accusers the tempting fruit of his criminal passion, the embalmed image of an archetypal form of loveliness. The text known as "Lolita, or the Confession of a White Widowed Male" is a skillful, indeed seductive, example of the fine art of copping a plea.

Humbert's prison memoir is, then, a sophisticated appeal for the reader's clemency and complicity on behalf of a penitent "nympholept" (17). But every sentence penned by Humbert also belongs to Vladimir Nabokov, who has created the prose and poses that compose the rhetorical performance of the self-styled prisoner of love. *Lolita* is thus a double-voiced discourse to an extent that far exceeds Humbert's own capacity for deliberate chicanery and deceit. Nabokov's novel impersonates the self-betraying discourse of an exemplary transgressor, much like Poe's criminal soliloquizers and Dostoevsky's miserable monologists. Nabokov the ventriloquist feeds Humbert the seductive sentences of a lyrical dementia that is for some readers quite contagious, composing a text replete with scenes that one might aptly "accuse of a sensuous existence of their own," despite John Ray, Jr.'s conviction that only "a certain type of mind might call [them] 'aphrodisiac'" (5, 4). An aesthetic and moral intelligence too supple for Ray's naive and didactic mind to grasp has conceived the alluring textual body of *Lolita*. How, though, might one separate Nabokov's voice from the articulate voicings of his creature Humbert, the self-serving apologist of transgressive romantic passion? That is the knotty question I ask my students to untangle.

There is a good deal of literary precedent behind the symptomatic linguistic pathology that is put on display in Nabokov's *Lolita*. By way of prologue to *Lolita* in my course The Literature of Madness, I assign texts beyond those which figure in Humbert's deliberate allusions to Poe. I pay particular attention to Poe's hyperarticulate narrators in such criminally insane monologues as "The Black Cat" and "The Tell-Tale Heart." In those grisly tales, Poe exposes not only the ill-concealed nervousness and strained logic of guilt-laden consciences but also the obsessive, homicidal projection of self-hatred onto mirror images of the self (the cloyingly domesticated cat; the shrouded eye/I of a watchful old man). Another pair of gruesome Poe monologues, "Berenice" and "Ligeia," features neurasthenic, supersensitive narrators whose intensity of interest feeds vampirishly on certain ineffable characteristics of loved ones who are drained of vitality by such unwonted attention. The narrator of "Ligeia" strives vainly to define precisely the hidden secret of his beloved's attractiveness, parsing her body like a mystic text to find proof of Lord Bacon's theorem: "There is no exquisite beauty without some *strangeness* in the proportions" (*Complete Tales* 655). Poe's narrator, Humbert-like, ghoulishly superimposes the features of his lost Ligeia onto the second wife, who replaces Ligeia in his bridal chamber (see Peterson, "Nabokov").

Humbert, who so memorably introduces himself to his readers as a visionary artist and madman, the "nympholept" who can discern "by ineffable signs . . . and other indices which despair and shame and tears of tenderness forbid me to tabulate—the little deadly demon among the wholesome children" (17), is kinsman to Poe's maudlin connoisseurs of refined perceptions. Humbert's bathetic self-presentation as a "lone voyager" and "enchanted hunter" of esoteric pleasures is intended, like the plangent appeals of Poe's monomaniacs, to attract the compassion (and envy) of the insufficiently imaginative reader. As in Poe's monologues, however, the fancy prose style barely cloaks something murderous. It is no mere coincidence that Humbert's elegant cri de coeur has at its center, like Poe's *Tales of the Grotesque and Arabesque*, rather lurid sexual aberrations and an ill-concealed hostility toward despised doubles (Quilty and Gaston Godin).

Yet nothing in Poe's prose can quite match the confidence, the controlled wit, the tonal volatility of Humbert's confession. And that is why I ask my students to read Dostoevsky's major confessional monologues before reading *Lolita*. "Notes from the Underground" and "A Gentle Creature" display Dostoevsky's genius for capturing the inextricable contradictions, the elaborate rationalizations that result when propositions about the self are embedded in sentences that perform the anxieties of an ever-vigilant self-consciousness. Dostoevsky presides over the self-canceling assertions of the underground man's wounded ego and the guilty widower's battered self-respect. In each confession, the narrator desperately clings to romantic ideas about heroic repudiations of rational self-interest only to have shameful traces of compulsive and self-destructive behavior emerge in the autobiographical testimony. Despite his announced contempt for Dostoevsky, Nabokov kept returning in his own fiction to the precedent of the extended confessional monologue (see Connolly, "Madness"; Peterson, "White (K)nights"). And he never returns to it more effectively than in *Lolita*, where the supremely self-conscious style of interaction with his readers makes suspect every pretense of sincere confession Humbert attempts. Elizabeth Bruss gives a shrewd account of Humbert's syntactic undoing (which applies equally well to Dostoevsky's monologists): "The glance with which he fixes his readers, the alternate accusations and supplications which reach out to us from his pages, are unhealthy, symptomatic of everything he would deny about himself" (157).

As a practical exercise in uncovering Nabokov's subversive presence within Humbert's carefully monitored manipulative prose, I ask my students to pay particularly close attention to two of Humbert's bravura performances of strategic self-defense. As a first exhibit, I put before them the notorious scene of "innocent" stolen pleasure—Humbert's carefully engineered "lap-dance" with Dolores Haze—in part 1, chapter 13. Humbert makes a direct appeal to his reader's maturity and sophistication: "I want my learned readers to participate in the scene I am about to replay; I want them to examine its every detail . . . viewed with what my lawyer has called, in a private talk we have had, 'impartial sympathy'" (57). Note that the bold invitation to cross-examine the testimony has a proviso attached to it; the reader is asked to participate in a scandalous encounter but also to rise to the oxymoronic height of "impartial sympathy." Next, Humbert quite literally sets the scene with a main character, "Humbert the Hummer," being approached in a sunlit living room with a "candy-striped davenport" by a little painted lady, pretty in pink with a "banal, Eden-red apple" (57–58). These are the props with which situation comedies are staged, and clever Humbert knows it well. The reader, presumably charmed and morally disarmed, is now prepared to play voyeur as Humbert replays the grapple for the apple that leads to the "magic friction" and the prolonged release (in breathless run-on sentences) of Humbert's "hidden tumor of unspeakable passion" as he grasps the "safely solipsized" Lolita (59, 60). Humbert's allegedly innocuous pleasure requires not only the transubstantiation of hazy Dolores into "Lola the bobby-soxer" but also the exotic accompaniment of a popular ditty about "Carmen, my little Carmen" and a flagrantly orientalist fantasy in which "Humbert the Hound" is transformed into a "radiant and robust Turk" in his "self-made seraglio" (59–60). How could the amused and bemused reader deny Humbert this harmless "honey of a spasm without impairing the morals of a minor" (62)? How might Nabokov's presence be felt within this skillful, if amoral, erotic hallucination that Humbert has provided for the compliant reader's participation?

Good readers should note that Humbert's assertion that no harm was done, that nothing was possessed other than a fanciful Lolita while "the child knew nothing" (62), is undone in a postclimactic episode. The phone rings and Humbert observes, "There she stood and blinked, cheeks aflame, hair awry, her eyes passing over me as lightly as they did over the furniture. . . . Blessed be the Lord, she had noticed nothing!" (61). The flushed features of Dolly's carnal excitement make a brief appearance in Humbert's text, only to be quickly ignored. Much earlier in the action, Nabokov drops a rather disruptive prop into Humbert's carefully managed seduction scenario. Dolores wants to show Humbert a "Picture of the Week," for which he can only manage to display tepid interest: "Dimly there came into view: a surrealist painter relaxing, supine, on a beach, and near him, likewise supine, a plaster replica of the Venus di Milo, half-buried in sand" (58). Here we have, in a snapshot, Nabokov's witty commentary on the fraudulent, delusional romance that Humbert himself is conducting with a cheap replica of a former prototype of beauty. Even Dolores Haze recognizes a parody when she sees one. Perhaps Nabokov's readers, too, can be expected to recognize in this visual clue the insanity that can result when live bodies are made to bear the imprint of dead archetypes.

A second and even more incriminating exhibit of Humbert's incurable manipulation of life to accord with his fantasies occurs in a scene that unwary readers often read as a sure sign of Humbert's redemption. In part 2, chapter 29,

Humbert finally tracks down his lost love in the bloated and blotched form of the pregnant Mrs. Richard F. Schiller. In singing prose that "can conjure up a tendresse" (to quote John Ray [5]), Humbert confesses his profound regret and admits to an undying, mature love for a now "hopelessly worn" Lolita with ruined looks: "and I looked and looked at her, and knew as clearly as I know I am to die, that I loved her more than anything I had seen or imagined on earth, or hoped for anywhere else" (277). But as Humbert's redemption song continues it becomes clear that for Humbert what he truly loves is, as before, what he imagines he sees:

> You may jeer at me, and threaten to clear the court, but until I am gagged and half-throttled, I will shout my poor truth. I insist the world know how much I loved my Lolita, *this* Lolita, pale and polluted, and big with another's child, but still gray-eyed, still sooty-lashed, still auburn and almond, still Carmencita, still mine; *Changeons de vie, ma Carmen, allons vivre quelque part où nous ne serons jamais séparés.* (278)

Could there be a better example of how language as a rhetorical performance can give the lie to the intended meaning of a stated proposition? Dolores Schiller is conjured back into the shape of "a little Carmen" before she can be clutched to Humbert's breast. In the full passage, Nabokov makes it abundantly clear that Humbert's purported moral progress is actually a reversion to his besetting sin of nympholepsy. Even as he contemplates the womanly body of the former Lolita, Humbert still needs to imagine her as "the faint violet whiff and dead leaf echo of the nymphet I had rolled myself upon with such cries in the past; an echo on the brink of a russet ravine" (277). Desperate to reclaim the phantom of a phantom, Humbert, like Poe's lyrical speaker in "Annabel Lee," still lies down by the side of his darling, his vanished bride, with nothing but words to play with.

We learn on the last page of Humbert's memoir that he has reread it and finds in its twists of phrase a "slippery self eluding [him], gliding into deeper and darker waters than [he cares] to probe" (308). He is, in fact, no more in command of his solitary confession than Dostoevsky's strenuous self-deluding autobiographers, though he is a more accomplished rhetorician who aims to mute his murder of a double and his rape of a child in the sobbing sonorities of elegiac poetry. But Humbert's confession is simultaneously Nabokov's seriously playful novel that skillfully parodies the solipsistic melancholy of Poe's haunted lovers and exposes Humbert's "logodaedaly," his verbal conjury, for the incurable and insatiable lyrical madness it is (249). Nabokov's novel is, among its many claims to fame, an innovative and extremely subtle variant of a genre much favored by Poe and Dostoevsky—the double-voiced confessional monologue. For readers on the lookout, there is something not quite right about Humbert's too artistically wrought proclamations of love and repentance. The alluring body of text, hailed on the cover of the Vintage International edition of

Lolita as "the only convincing love story of our century," embalms the scented corpse of an imaginary relationship. With Nabokov's help, Humbert's prose poem emits an air of sweet corruption. Humbert, on finally rereading his story, probably realized best what his rhetoric had wrought: "It has bits of marrow sticking to it, and blood, and beautiful bright-green flies" (308).

Teaching *Lolita* as a Post-Romantic Text

Claudia Moscovici

Isaiah Berlin begins his introduction to Romanticism with the resounding claim, "The importance of Romanticism is that it is the largest recent movement to transform the lives and the thought of the Western world" (1). One can easily interpret Berlin's thesis to generate the general agreement that Romanticism was important to Western culture and that it influenced modernism. This argument is uncontroversial but also uninteresting; several critics have said the same before him, and he would not need to write a book on Romanticism in 1999 to prove this point. Berlin is making a more significant and bolder claim. He traces the roots of Romanticism to help us see how it affects us—and should affect us—today. Given that we tend to think of Romanticism as a cultural movement (or movements) whose time has long passed, the stronger version of Berlin's thesis needs to be explored further.

Initially, the claim that Romanticism is in some sense alive today may seem—to say the least—a bit of an exaggeration. Since modernism and postmodernism have taken the cultural stage, Romanticism appears to have taken a bow. A visit to any museum of contemporary art should suffice to convince even those who are most nostalgic. If we step into such a museum, we can still see art that resembles the geometry of Piet Mondrian, the colorful flourish of Jackson Pollock, or the pop readymades and silk screens of Andy Warhol, but we are not likely to spot any contemporary Eugène Delacroix. And, if by some odd chance we did, we would dismiss the paintings as anachronisms, something we would pay ten euros for, the way we do for impressionist sketches sold on the streets of Montmartre.

Those who wish to preserve the Romantic spirit in literature face the same barrier as those who long for it in art. Reading Gustave Flaubert is one thing, but writing like him today is quite another. No writer is likely to get critical attention—except perhaps in the less welcomed form of ridicule—by writing in a lyrical, ornate, and Romantic style. Romantic works in general appear to be a thing of the past, relegated to the museums, history books, and courses that cling to the tradition of the Western canon.

Even in those cases where the impassioned lyricism made famous by the Romantics continues in realist and modernist literature, it tends to be safely protected from criticism by a shell of irony. I am thinking of Vladimir Nabokov's *Lolita* in particular, a novel that has been rightfully called the best love story of the twentieth century. For who can resist being moved by Humbert Humbert's obsessive, hopeless passion for the little nymphet, Dolores Haze? While the subject of a middle-aged man falling in love with a preadolescent girl is not likely to arouse universal sympathy, the beginning of Lolita is hauntingly romantic:

Lolita, light of my life, fire of my loins. My sin, my soul. Lo-lee-ta: the tip of the tongue taking a trip of three steps down the palate to tap, at three, on the teeth. Lo. Lee. Ta.

She was Lo, plain Lo, in the morning, standing four feet ten in one sock. She was Lola in slacks. She was Dolly at school. She was Dolores on the dotted line. But in my arms she was always Lolita.   (9)

Passion is not the only Romantic theme, but it is certainly the central one. Few writers have conveyed passion with such an erotic and emotive power as Nabokov, where the most viscerally physical aspect of love seems inseparable from a longing for a union with the beloved that touches on the transcendent. "Nabokov writes prose the only way it should be written, that is, ecstatically," John Updike is quoted as saying on the back cover of the Vintage International edition of *Lolita*. Indeed, Nabokov's intense lyricism, his intricately ironic style, his focus on a love that is intensified by the taste of taboo, and, above all, his expression of a sensuality that is inseparable from emotion, recall novels such as Flaubert's *Madame Bovary*. Flaubert had to convey Romantic themes in a realist manner protected by a thick layer of cynicism to disassociate himself from a late Romanticism that was already passé. Similarly, Nabokov was compelled to transform ecstatic passion into pathology, lyricism into a hallucination of unrequited and absurd desire, to make Romantic themes palatable to an audience used to the cynicism and textual play of modernist literature.

This essay discusses how I have taught *Lolita*—in comparative literature courses and philosophy freshman seminars—as part of the tradition of Romanticism, as much as that of modernism: namely, as one of the few novels that manages to preserve Romantic tropes and themes in a way that makes them seem vital to modern times.

Background Reading in Romanticism

I introduce *Lolita* as a post-Romantic novel after students have read William Wordsworth's *Preface to the Lyrical Ballads*—which M. H. Abrams has called "the manifesto of British Romanticism" (*Mirror* 100)—as well as Flaubert's *Madame Bovary*. Along with these works, I assign the introduction of Martha Nussbaum's *Upheavals of Thought* to set the stage for a class discussion about the role played by emotion in art and literature, particularly during the Romantic movement. The class examines how expressive models of art such as the ones presented by the Romantics emphasize the complexity of emotion and the manner in which, as Nussbaum explains, they are related to value judgments, beliefs, tastes, knowledge about the world, and reasoning. Students also talk about the link between emotion and artistic expression by giving contemporary examples to draw a bridge between what may seem an abstract philosophy of emotion and our lives.

Then we return to Wordsworth's *Preface* to see how expressive theories of art are even more complex than emotion because they are a form of processed emotion, shaped by figurative language, irony, tone, and encoded clues for reader identification or distance, all of which complicate and mediate the expression of emotion.

This background introduction to Romanticism as a movement focused on emotion—emotion understood as something complex and related to ethics—is helpful, I believe, to teaching and understanding *Lolita*, a complex, wonderfully moving novel that nonetheless lends itself to strong emotions and to one-dimensional moralist readings. The subject of incest and of an older man making love to a preadolescent girl is troubling even today, and it was much more so in the America of the early 1950s, when the novel was originally published. In fact, during the McCarthy era of political and moral conservatism, the sexual content of the novel and taboo subject made it unpublishable in the United States. *Lolita* first appeared in print in France, where it was a huge and immediate success. But there too it was received in a somewhat one-dimensional manner. Many readers celebrated the violation of taboo and started fashioning themselves after its main characters. In his autobiographical writings, Nabokov documents receiving dozens of letters from men happy to have found their Lolitas, not the least of them being the French novelist Alain Robbe-Grillet, who adored the novel and whose young wife dressed "à la Lolita."

Philosophical and Literary Analysis

From the background discussion of Romanticism and of the reception of *Lolita*'s publication, we move on to a philosophical and textual analysis, focusing in particular on the novel's extraordinary style. Like Flaubert, Nabokov is one of the great stylists of his century. To begin this exploration of the possible relation between aesthetics and ethics, I assign the introduction of Nussbaum's *Love's Knowledge* or *Poetic Justice*. Both books focus on how novels encourage us to reflect on our ethical assumptions about life because of their aesthetic richness, which makes them not life.

Then we return to *Lolita*, to see how its style—paying particular attention to its combination of lyricism, irony, and humor—leads us to approach the moral transgressions it describes with special care. For example, once we look more closely at its mode of representation, it is difficult to read *Lolita* from a feminist perspective in the old sense of the term, as a novel in which a young girl is victimized by an older man. In almost every erotic scene, although Lolita has little passion (associated with will and desire), she nonetheless exercises a lot of agency. She is, indeed, very young and desires very little the man who is mad with desire for her. Yet it is she who seduces him in a scene so removed from more conventional descriptions of the little vixen that it is absolutely endearing. The humor and irony of this scene are attenuated by its gentleness, since

Humbert pretends to know nothing about love and indulgently allows Lolita to "teach" him.

Humor and irony are inseparable in the seduction scene, since the irony—the twist that the seducer is seduced—is humorous. The scene begins in a traditional manner, with the older man envisioning having a helpless, passive, and innocent girl embellished with the symbols of innocence—she is wearing one sock and holding a velvet ribbon in her hand: "Naked, except for one sock and her charm bracelet, spread-eagled on the bed where my philter had felled her—so I foreglimpsed her; a velvet hair ribbon was still clutched in her hand" (125). Actually, Lolita is not altogether innocent, nor is she a little vixen.

As students tend to point out in class discussion and debate, the character of Lolita defies stereotypes and expectations. For instance, she had already had a sexual experience with a boy named Charley at summer camp, but she had not fully understood what sexuality meant, and, like a child, Lolita confused the boundaries between sexuality and childish play. In a reversal of passive and active, male and female, and child and adult roles, it is she who wants to teach Humbert a thing or two about lovemaking, but even there—and this is where the humor blends with the irony—she does it unknowingly, with puerile innocence:

> "You mean," she persisted, now kneeling above me, "you never did it
>   when you were a kid?"
> "Never," I answered quite truthfully.
> "Okay," said Lolita, "here is where we start."   (133)

Feminine innocence, Nabokov shows us, is not what the male imagination had concocted: passive, unknowing, unconscious. It is playful, active, confident of its own knowledge and powers—especially there where it lacks them.

As some of my students insist, however, masculine stereotypes still hold, and Humbert Humbert is not morally off the hook. He pursues Lolita constantly as a prey, with deliberate tenacity and full knowledge that what he is doing is wrong. Yet the student reaction tends to be more complex than this black-and-white morality; it is less judgmental and dismissive. Even when by legal standards Humbert is morally culpable, his self-awareness and self-deprecating humor disarm readers.

The class examines many textual examples of this phenomenon, including the episode in which Humbert plans the seduction of another little girl, the McCoos' daughter: "I exchanged letters with these people, satisfying them I was housebroken, and spent a fantastic night on the train, imagining in all possible detail the enigmatic nymphet I would coach in French and fondle in Humbertish" (35). This scene, which renders explicit Humbert's predatory intentions, foreshadows the first sensual act between Humbert and Lolita, of which the most striking feature—now that we have long known what the protagonist intends to do—is not Humbert's actions but the subtlety and understatement of the description:

As I looked on, through prismatic layers of light, dry-lipped, focusing my lust and rocking slightly under my newspaper, I felt that my perception of her, if properly concentrated upon, might be sufficient to have me attain a beggar's bliss immediately; but, like some predator that prefers a moving prey to a motionless one, I planned to have this pitiful attainment coincide with one of the various girlish movements she made now and then as she read.   (42)

After the first reading, some of my students, perhaps used to more explicit language in novels—one only needs to think of how Norman Mailer, John Updike, or Philip Roth would have described this scene—do not even realize what exactly is happening here. Subtlety of description softens the sexual brutality and gives a sense of the predator's inefficacy. Humbert is so human, vulnerable, and unskilled at seduction that he cannot be readily pegged as a villain. Perhaps that in itself manifests his narrative skill at seduction, since the lack of guile he simulates with Lolita is mirrored in his attitude as a narrator who is not in control of his circumstances, desires, or even the girl he seduces.

In his unrelenting irony and self-deprecation, Humbert appears as a character more to be pitied and laughed with (he is always smart enough to laugh at himself) rather than morally condemned. Another scene, for instance, shows him as an ineffectual seducer:

At last I was right behind her when I had the unfortunate idea of blustering a trifle—shaking her by the scruff of the neck and that sort of thing to cover my real *manège*, and she said in a shrill brief whine: "Cut it out!"—most coarsely, the little wench, and with a ghastly grin Humbert the Humble beat a gloomy retreat while she went on wisecracking streetward.   (55)

The power relations between Lolita and Humbert defy any simple discourse of victimization, turning on a combination of humor, self-aware criticism, irony, and the expression of intense passion to show Humbert as a man helplessly and hopelessly in love with a girl who, through her very lack of love for him, holds the reins of the relationship. In class we examine closely several of the unforgettably moving citations that express Humbert's passion. In one notable passage, Humbert recalls his passion for Annabel, his childhood love, describing his desire in unbelievably emotional terms:

She would try to relieve the pain of love by first roughly rubbing her dry lips against mine; then my darling would draw away with a nervous toss of her hair, and then again come darkly near and let me feed on her open mouth, while with a generosity that was ready to offer her everything, my heart, my throat, my entrails, I gave her to hold in her awkward fist the scepter of my passion.   (15)

Passion, Nabokov suggests, is exactly how the Romantics had conceived it: an overwhelming force at the center of human existence where the most intense emotions are inseparable from the most fervent, voracious, and insatiable physical desire. Passion is transcendental, as the Romantics also indicated, only in a human way. It places a human being—a girl, a woman, a mistress, a muse—at the center of human existence and declares love for her as the highest, most enduring, and most creative human endeavor. Yet, as my students have noticed, Nabokov's return to Romantic assumptions is sandwiched between paragraphs that express astonishing cynicism and even misogyny.

Right before chanting in a lyrical manner his love for Annabel, the narrator recalls the loss of his mother early in life: "My very photogenic mother died in a freak accident (picnic, lightning) when I was three, and, save for a pocket of warmth in the darkest past, nothing of her subsists within the hollows and dells of memory" (10). Nobody can accuse Nabokov of committing the most serious romantic error—namely, of being too earnest and sentimental—which is why our class discussion turns a lot on tropes. Irony, or the winks to the sophisticated implied reader that the narrator does not always mean what he says; a keen sense of humor; and cynicism, which many students associate with intelligence, all place the novel well within the acceptable boundaries of modernist literature. By virtue of its very artistry, the novel remains morally complex. The heated debates students have about it in class attest to its irresolvable complexity.

On the one hand, *Lolita* is not an amoral novel that condones incest and sleeping with a child, as some readers have gleefully interpreted it. Students rarely miss the fact that the most moving scene of the novel is not the one describing Humbert's passion, but the one showing Lolita's childlike helplessness, loneliness, and dependency on her lover/father: "At the hotel we had separate rooms, but in the middle of the night she came sobbing into mine, and we made it up very gently. You see, she had absolutely nowhere else to go" (142). The sad ending features a Lolita marked by her incestuous affair at least as much as her stepfather, who will always yearn for an impossible love.

On the other hand, *Lolita* is not a moralist novel that only depicts a child's victimization. As our class textual and ethical analysis reveals, Humbert's self-deprecating humor attenuates his culpability and power of conquest; the helpless and hopeless nature of his passion is conveyed through a lyricism that moves us; the irony gives spellbinding twists to stereotyped roles and unexamined moral assumptions; and the comic tone of the novel only highlights its underlying tragic nature. *Lolita* is, at least in part, a post-Romantic novel that expresses in an exquisite, thought-provoking style a passion that we know to be doomed from the very start.

Art as Pedagogy in *Lolita*

Ellen Pifer

The word "realistic" is a term students routinely employ to designate features of a text they find plausible or familiar, that is, elements that neither surprise nor shock them. No wonder they are baffled by a novel whose scandalous subject—the passion of a middle-aged European male for a twelve-year-old American girl—may be the least shocking thing about it. Encountering *Lolita*'s daring design, students often find themselves at a loss; their familiar categories fail. That John Ray, Jr., PhD, who pens the novel's foreword, turns out to be an invented character is only the first of the false leads with which they must grapple. (A handful of students inevitably confess that they skipped Ray's foreword, having assumed it was yet another academic preface to an assigned "classic.")

Upending the conventions of literary realism, *Lolita* calls for distinctions that lie outside the conventional poles of art versus life, fiction versus reality. Just as Humbert draws attention from the outset to the "fancy prose style" of his narrative, so the design of *Lolita* foregrounds the processes of fiction making by which the novel's reality has been fabricated (9). Vladimir Nabokov's well-known disdain for the pedagogical uses of literature notwithstanding, students charged with exploring the art of *Lolita* receive a valuable lesson in epistemology. For if, as this novel persuasively suggests, reality is what human beings discover through the fictions they construct, then fiction is not—as conventionally assumed or defined—opposed to truth, but rather it is the means by which truths are discovered. Still, as Nabokov suggests everywhere in his work, the fictions that human beings construct and create operate at different levels of consciousness. Not all are equally telling or incisive. Some are generous and vital; others, borrowed or base. The term "average reality" sums up, for Nabokov, what we conventionally refer to as reality—a landscape dotted with familiar signposts: the received ideas, attitudes, and issues that constitute collective life ("On a Book" 312). To Nabokov, this collective or shared reality, reduced to the most common denominators of human awareness and perception, is reality in its least compelling form—particularly as a subject for art. The drama that takes center stage in his work is that of individual consciousness coming to grips with perceived events, people, and phenomena. Crucial to this process is the way in which a character's unique desires and perceptions animate the world he or she perceives as real.

If a Nabokov novel calls for distinctions that lie outside the conventional polarities of art and life, fiction and reality, what might they be? To begin, let us recognize all constructs of reality as fictions of varying kinds and degrees. Let "fiction" with a lowercase *f* signify Nabokov's average reality, the collective world of common denominators that we all share in our daily lives. Then let "Fiction" with a capital *F* signify the more intimate and compelling reality that is uniquely meaningful to each individual. Here elements of average reality may take on grave importance or prove a matter of indifference as individual consciousness subjectively registers and reflects phenomena according to its own lights. Finally, let us distinguish between two levels of Fiction operating in Nabokov's text. In addition to creating awareness of the way a character's perceptions—most particularly those of his first-person narrator—shape or construct the reality registered by consciousness, *Lolita* signals the presence of an author existing beyond the world of the characters, shaping and manipulating the ultimate design, the Fiction, that is the novel.

Since Humbert serves as *Lolita*'s first-person narrator, we begin by examining both his "fancy prose style" and the way it registers the reality, or Fiction, he perceives. Crucial to our examination is a distinction that Humbert at times tries to finesse but ultimately cannot deny: the distinction between the "North American girl-child named Dolores Haze"—the offspring of Charlotte Haze and her dead husband, Harold—and the magical nymphet Lolita, whose name and image spring from Humbert's overweening imagination (283). Like his literary predecessors, a long line of romantic dreamers from Don Quixote to Jay Gatsby, Humbert suffers the fatal affliction of infinite desire. His fantasies are fueled by an ideal image wedded to an impossible dream. Imagination is the magic carpet that transports him to "that intangible island of entranced time where Lolita plays with her likes" (17).

In rare moments of lucidity Humbert acknowledges his solipsistic perception: "What I had madly possessed," he states in a well-known passage, "was not she, but my own creation, another, fanciful Lolita—perhaps, more real than Lolita; . . . and having no will, no consciousness—indeed, no life of her own" (62). His sexual desire originates not in some physical or biochemical reflex but in the romantic quest for the ideal, what he calls "the great rosegray never-to-be-had" (264). Humbert's solipsism not only provides a key to the romantic nature of his obsession but also underscores the duplicity of his attempts to cast himself as the passive prey of the nymphet's "demoniac" power. In defining his nympholepsy he distinguishes between "human little girls," mere "wholesome children," and those "chosen creatures" who "reveal their true nature" as "not human, but nymphic (that is, demoniac)." But as Humbert himself reveals, it is the potent force of his imagination that lends "fantastic power" to the nymphet's "shifty, soul-shattering, insidious charm" (16–17).

While students readily concede that the Fiction Humbert registers and recounts in his narrative is a strange brew of imagination and obsession, they are less attuned to the popular fictions to which Dolly Haze and her mother eagerly subscribe. These midcentury constructs are not so different, after all, from those perpetrated by the media and advertisements of culture today. Taken at face value, the way in which popular fictions rule the perceptions of Charlotte Haze and her daughter offers comic relief to the novel's darker themes of betrayal and child abuse. But behind the satiric thrust, careful readers will discover a useful introduction to the epistemological lesson embedded in *Lolita*. When, for example, Charlotte snags handsome Humbert for a husband and enters a brave new world of married bliss, she pictures their "joint" future "as one of those southern boulevards at midday that have solid shade on one side and smooth sunshine on the other, all the way to the end of a prospect, where pink mountains loom" (77). That this sunny suburban paradise bears no resemblance to Ramsdale's New England landscape—or to any other prospect existing outside a realtor's brochure—does not give Charlotte pause. While she thrills to her new life with the "zest of a banal young bride," Humbert is faced with performing the nightly duties of an ardent bridegroom (77). Strenuously applying his imagination to the task at hand, he mentally gleans in the full-blown form of "big Haze" a "dim first version of Lolita's outline" (51, 76).

The faith that Dolly Haze brings to the fictions of advertising and movie magazines is no less ardent than her mother's devotion to decorating manuals. Capturing the quasi-religious nature of that faith, Humbert says, "She believed, with a kind of celestial trust, any advertisement or advice that appeared in *Movie Love* or *Screen Land*." He adds, "She it was to whom ads were dedicated: the ideal consumer, the subject and object of every foul poster" (148). Like her mother, Dolores Haze is transfixed by "adman visions" that pander to human longing for the sake of profit (155). But while Humbert expresses his unalloyed contempt for those who traffic in false promises and "foul posters," these "admen" help him advance his own predatory motives. After Charlotte's death, when Humbert and the twelve-year-old embark on their cross-country travels, he takes full advantage of Dolly's status as an "ideal consumer." Plying her with all manner of toys, frocks, and "gooey fudge sundaes," he manages to bribe the child into sullen silence about their criminal relationship (148).

Other ready-made fictions of American popular culture, such as group psychology and "progressive" theories of child rearing, help Humbert disguise his criminal passion. Several years after their cohabitation begins, he enrolls Lolita in a private girls' school in the town of Beardsley, where he has accepted a teaching post. When headmistress Pratt meets with Humbert, she urges this supposedly "old-fashioned European" father to allow Dolly to explore her repressed sexuality (194). Pratt's indifference to other possible sources of the child's "antagonistic, dissatisfied, cagey" behavior is monumental (196). Repeatedly addressing Humbert as "Mr. Haze," she fails to note that he is not even Dolores Haze's biological parent. As the scene progresses, Pratt's failure to detect any trace of Dolly's actual situation becomes increasingly less comic and more alarming. The disparity between Pratt's view of reality and Humbert's— between the stereotypes disseminated by average reality and the searing intensity of Humbert's private vision—proves fatal to the child's welfare.

Complicating our perception of Humbert's Fiction is his intermittent awareness of some mysterious agency designing his fate. In the Enchanted Hunters hotel, where the doomed child's own fate is sealed, Humbert registers an awareness of past, present, and future events as he signs the hotel guest book. In "the slow clear hand of crime," he records his name as "Edgar H. Humbert," sustaining the pattern of allusions to Edgar Allan Poe and his child-bride introduced at the outset of the novel. Then, as Humbert anticipates the "crime" against the child that he is about to commit, he recalls with a pang her dead mother, on whose grave he envisions a single raindrop falling like a tear from heaven. Instantaneously shifting from the recent past to the dreaded future, Humbert's awareness registers an image of "Lo" in the hotel lobby, "leaving the dog as she would leave me some day." Whether his insight stems from retrospective knowledge, as a narrator looking back on events, or from a fateful imagination, we cannot be sure. But when the number of the hotel room turns up as "342!"—the number of the Haze household's street address—the blatant coincidence puts readers on the alert (118).

The number 342 signals only one of many "coincidences" calling attention to the design, or artifice, of *Lolita*. Take, for example, the "conflagration" that conveniently burns down the McCoo house on the day that Humbert arrives in Ramsdale. A "distraught" and now homeless Mr. McCoo informs Humbert that a "Mrs. Haze of 342 Lawn Street" has generously "offered to accommodate" him (35). Humbert is at once "angry, disappointed and bored" (36), having been lured to the prospect of rooming at the McCoos' by a colleague's account of their "two little daughters, one . . . a girl of twelve" (35). Indeed, he has just spent a "fantastic night on the train, imagining in all possible detail the enigmatic nymphet I would coach in French and fondle in Humbertish." News that the McCoos' "house had just burned down" makes him wonder whether the fateful fire was ignited by "the synchronous conflagration that had been raging all night in my veins" (35). As Humbert soon surmises, however, the "agent of fate" guiding him to the Haze household operates on a higher plane altogether (103).

Later in the novel, when Charlotte Haze is run over by a car, Humbert detects, along with his own "vile contribution" to the event, the "intricacies of the pattern (hurrying housewife, slippery pavement, a pest of a dog, steep grade, big car, baboon at its wheel)" arranged by the "synchronizing phantom" directing his fate (103). Entrapped in a Fiction constructed by his author, Humbert, as a character, can only glean the ghost of a higher power controlling his destiny. Nabokov's readers, of course, have a clearer view of the agency at work. Challenging the conventions of literary realism, Nabokov invites readers to contemplate the relation of fiction, and Fiction, to reality in a new way. What moves or delights us in *Lolita* may strike us as profoundly meaningful and even true to life, but these effects are in no way dependent on that most persistent of all fictions governing average reality: the fiction of unmediated reality.

The distinction between the individual's private world, or Fiction, responsive to the personal dictates of will and imagination, and the public world of shared fictions—of social contracts and legal constructs constituting collective life—proves crucial to reading *Lolita* in yet another way. It helps account for the moral awakening that gradually dawns on Humbert in the course of his narrative, as his arduous efforts to defend himself give way to confessions of remorse and even self-condemnation. Near the end of the novel he frankly acknowledges that he has broken all "laws of humanity"—those vital fictions by which civilized individuals agree to live (306). As surely as he has broken these moral and civil laws, Humbert knows that "something within" Lolita had also "been broken by me" (232). Inflicting his private Fiction of the nymphet—a mythical creature who must "[n]ever grow up"—on an immature "girl-child" who has every right to do so, he has stunted the child's growth and freedom (21, 19). In entomology, as Nabokov the lepidopterist well knew, a *nymph* signifies the "immature stage" of an insect that "does not undergo complete metamorphosis" (Johnson and Coates 36 [Zoland]). Because a girl-child, unlike the *nymph* or the fantasized nymphet, is destined to metamorphose into a full-blown woman, time itself becomes Humbert's enemy. By the time that Lolita turns fourteen, he is keenly aware of her "advanced age" (230).

What Humbert dreads even more than Lolita's growing up is her possible flight from captivity. Only after she succeeds in escaping him does he acknowledge her right to liberty and the innocence he betrayed. In the end it is his own conscience that condemns him for his transgressions against the "poor, bruised child" he exploited (283). Because of him, he says, "a North American girl-child named Dolores Haze had been deprived of her childhood by a maniac" (283). In this recognition, tragically belated though it is, Humbert breaks through his solipsistic vision of the nymphet to an awareness of the child's autonomous identity. In this liberating act of imagination he removes her from his "self-made seraglio" to her rightful domain: the vast North American continent over which his despotic will can claim no authority (60).

Scurrilous as Humbert is, he is hardly alone in his desire to fit other people into his private world, as though his fellow creatures were characters in a text of his own making. Aware of this principle, if not the full reach of its implications, he observes:

> [W]e are inclined to endow our friends with the stability of type that literary characters acquire in the reader's mind. . . . Whatever evolution this or that popular character has gone through between the book covers, his fate is fixed in our minds, and, similarly, we expect our friends to follow this or that logical and conventional pattern we have fixed for them.   (265)

Recognizing that Humbert is just such a character, whose "fate is fixed" between "book covers," *Lolita*'s readers may find his analogy revealing: the world that Humbert shares with his fellow creatures, those images of human beings reflected in *Lolita*'s text, is one over which his private Fiction does not hold sway. Like real human beings, they owe their existence to a higher agency.

By calling attention to the fabricated nature of the worlds he constructs in his novels, Nabokov, unlike his narrator, acknowledges the limits of his private universe of Fiction. In *Lolita*, as in his other works, the devices of self-conscious artifice point to the circumscribed realm of the author's authority. It is Humbert, not his author, who errs by conflating his private universe of perception with the larger world he inhabits. The folly that results in Humbert's betrayal of the child's rights is rooted in his failure to distinguish between his private reality and the constructs of average reality by which human beings agree to coexist. Humbert knows that he can never restore to the child the liberty of which he deprived her. Yet the image of the "North American girl-child named Dolores Haze" comes vividly to life within the pages of his memoir, garnering whatever partial redemption readers are willing to grant him. In any case, Humbert's awakening to the child's reality proves crucial to the ethical and aesthetic effects of a novel that promotes, at every level, the reader's awareness of its status as a work of fiction. Nabokov, we know, took every opportunity to challenge the notion that art should serve a didactic purpose. Still, *Lolita* is a novel as enlightening as it is disturbing, as profound as it is playful. Here, one might say, art is pedagogy—not by serving up ready-made answers to moral and ethical problems but by compelling readers to ponder the ways in which fiction is created and reality called into being.

In the process of reinventing America so brilliantly in *Lolita*, Nabokov, at that point already the author of eight Russian novels and two in English, did more than turn himself into an American writer. As novelists from John Updike to John Barth to Edmund White have testified, Nabokov infused the American language with new vitality. His contribution to American letters does not stop there, however. Fueling the stylistic originality, precise wit, and verbal audacity of his art is a charged vision of fiction's essential relation to human reality. If the experience of teaching *Lolita* is any indication, this vision has profound implications for the way we read and teach not just this novel but American literature as a whole. Undermining the assumptions of a technologically saturated culture that finds literature a poor cousin to science and mathematical calculation, *Lolita* testifies to the essential role that art plays in our lives.

Russian Cultural Contexts for *Lolita*

Julian W. Connolly

Although many readers might view *Lolita* as Vladimir Nabokov's most American novel, they might not be aware that the author made significant use of important Russian literary and cultural elements in the creation of the work. This essay aims to help students understand Nabokov's use of Russian cultural elements, from folk beliefs about the mythological creature *rusalka* ("water nymph") to works by such major nineteenth-century Russian authors as Aleksandr Pushkin, Nikolay Gogol, and Fyodor Dostoevsky.

According to East Slavic folk belief, *rusalki* (the plural form of *rusalka*) were female spirits who lived in rivers and ponds and often lured mortal beings into their watery realm or tickled them to death. In many areas, these spirits were believed to be the souls of unbaptized or stillborn babies and drowned maidens, sometimes women who had committed suicide because of unrequited love (see Ivanits 75). In the southern regions of Russia and in Ukraine, these nymphs were regarded as "ethereal beauties," but, despite their beauty, the local peasants "entertained no doubts that *rusalki* were connected with the unclean force." Indeed, in Kaluga province it was believed that the nymphs "received their beauty and eternal youth directly from the devil" (Ivanits 75).

The combination of seductive beauty and lethal danger in the *rusalka* figure exercised a powerful appeal on the Russian literary imagination, and writers from Pushkin to Gogol and Ivan Turgenev incorporated folk beliefs about the *rusalki* in their work. Two texts are particularly relevant to a discussion of Nabokov's use of the *rusalka* theme in *Lolita*. In Gogol's short story "A May Night, or The Drowned Maiden" (1832) the male protagonist is charged by an unhappy water nymph with the task of picking an evil witch out of a group of *rusalki* who have emerged from the water to sing and dance innocently. The hero Levko notices that one of the maidens is not as translucent as the others, and he seems to detect something malevolent in her look; he then succeeds in identifying that figure as the witch.

There may be an echo of the *rusalka* and the incident in Gogol's story in the descriptions of the nymphet that Humbert Humbert offers in *Lolita*. He begins by saying that between the ages of nine and fourteen "there occur maidens who, to certain bewitched travelers, twice or many times older than they, reveal their true nature which is not human, but nymphic (that is demoniac)" (16). He then asserts that one has to be "an artist and a madman" to "discern at once, by ineffable sights . . . the little deadly demon among the wholesome children; *she* stands unrecognized by them and unconscious herself of her fantastic power" (17). Dolly Haze, of course, is identified by Humbert as just such a demonic nymphet.

Yet this identification of Dolly with demonic powers of enchantment is not presented to the reader by Nabokov as objective fact. The attribution is solely

Humbert's fantasy; he projects this infernal nature onto the figure of an innocent child. It was paramount for Nabokov to assert the essential innocence of
the child in his work, and although he does not put Dolly Haze in the role of the
rusalka, he does incorporate several elements of the *rusalka* theme in *Lolita*. To
appreciate this reference in full, we must turn to a second Russian literary text,
Pushkin's unfinished drama *Rusalka*.

Pushkin's drama centers on the fate of a miller's daughter who is seduced
and abandoned by a prince. Grief-stricken over his decision to betray her for
another woman, the young maiden, pregnant with the prince's child, throws
herself into a river and drowns. Haunted by remorse, the prince begins to frequent the shore of the river where his lover died, and the dead woman, who has
been transformed into the queen of the water nymphs, longs for vengeance.
Consequently, she sends her daughter—the prince's child—ashore to inter-
cept the prince. Pushkin's fragment ends with the prince catching sight of the
"beautiful child." Although the writer worked on the piece in 1829 and 1832, it
remained unfinished at the time of his death in 1836.

Nabokov, who had published a short poem entitled "Rusalka" in his verse collection *The Empyrean Path*, was intrigued with Pushkin's fragment and decided
to write an ending for the piece in the late 1930s. In Nabokov's continuation of
the Pushkin original, the prince is initially unable to identify this beautiful child
who has caught his attention, but then he comprehends who her mother is, and,
despite his trepidation, he follows the girl into the water. What occurs thereafter
is unknown, and Nabokov concludes the scene with the cryptic stage direction:
"Pushkin shrugs his shoulders" (Nabokov, *Stikhotvoreniia* 361). According to
Brian Boyd, Nabokov contemplated using his completed text to conclude the
second part of his novel *The Gift* (*Russian Years* 516–17). Since Nabokov never
finished the second part of the novel, he eventually published this continuation
of *Rusalka* as a freestanding piece in the journal *Novyi zhurnal* in 1942.

What is important for our reading of *Lolita* are the relationships among the
prince, the dead mother, and the child. In Pushkin's text, the prince loved the
miller's daughter but abandoned her for another woman; the abandoned woman
then has a child unbeknownst to the prince and uses that child to entice her
unfaithful lover to an untimely end. In *Lolita*, Nabokov condenses the romantic relationships in a distinctive way: the protagonist woos and weds a woman
(Charlotte Haze), but his real interest is directed toward another female, the
woman's own daughter. In both texts, the jilted woman dies soon after discovering her lover's betrayal, and at this point Nabokov significantly reworks Pushkin's plot. In Pushkin's drama, the dead woman burns to avenge her betrayal
and uses her daughter as agent for this revenge. In Nabokov's novel, Charlotte
simply disappears and seems to leave her daughter alone and unprotected. But
perhaps the situation is more subtle than initially meets the eye.

To begin with, we should note that Charlotte is repeatedly linked with images
of water (see Alexandrov, *Nabokov's Otherworld* 178–80) and is actually called
a mermaid by Humbert twice (86, 132). Significantly, when Nabokov translated

the text into Russian, he used the word *rusalka* for the second of these references (156). In what is clearly a transformation of the *rusalka* myth, Humbert
considers drowning Charlotte to gain access to her daughter. Although drowning is the means by which mortal women became *rusalki* in Russian folklore,
these women drowned themselves; they were not drowned by others.

Yet Charlotte stands apart from the betrayed woman in the Pushkin drama.
She is not depicted as a figure of vengeance who would use her daughter to get
back at the man who betrayed her. On the contrary, her intentions while still
alive were to keep her daughter away from Humbert's predations. Indeed, this
association between Charlotte and Dolly's eventual escape from Humbert is
reinforced in a sentence that may suggest a kind of spectral presence for the
dead Charlotte, if not as a vengeful *rusalka*, then as a grieving mother. When
Humbert is checking into the Enchanted Hunters hotel, where he hopes to take
his full pleasure with his unsuspecting victim, a remarkable passage details a
series of events that transpire in rapid succession: "A key (342!) was half-shown
to me . . . Lo, leaving the dog as she would leave me some day, rose from her
haunches; a raindrop fell on Charlotte's grave . . . and the doomed child went in
followed by her throat-clearing father" (118–19). In this sequence, the raindrop
falling on Charlotte's grave stands out as the only event that does not occur in
the hotel. The image of the falling raindrop may suggest a falling tear, perhaps
shed by Charlotte as she contemplates the fate of her "doomed child."

On the other hand, if Vladimir Alexandrov is correct when he argues that
"Charlotte's spirit appears to abet" Humbert's decision to go to the Enchanted
Hunters hotel, where Quilty will glimpse Dolly and thus set in motion the elaborate plot to steal her away from Humbert (*Nabokov's Otherworld* 180–81), then
Charlotte's spirit does transcend merely mourning her daughter's plight. Charlotte becomes a spirit of liberation, helping her daughter escape the clutches of
the obsessed pedophile, and thus Nabokov has again worked a transformation
of the original Pushkinian *rusalka* plot. The problem with this interpretation is
that Quilty is not a particularly savory character. Would Charlotte really consider him an appropriate savior for her daughter? Yet it might be possible that,
as Efim Kurganov argues, Charlotte's willingness to abet Quilty in his campaign
against Humbert indicates a desire to punish Humbert, and such a desire would
bring her closer to the original *rusalka* image (59–60).

In any event, Nabokov's treatment of Dolly Haze rescues the child from any
hint of the demonic character ascribed by Russian peasants to the *rusalka* and
by Humbert to her as a prototypical nymphet. In fact, the writer's sympathy for
the image of the abused child is so deep that he invokes the work of another
Russian author, Dostoevsky, to bolster his case that the suffering of the child
should not be ignored or diminished. By the time he wrote *Lolita*, Nabokov felt
that Dostoevsky's work was seriously flawed in the way it seemed to focus the
reader's attention (and potential empathy) on the figures of rank criminals rather
than on the vulnerable female figures they encounter. Nabokov at the outset of
his career seemed to find much of interest and inspiration in Dostoevsky's work

(see Connolly, "Madness"), but by the time he began teaching Russian literature at Wellesley College and Cornell University, he developed a more critical attitude toward his predecessor. In September 1946, Nabokov wrote to Edmund Wilson that he had been rereading Leo Tolstoy and Dostoevsky: "The latter is a third rate writer and his fame is incomprehensible" (*Dear Bunny* 197). The lecture notes preserved from his teaching at Cornell offer more detailed insight into the specific flaws Nabokov detected in Dostoevsky's writing (see *Lectures on Russian Literature* 97–135). Among other things, Nabokov perceived in Dostoevsky a deplorable tendency toward didacticism at the expense of art, a weakness for sentimental clichés, and an over-reliance on melodramatic stage effects. In a 1963 interview he offers a summary dismissal of Dostoevsky: "He was a prophet, a claptrap journalist and a slapdash comedian. . . . [H]is sensitive murderers and soulful prostitutes are not to be endured for one moment—by this reader anyway" (*Strong Opinions* 42).

The comment about "sensitive murderers and soulful prostitutes" is a reference to *Crime and Punishment* and an echo of a more detailed analysis of a sentence in *Crime and Punishment* that he gave in a lecture at Cornell: "But then comes this singular sentence that for sheer stupidity has hardly the equal in world-famous literature." He then reads the sentence—"The candle was flickering out, dimly lighting up in the poverty-stricken room the murderer and the harlot who had been reading together the eternal book"—and subjects it to a scathing critique (*Lectures on Russian Literature* 110). What he finds most objectionable about the sentence is its linkage of a "filthy murderer" and an "unfortunate girl." Not only does he find it reprehensible that Dostoevsky would link the "inhuman and idiotic crime" of Raskolnikov with the "plight of a girl who impairs human dignity by selling her body" (110), but he also notes that while Dostoevsky describes in great detail Raskolnikov's crime, his muddled motives, and so on, the novelist tells the reader almost nothing about Sonya's acts as a prostitute. Nabokov sums up this elision as "a glorified cliché": "The harlot's sin is taken for granted. Now I submit that the true artist is the person who never takes anything for granted" (113).

I argue that Nabokov's indignation over Dostoevsky's handling of the Raskolnikov-Sonya relationship played a role in the design of *Lolita*, which was written during his years at Cornell. The novel contains several threads of an anti-Dostoevsky polemic, primarily centered on the relationship between Humbert Humbert and Dolores Haze and on the way Humbert as narrator treats Dolly as the subject of his narration. Several critics have noted that the theme of sexual child abuse in *Lolita* recalls a series of parallel situations depicted in Dostoevsky's work: in *Crime and Punishment*, for example, Arkady Svidrigailov is reputed to be a child abuser. Even more important, however, is the figure of Nikolai Stavrogin in the novel *The Devils*, and an interesting assignment for students would be to read "At Tikhon's," the chapter in *The Devils* in which Stavrogin implicates himself in the sexual abuse of a child who was roughly the same age as Dolly Haze when Humbert first saw her (Humbert himself writes that he felt a "Dostoevskian grin dawning" as he contemplated the fact that by marrying Dolly's mother he would be able to have ready access to the child [70]).[1]

There are two key points that the reader should observe when comparing *Lolita* and *The Devils*. First, just as Nabokov commented with indignation the relative lack of authorial attention given to Sonya and her plight, so too we should note—as the scholar Katherine O'Connor has—that Matryoshka, the little girl mentioned in Stavrogin's confession, hardly exists "as a living personality"; she is, in fact, "virtually expendable as a truly individualized character" (68). In *Lolita*, Nabokov set out to remedy this recurrent disregard for the living personality of the child in a particularly subtle way. He created a narrator who initially seems to reproduce Dostoevsky's fundamental error: Humbert focuses almost exclusively on *his* suffering, *his* "crime," and he allows the reader almost no direct access to the inner condition of his victim. Indeed, he confesses near the end of the novel that he "did not know a thing about [his] darling's mind and that quite possibly . . . there was in her a garden and a twilight, and a palace gate" (284). Nevertheless, through Humbert's often exasperated descriptions of Dolly, Nabokov provides a great deal of information about the girl's tastes and interests, from the specific types of magazines and movies she enjoys to the types of roadside attractions that pique her curiosity. Above all, we discover that behind Humbert's image of "this Lolita, *my* Lolita," there exists a valiant, spirited child who struggles to assert her independence and find her freedom, much like a distant hill Humbert observes "scrambling out—scarred but still untamed—from the wilderness of agriculture that was trying to swallow it" (40, 153).

The second point of comparison between Stavrogin's and Humbert's confessions is that, although in both novels the narrator-confessor is acutely aware of the potential response of his anonymous audience and seeks to manipulate that response for his own ends, Stavrogin's confession remains obsessively concerned only with his own desires and needs, whereas Humbert's confession ultimately serves another purpose. Many readers of *Lolita* would agree that in the final stages of the narrative Humbert desires not merely to explain his atrocious behavior but also to atone or compensate in some small way for the damage he has inflicted on Dolly. Humbert's confession, unlike Stavrogin's, is not just a tool for self-display and self-laceration. Through it, Humbert hopes to move beyond his personal woes and to enshrine the object of his obsession in the involute realm of immortal art. Thus Nabokov, in both his manipulation of the *rusalka* theme and his treatment of elements from Dostoevsky's fiction, seeks to rework classic Russian texts and to offer his readers a fresh, original, and indeed unprecedented work of art.

NOTE

[1] The controversial chapter from *The Devils* was not accepted for publication at the time the novel was first released; it was not published until 1922.

Teaching *Lolita* through Pushkin's Lens

Priscilla Meyer

If students have been introduced to Vladimir Nabokov's novel *Lolita* by Stanley Kubrick or Adrian Lyne, they are likely to focus on plot, on Lolita's captivity and abuse. It is always a challenge to steer discussion from students' identification with characters toward the author's construction of a work of art. Reading Aleksandr Pushkin's *Eugene Onegin* before reading *Lolita* accentuates the specifically literary aspects of the novel. Students can readily believe that *Onegin* will be relevant when they heft Nabokov's translation and commentary and realize that his preparation of it (1950–57) overlapped with his writing of *Lolita* (1947–54).

In his foreword to *Onegin*, Nabokov identifies two distinct types of translation: the literal and the "paraphrastic." He defines paraphrastic translation as "a free version of the original with additions and omissions prompted by the exigencies of form and the conventions attributed to the consumer" (1: vii–viii). His translation of *Onegin* forgoes rhyme and meter for strict literalism; *Lolita* takes paraphrastic translation to an extreme. This juxtaposition suggests that *Lolita* can be read as a translation through space and time of a Russian literary monument of the 1820s into an American one of the 1950s, parodying the idea of adapting the original to the conventions of the consumer. Aware that he is an ideal bridge between the English-speaking world and Pushkin's, Nabokov writes the most Russian *Onegin* possible in his English translation and produces its most American paraphrase in *Lolita*; he uses both methods of translation to close the cultural gap between the producer (Pushkin) and the consumer (the American reader circa 1950). Thus Nabokov pays homage to the greatest Russian poet's masterpiece and enriches the American tradition by smuggling Pushkin's art, concerns, and frame of reference into a new Russo-American synthesis.

In *Speak, Memory,* Nabokov writes of "folding the magic carpet" in such a way as to reveal the coincidence of pattern in life, which he considers the essence of the artist's task (139). The neat hundred-year interval between Pushkin's birth and his own (1799, 1899) is just the kind of fatidic coincidence that fascinated both Pushkin and Nabokov. In the commentary to his translation of *Onegin*, Nabokov describes the Summer Garden in Saint Petersburg, adding, "There, a hundred years later, I, too, was walked by a tutor" (2: 41). Nabokov, an exiled poet, the impoverished descendant of an ancient liberal, artistic, aristocratic family, would identify strongly with Pushkin. But Nabokov, unlike Humbert, who compares himself with Vergil, Petrarch, Dante, and Edgar Allan Poe, modestly refrains from saying so explicitly. *Lolita*, however, demonstrates their shared literary aesthetics.

That *Lolita* is a parody of a free translation of *Onegin* may sound startling, but even though the novels appear to be so disparate, their plots are similar. The principal action of both novels spans a little over five years: *Onegin* begins in the winter of 1819 and ends in the spring of 1825; Humbert meets Lolita "more than five years before" (289) he shoots Quilty. The feelings of the parodically romantic heroes (Onegin and Humbert) for the heroines (Tatyana and Lolita) are juxtaposed to the authorial persona's relation to his muse, who is associated in both novels with the goddess Diana, the moon, and Gottfried Bürger's "Lenore" (about which Nabokov has much to say in his commentary). The heroines undergo a metamorphosis from provincial miss to experienced, inaccessible grown woman. At this point Pushkin's and Nabokov's heroes return from prolonged (two- or three-year) travels and offer their love, only to be rejected. Tatyana fails to recognize the change in Eugene, who is at last capable of genuine love; she thinks he merely wants to boast of a society conquest. Lolita likewise misunderstands Humbert's proposal that she come away with him forever: "you mean you will give us [us] that money only if I go with you to a motel" (278). Furthermore, Onegin and Humbert kill Lensky and Quilty in duels that are farcical because of the parodic purpose of the victims: first and foremost, they represent the Bad Writer—*Lensky* is Pushkin's representation of the naive Romantic pseudo-poet, and Quilty is Humbert's projection of hack writer-pornographer—versions of themselves that they want to cast off. The superficially realistic boy-loses-girl plot is a transparently metaphorical representation of the true subject of both novels: the interrelation of literary aesthetics and life.

Nabokov establishes the same elegant symmetry in *Lolita* that he charts in his commentary to *Onegin*. The "Pursuit Theme" of Onegin by "Pushkin" (2: 78) is taken up in the symmetrical East-West, West-East chase of Humbert by Quilty and Quilty by Humbert. Humbert's romance with Lolita begins with Charlotte's letter and ends with Lolita's, just as Tatyana's and Onegin's letters frame their love story. It is a lesson in narrative construction as well as in cultural translation to have students compare the two sets of manageably short letters—the author's and narrator's implicit presence in each, psychological and linguistic; their dialogic relationship to the addressee; the social context of the forwardness of the confessions; their differing uses of French.

Once having read both *Onegin* and *Lolita*, students will be amused to discover how Nabokov updates, translates, and then parodies Pushkin's characters, literary references, and cultural universe. Pushkin emphasizes the importance of critical distance for the reader and the author: Tatyana projects her reading of sentimental novels onto Onegin, Onegin plays the role of a Byronic hero, Lensky falls prey to German Romantic ideas of the ideal, while "Pushkin" disclaims any resemblance to his hero or poetic relationship to Byron. Nabokov lowers Lolita's reading to comic books and teen magazines, connects Quilty to several German sources including Bürger's poem "Lenore," and has Humbert fill his own narrative with references to Poe. Rather than Pushkin's innocent, though tragic, projections of literature onto life, Nabokov creates the far more shocking projection of Humbert's nympholepsy onto the helpless Dolores Haze, a vile parody of the poet-muse relationship.

Reading *Lolita* through Pushkin's lens places Nabokov's American novel in its invisible but essential Russian context, identifying the questions both writers address in creating a literary tradition—the defining role of intertexts, the problem of the reader's projection of self into a fictional world, the primacy of language in defining a literary character.

Class discussion of literal translation raised by Nabokov's commentary on and controversial translation of *Onegin* heightens awareness of Nabokov's play with colliding stylistic levels, Humbert's formal European English and Lolita's American kid idiom. In his search for the basis of a truly national Russian literary language, Pushkin roamed the villages around his estate collecting peasant sayings and laments. Nabokov, when "inventing America" for *Lolita,* "traveled in school buses" to steep himself in the intonations of American schoolgirls (Gilliatt 280). His analogue to the Russian folk language that Pushkin blends into *Onegin's* narrative is brilliant. In America, which lacks a peasantry, children represent a source of a living oral tradition uncontaminated by literacy; their speech is juicy raw material for the construction of a new national literature.

In *Lolita,* this popular speech, which includes the language of movies, radio, and ads, is contrasted with Humbert's elevated periphrastic manner ("You talk like a book, *Dad*" [114]). Nabokov juxtaposes the two extremes to highlight the discrepancy between them:

> You will dwell, my Lolita will dwell (come here, my brown flower) with thirty-nine other dopes in a dirty dormitory.   (151)

> *Nous connûmes* (this is royal fun) the would-be enticements of their repetitious names—all those Sunset Motels, U-Beam Cottages, Hillcrest Courts . . .
>   *Nous connûmes* the various types of motor court operators, the reformed criminal, the retired teacher and the business flop. . . .   (146)

Pushkin characterizes Tatyana by her blend of simple spoken Russian with the language of the French novels she reads and Eugene by the foreign words from English, French, and German used in his Saint Petersburg milieu. Humbert tries to address Lo in her own language, blending her popular magazine lingo with his educated language:

> "Come and kiss your old man," I would say, "and drop that moody nonsense. In former times, when I was still your dream male [the reader will notice what pains I took to speak Lo's tongue], you swooned to records of the number one throb-and-sob idol of your coevals [Lo: "Of my what? Speak English"].   (149)

And Lo, usually when being devious, occasionally speaks Humbert's language:

> "Well, speak," said Lo. "Was the corroboration satisfactory?"   (204)

"I choose? *C'est entendu?*" She asked wobbling a little beside me. Used
French only when she was a very good little girl.   (209)

Humbert's periphrastic speech also serves a euphemistic purpose. He refers
to his penis as "my life," mentions fellatio three times indirectly (e.g., he has Lo
earn "the hard and nauseous way" permission to be in the school play, or, as he
puts it, "to participate in the school's theatrical program" [187]), and has intercourse with her when she is sick but obscures this Dostoevskian grotesquery
with Latin and lyricism:

At first she "ran a temperature" in American parlance, and I could not resist the exquisite caloricity of unexpected delights—Venus febriculosa—
though it was a very languid Lolita that moaned and coughed and shivered
in my embrace.   (198)

Thus through euphemism Humbert transforms the pervert into the "bewitched
traveler" (Tamir-Ghez, "Rhetorical Manipulation" 186).

Like Pushkin, Nabokov frequently highlights his use of foreign words and
the deliberate collision of stylistic levels (Weil 279) to resolve their polarization
through the vivid evocation of the everyday, conventionally considered inappro-
priate subject matter for lyricism, in which high and low elements are combined
in a poetry low on tropes and high on alliteration. Compare Pushkin's picture
of Russian provincial winter with Nabokov's lyrical evocation of American suburban summer:

A joyful crew of boys
Loudly cut the ice with their skates
A heavy goose with red feet, planning
to swim on the bosom of the waters,
Steps carefully onto the ice,
Slips and falls.   (1: 202; ch. 4, st. 42)

In the middle distance, two little maidens in shorts and halters came out of
a sun-dappled privy marked "Women." Gum-chewing Mabel (or Mabel's
understudy) laboriously, absent-mindedly, straddled a bicycle, and Marion, shaking her hair because of the flies, settled behind, her legs wide
apart; and, wobbling, they slowly, absently, merged with the light and
shade.   (84)

The two worlds represented by the stylistic poles are brought together by the
vision of the poet, thereby elevating the low subject matter (gum, flies, kids,
bikes, shorts) and revivifying elevated poetic diction with the simple word (note
the absence of periphrase or barbarisms in these descriptions). By placing these

and several other languages in proximity, Pushkin and Nabokov create a "system of languages that mutually and ideologically interanimate each other. . . . The author . . . cannot be found at any one of the novel's language levels: he is to be found at the center of organization where all levels intersect," a principle that obtains in the realist novel in general (Bakhtin 47–49).

Literary translation involves cultural translation—the interpretation of one culture by another. In *Lolita* America is seen through foreign eyes; the New World is presented through the filter of the Old. Like Nabokov, Humbert leaves France for America in 1940. For Nabokov, the move from Europe to America entailed changing his medium from Russian to English. Humbert's career reflects Nabokov's in this respect too: in France, Humbert writes a history of English poetry in French; in the United States, he compiles a manual of French literature for English-speaking students (16).

Humbert's view of his newly adopted country is heavily influenced by European art and by Romanticism in particular. Admiring the American countryside, he speaks of the "Chateaubriandesque trees" (145), superimposing French fictional trees on whatever elms, maples, and oaks he may be observing. Humbert describes "the average lowland North-American countryside" in terms of another object from his European past, "those painted oilcloths which were imported from America in the old days to be hung above washstands in Central-European nurseries" (152). While Humbert says that these models of natural scenes faded "the nearer I came to know them," he nonetheless writes of "Claude Lorrain clouds" and "a stern El Greco horizon" (152).

Humbert's inability to see the American trees for the French Romantic forest, the distorting of his present experience by his European literary baggage, resembles the problems facing Russian culture at the time when the modern Russian novel was struggling with the assimilation of European models. The problem is central to *Eugene Onegin*, whose characters' fates are determined by their superficial assimilation of German Romantic philosophy (Lensky) or Romantic novels (Tatyana, Onegin).

Both Nabokov and Pushkin urge the reader to distinguish among hero, narrator, and author by seeming to confuse the persona with themselves: as Nabokov indicates the crucial distance between Humbert the narrator and himself, "Pushkin" lives in Pushkin's Saint Petersburg and has Pushkin's friends, but his persona cannot be equated with the actual, historical author.

Because projection is the basis for the concept of the poet's muse, as well as for plots about doubles, the Romantic poet is in constant danger of solipsism. Nabokov is particularly concerned to reveal this solipsistic potential of romanticisms of all stripes as a false variant of his own faith in the world of the imagination. If the imagination is allowed to behave purely projectively without the natural scientist's regard for the perceived object, the object is liable to any perversion. This is the motivation for the abundance of perverts in Nabokov's (allegedly perverse) work.

Pushkin is concerned with the same problem. Discussing the process of literary creation, he contrasts his own methods with those of Onegin's friend, Lensky, who regularly rushes over to Olga with his latest impassioned madrigal:

> but I, when loving, was stupid and mute.
>
> Love passed, the Muse appeared,
> And the dark mind cleared up.
> Once free, I seek again the concord
> of magic sounds, feelings, and thoughts;
> . . . .
> and soon, soon the storm's trace
>   will hush completely in my soul:
> *then* I shall start to write a poem
>   in twenty-five cantos or so.   (1: 124; ch. 1, sts. 58–59)

Pushkin's ideas about the creation of literature, which form the core of *Onegin,* are contained in this "Love passed, the Muse appeared." Nabokov's note to this part of *Onegin* is his own credo as well:

> Pushkin expresses here his concepts of the workings of the poet's mind, in four stages:
>
> 1. Direct perception of a "dear object" or event.
> 2. The hot, silent shock of irrational rapture accompanying the evocation of that impression in one's fancies or actual dreams.
> 3. The preservation of the image.
> 4. The later, cooler touch of creative art, as identified with rationally controlled inspiration, verbal transmutation, and a new harmony.   (2: 211)

Humbert's attempt to cast his sexual obsession with Lolita as the relation between a poet and his muse is Nabokov's metaphor for the violation of the ideal of artistic critical distance.

Nabokov's note to chapter 1, stanza 38, on the quest for the source of Onegin's ennui contains his position paper in miniature:

> To this quest Russian critics applied themselves with tremendous zeal, accumulating in the course of a dozen decades one of the most boring masses of comments known to civilized man. Even a special term for Onegin's distemper has been invented (*Oneginstvo,* "Oneginism"); and thousands of pages have been devoted to him as a "type" of something or other (*e.g.,* of a "superfluous man" or a metaphysical "dandy," etc.). . . . . Thus a character borrowed from books but brilliantly recomposed by a great poet to whom life and library were one, placed by that poet within a brilliantly

reconstructed environment, and played with by that poet in a succession
of compositional patterns—lyrical impersonations, tomfooleries of genius,
literary parodies, and so on—is treated by Russian pedants as a sociological
and historical phenomenon typical of Alexander I's regime (alas, this tendency to generalize and vulgarize the unique fancy of an individual genius
has also its advocates in the United States).   (2: 150–51)

The student who learns to identify the difference between solipsistic and
creative projections in art and life will be armed against their confusion, which
creates the brilliance of, and causes the tragedies in, both *Onegin* and *Lolita*.
To help students assimilate Pushkin's version of how you are what you read,
I have them write their own parody of *Eugene Onegin* before reading *Lolita*.
They are asked to translate Onegin into the United States (or their country of
origin) of the current decade. This assignment gives them the experience of
being the author of a parody, of seeing the characters and plot from the author's
point of view, so that when they finally read *Lolita*, they experience Nabokov's
novel as authors themselves and can identify his devices more readily. After
we have discussed *Lolita*, I ask them to identify parallels with *Onegin*. In a
seminar on Nabokov, this exercise has the added benefit of explaining the Olga-
Chernyshevsky-Rudolph triangle in *The Gift* as a parody of the Olga-Onegin-
Lensky one and of identifying the novel's closing *Onegin* stanza.

With Pushkin's help, students achieve a reading of *Lolita* with heightened
awareness of language. For Nabokov, the novel's tragedy is both the loss of his
beloved Russian language (Steiner 123–25) and the debasement of the world of
the imagination. The clash between Europe and America underlying Humbert's
projection of his world onto Lo's shows nymphancy to be Humbert's perverse
metaphor for metamorphosis, one of Nabokov's treasured themes. *Onegin* highlights the difference between Humbert's memoir, which treats his attempt to
freeze the past he has lost as a neurotic condition, and Nabokov's novel, which
celebrates the possibility of incorporating what has been lost by creating a synthesis of Russia and America.

From Bauer's Li to Nabokov's Lo:
Lolita and Early Russian Film

Galya Diment

Since the release of Stanley Kubrick's *Lolita* in 1962 and the publication of Alfred Appel's *Nabokov's Dark Cinema* in 1974, the topics Vladimir Nabokov and cinema and, more narrowly, *Lolita* and cinema have become common in scholarship and courses on Nabokov. My interest, however, is in Nabokov and a different kind of cinema, prerevolutionary Russian cinema, in particular the work of Evgenii Bauer (1865–1917). The most popular and prolific director of Nabokov's youth, Bauer made more than eighty films (many of which did not survive) in less than five years—from 1913 until his sudden death between the two revolutions of 1917. Given students'—as well as my own—interest in film, I teach early Russian and Soviet cinema almost every year. I never fail to mention to those who are familiar with Nabokov how often Nabokov's oeuvre, including *Lolita*, appears to echo Bauer's films. Teaching Nabokov's *Lolita* and Bauer's films side by side furthers the exploration of Nabokov's deep Russian roots and demonstrates how crucial his formative experiences with Russian art and culture were both for his Russian and his American works. It also brings a new angle into the discussion of cinematographic elements in Nabokov's prose and thus serves as a helpful prequel to Nabokov's "dark cinema," as mapped out by Appel.

Nabokov's childhood coincided with the infancy of Russian cinema. *Sten'ka Razin*, the first film made by a Russian director (Vladimir Romashkov) and produced by a Russian studio (Drankov Company), appeared in 1908, when Nabokov was nine. In *Speak, Memory*, he describes how, in 1915 and 1916, he and his beloved "Tamara" (Liusia Shulgina) would go to one of the two movie theaters on Nevsky Prospect ("The Parisiana" and "The Piccadilly") during cold winter days when they needed a warm (and conveniently dark) place to be together. They would sit in the last row of seats, and though they probably paid scarce attention to the screen, they still noticed that

> [t]he art was progressing. Sea waves were tinted a sickly blue and as they rode in and burst into foam against a black, remembered rock . . . there was a special machine that imitated the sound of the surf, making a kind of washy swish. . . . As often as not, the title of the main picture was a quotation from some popular poem or song and might be quite long-winded. . . . Female stars had low foreheads, magnificent eyebrows, lavishly shaded eyes. (236)

Nabokov frequently mentions the experience of watching silent films in his early Russian works. Among the better-known examples are the oft-cited scene in *Mary*, where Ganin recognizes himself as an extra in a German film

(20–21), and Luzhin's emotional reaction to watching his very first movie in *Defense* (191–92). Among less-discussed instances is a remarkable poem, "Cinematograph" ("Kinematograf"), which Nabokov wrote in 1928 and published in the émigré paper *Rul'* ("Rudder"; 25 Nov.). The poem starts with a declaration of love: "I love these circuses of light, increasingly more hopelessly and more tenderly" ("Liubliu ia svetovye balagany / vse beznadezhnee i vse nezhnei"); proceeds to marvel at the magic of the cinematographic deception: "Here is a moonlit bedroom / just look how this shawl falls on the rug / Without seeing the bright lights on the set / or hearing the voice of the irritated director" ("Vot spal'nia ozarennaia. Smotrite, / kak eta shal' upala na kover. / Ne viden oslepitel'nyi iupiter, / ne slyshen razdrazhennyi rezhisser"); and ends with an abrupt dissolution of the vision: "And here is the end. . . . The invisible piano dies out. / . . . / . . . the invention melts away" ("I vot—konets . . . Roial' nezrimyi umer / temno i neznachitel'no pozhiv. / Ochnulsia mir, prokhladoiu i shumom / rastaiavshuiu vydumku smeniv") (*Krug* 105–06; my trans.).

I firmly believe that Nabokov's keen interest in gestures, so evident in all his novels, was, in fact, spurred by the silent films of his youth, where gestures played an all-important communicative role. It is, therefore, surprising that Nabokov's exposure to early Russian film has remained a blind spot in Nabokov studies. In Appel's book, the actor Ivan Mozzhukhin does make a brief appearance (as "Mosjoukine," the spelling he adopted after leaving Russia) but only in his sole American role, in the 1927 film *Surrender* (274). In her article "Nabokov and Cinema," Barbara Wyllie catalogs possible influences on Nabokov's formative years as an artist, but she does not mention the significance of the first films Nabokov watched as a young man growing up in Russia. Instead, she directs us toward pondering the possible impact in later years of "German Expressionist as well as Soviet and European avant-garde film, the epics of Cecil B. DeMille and D. W. Griffith, Mack Sennett's slapstick comedies" (221).

While foreign films were very popular among early moviegoers in Russia, by the time Nabokov was old enough to appreciate movies, the First World War had largely put an end to new foreign imports. It fell to the local talents, therefore, to produce enough films to support the studios and their theaters, as well as to satisfy the increasing craving for escape that people in wartime inevitably develop. This situation explains the head-spinning number of films that directors like Bauer, Iakov Protazanov (1881–1945), Petr Chardynin (1873–1934), and Vasilii Goncharov (1861–1915) were making during the war years. It was the era of two of Russia's megastars, Vera Kholodnaia (1893–1919) and Mozzhukhin (1889–1939), the latter described by Nabokov as "[t]he favorite actor of the day . . . whom Tamara and I had so often admired on the screen" (*Speak, Memory* 237, 247). (Young Nabokov annoyed Mozzhukhin when he inadvertently interrupted a film shooting taking place in early 1918 in Crimea.)

It was equally the era of Bauer, who was already in his forties when he started working in film. Bauer still remains an obscure figure in the history of cinematography. He graduated from Moscow's Institute of Painting, Sculpture, and

Architecture and, as did many future directors, first made his mark as a set designer, specializing in artistically impeccable and opulent art nouveau sets. He worked for Drankov and Pathé studios before he moved in 1913 to Khanzhonkov Production Company, where he became the most successful and acclaimed director of the war years. Bauer died in June 1917, after breaking his leg on a set in Crimea and, while bedridden, developing pneumonia. Several months later, with the advent of the Bolshevik revolution, his name and films would become virtually purged, and it has only been since the early 1990s that he has begun to receive his due as one of the world's most remarkable directors of that early era.

Among all the directors working at the time, Bauer was probably the closest to sharing young Nabokov's sensibilities and interests. Unlike Goncharov, who often focused exclusively on Russian peasants, or the very solidly middle-class Protazanov, Bauer was preoccupied with the upper social crust of the Russian society, which, as we know, was the immediate milieu of the Nabokov family. If only for that reason, Bauer's films should be an obligatory element for anyone who wants to get a sense of what Nabokov was likely to see and be surrounded with in the Saint Petersburg of his youth. I use Bauer's films every time I teach *Speak, Memory*. But beyond this general interest, there is a significant commonality of themes and even techniques. A supreme artist and a precocious filmmaker, Bauer was firmly rooted in Russian and European modernism. While many of the films Bauer made are on the surface melodramas similar to other typical cinematographic staples of the 1910s, they brim with dark psychological twists and turns of the kind that Nabokov appreciated.

These twists often stemmed from Bauer's preoccupation with the obsessive—and frequently criminal—behavior caused by men's desire to possess, preserve, and immortalize the beauty of the objects of their passion, even if that meant extinguishing their lives first. In *Smert' na zhizn'* ("Death for Life") a husband, played by Mozzhukhin, kills his wife and then keeps her embalmed body in a cellar to prevent aging and decay and thus preserve her beauty for eternity. In *Umiraiushchii lebed'* ("Dying Swan"), a painter strangles his model, a ballerina who stars in Camille Saint-Saens's *Dying Swan*, to bring verisimilitude to her pose and thus truly immortalize her art through his. Both films have immediate relevance to *Lolita*. Humbert would also love to prevent aging in his Lo, but, very much needing her alive, he has to settle instead on taking full advantage of Lolita before she "ages." And while he may be responsible just for ruining her life, not for her eventual demise, it is that very same "refuge of art" that Humbert, like the painter in "Dying Swan," offers to both himself and the object of his obsession as "the only immortality" the two of them can share (309).

There are, however, three other Bauer films that are even more productive when taught side by side with *Lolita*—*Grezy* ("Daydreams"), *Posle smerti* ("After Death"), and *Za schast'em* ("For Happiness"). All three films are readily available on either VHS or DVD. Together with "Dying Swan," these are the films that came out during the very peak of Nabokov's relationship with Shulgina, and, given how often they frequented movie houses at that time and how prominent Bauer was, it is hard to imagine that they would have missed them. Since, like Bauer, the films remain obscure, short summaries may be in order.

In "Daydreams," Sergei Nedelin (played by Aleksandr Vyrubov), a wealthy man, is despondent on losing his young wife, Elena, until he spots a woman on the street who looks very much like her. He follows the woman into a theater, where she turns out to be an actress performing in Jakob Meyerbeer's *Robert le Diable* ("Robert the Devil"; 1831). Nedelin is profoundly affected by the scene at the end of act 2 where the actress playing a dead nun masquerading as a maiden appears to be rising from her grave. He subsequently woos her, and they soon become engaged, upon which he proceeds to make his fiancée try on his dead wife's dress and copy her hairstyle. While the actress's vulgarity and common ways now and then repel him, Nedelin is obsessed with the desire to re-create his wife in another woman. The tale ends tragically, of course. His fiancée resents being treated as just the dead wife's look-alike and ridicules Nedelin for being a slave to his wife's memory, which he calls sacred. In the ultimate gesture of insult, she retrieves Elena's dark braid from a box where Nedelin has preserved it and, waving it around, mocks him for worshipping the "flea-breeding" hair of a dead woman. Enraged, Nedelin strangles his fiancée with the very braid she was taunting him with.

It is perhaps easy to imagine how both young Nabokov and his "Tamara" felt about such over-the-top melodramatic elements in Bauer when they would take a break from their own immediate love story to watch his. And yet any reader well acquainted with Nabokov will recognize several aspects of this film as similar to major themes in his works. Most significant, in "Vozvrashchenie Chorba" ("The Return of Chorb"; 1925), a bereaved husband, desiring to immortalize the image of his late wife and their love, re-creates their first night together in a dinky hotel by hiring a prostitute who vaguely resembles her. Particularly observant readers may note an interesting hair motif in the story, when a strand of the prostitute's—here blond—hair, left there on a previous stint in the same room, is noticed by Chorb's wife during their initial stay at the hotel.

And then there is the Annabel storyline of *Lolita*. Humbert Humbert is plainspoken about what he has been trying to do with the memory of Annabel, declaring that he "broke her spell by incarnating her in another" (15). Before he found a close match in Lolita, he had embarked on a series of more (Monique) or less (Marie) successful attempts at incarnation, mostly with prostitutes. Then, like Nedelin, he committed a grave blunder by linking his life with someone who, because of her good "imitation . . . of a little girl," he deemed close enough (25). Unlike Nedelin, Humbert never strangled his failed attempt at reincarnation, but he did seriously consider it: "I now wondered if Valechka . . . was really worth shooting, or strangling, or drowning" (29). Even a faint hair motif can be perceived in *Lolita* when Humbert, on his way to Pavor Manor, notes the only physical attribute of Lolita's that has been preserved in the car—

"a three-year-old bobby pin of hers in the depths of the glove compartment" (293), next, probably, to Chum, with which he intended to execute Quilty.

Interestingly enough, Humbert and Bauer may have the same antecedent in structuring their narratives: Edgar Allan Poe. As Appel points out, "Poe is referred to more than twenty times in *Lolita*, far more than any other writer" (Notes 331). Humbert's allusions to Poe's life (his marriage to his thirteen-year-old cousin Virginia [43]) and works are, in fact, at the heart of his plea for our sympathy and understanding; the title of Poe's poem "Annabel Lee" even serves as a bridge between Lolita's "precursor" (9), Annabel Leigh, and Lolita: "Annabel Haze, alias Dolores Lee, alias Loleeta" (167; see Appel, Notes 330–33). Humbert's identification with Poe is so intimate that he now and then gives his name to strangers as "Mr. Edgar H. Humbert" (75). Bauer's indebtedness to Poe is no less obvious. In "Dying Swan," there is a remarkable scene where the ballerina's prophetic dream ends in a very Poe-like manner, with numerous disembodied white hands all trying to reach her neck. "Daydreams" harks back to Poe's "Ligeia" (1838) both in its theme of the untimely loss of a beautiful young wife and the unsatisfactory experience with "the successor of the unforgotten Ligeia" (103). Even more striking, though, is the appearance of "huge masses of long and disheveled hair . . . blacker than the raven wings . . . of my lost love—of the lady—of the LADY LIGEIA" (108) as the story ends. (The same story carries a poem composed by Ligeia shortly before her death; the first line must have been quite amusing to Nabokov: "Lo! 'tis a gala night" [101].)

Comparing in class Nabokov's *Lolita* and Bauer's "Daydreams" provides an excellent vehicle for probing some of the more complex issues that *Lolita* raises in terms that students find easy to comprehend and respond to. Why do we tend to distinguish between plain crimes and crimes of passion? Is obsession a common human response to strong emotions or a sign of insanity? Is the essential "goodness" of Nedelin's love for his late wife and Humbert's love for Annabel compromised by the subsequent, or, more precisely, consequent crimes stemming from their attempts to reincarnate their lost lovers in others? Finally, to paraphrase Pushkin in *Mozart and Salieri*, can love and evil ever be compatible?

Bauer's "After Death" helps probe other aspects of the Lolita-Humbert relationship and, more specifically, the intricate tension between "reality" and perception, which is at the very core of both Nabokov's and Bauer's artistic philosophies. While Lolita is by no means an identical physical replica of Annabel, it hardly matters. As Humbert tells us:

> There are two kinds of visual memory: one when you skillfully recreate an image in the laboratory of your mind, with your eyes open . . . and the other when you instantly evoke, with shut eyes, on the dark innerside of your eyelids, the objective, absolutely optical replica of a beloved face.   (11)

There is an echo of the same theme as to which "replica" of the deceased beloved is truer to the woman's essence in "After Death." Like "Daydreams," this film is about the firm grip that the dead hold over the living. Based on Ivan Turgenev's story "Klara Milich" (1883; the other title of the story was, in fact, "Posle smerti"), the film follows a young man (Andrei Bagrov, played by Vitold Polonskii), an amateur scientist and photographer, who is still recovering from the death of his mother. Because he is grieving and also because he is painfully shy and afraid to be distracted from his scientific pursuits, Andrei spurns the attention of a young actress (Zoia Kadmina, played by Vera Karalli, who also stars in the "Dying Swan") even though he is strongly moved by her. When the actress commits suicide as a result of his rejection, Andrei, devastated by both guilt and love, becomes obsessed with trying to re-create her true image. Not satisfied with Zoia's photograph, he attempts to instill more life into it by employing a stereoscope and other scientific equipment in his laboratory to give it more dimensions. When science fails too, he shuts his eyes and relies, indeed, on the "dark innerside of [his] eyelids" for her to appear to him as a vision. Zoia obliges, and after a series of dreams and visions he dies of heart failure, clutching in his hand—strong glimpses of Poe here as well—a strand of dark hair, which, we are led to believe, entered the "real" world from Zoia's apparition.

The third film of particular relevance to *Lolita* is "For Happiness," Bauer's last completed film. Here a mother and a daughter, unbeknownst to each other, find themselves in love with the same man. The daughter, Li, played by a very young and petite Taisiia Borman, is probably supposed to be at least sixteen but looks fourteen or younger and would easily fit Humbert's definition of a "nymphet." Her mother (also Zoia, played by Lidiia Koreneva), a very rich widow who lost her husband ten years earlier, is involved in a serious relationship with a successful middle-aged lawyer (Dmitrii Gzhatskii, played by Nikolai Radin), but the two keep postponing making it public and getting engaged because Zoia fears that Li loved her father too much to accept a new man in her mother's life. The lawyer is therefore determined to make Li like him, and, alas, succeeds only too well. While he and Zoia readily attribute the warmth of Li's feelings to his progress in becoming a father figure, Li ends up rejecting her own suitor and declaring that her heart is given to Dmitrii Gzhatskii, without whose love she would die. Fearful that her frail daughter, who is already rapidly losing her sight, would go completely blind or even die, the mother begs her lover to marry Li. When he refuses and announces to Li that he is in love with her mother, the girl indeed enters the world of physical and emotional darkness. This is, of course, a reversal of the *Lolita* situation, where it is the daughter who is preferred to the mother and the mother who suffers a catastrophe after discovering the truth of the situation.

Looking at both "For Happiness" and *Lolita* facilitates an interesting discussion on the stereotype of mother-daughter relationships. Is Charlotte too selfish (obviously a cultural taboo for a mother) in putting her own needs before the needs and vulnerabilities of her child, thus failing to prevent the tragedy unfolding in front of her? Is the selflessness of Zoia's maternal love (the ideal cultural norm) any more helpful in averting the impending catastrophe? And, if we are brave enough to risk stepping into the territory usually covered by daytime TV soap operas and talk shows (of the type Lolita would probably watch), just what should mothers—and daughters—do in situations of this kind? (A successful answer to that question probably warrants extra credit.)

Lolita: Scene and Unseen

Brian Boyd

Students today often have more experience "reading" films than novels and naturally incline to watch the film of a book if there is one. They may also tend to accept a literary text rather passively, as if it were somehow a record of prior, even if fictional, events.

I approach *Lolita* by asking the class to dwell on a subscene in the novel, Humbert's first meeting with Lolita, and to consider actual and possible film versions of the scene to

> engage the skills undergraduates already have,
> block their inclination to think the film can substitute for the book,
> draw on the critical independence of mind they readily exercise once shown different ways of telling the same story, and
> develop their capacity to read and imagine actively.

Even apart from its recondite language and allusions, *Lolita* poses particular problems for students. The appeal of Humbert's intelligence, wit, and wry self-consciousness can seduce some, female as well as male, into seeing Humbert and Lolita's story almost entirely from Humbert's point of view. Some even go so far as to think that a girl as ordinary as Lolita is lucky to be loved so passionately by someone as discriminating and devoted as Humbert. Although students can be dislodged from such positions easily enough when asked to consider Humbert's recurring interest in other nymphets or in the possibility of "a litter of Lolitas" (300) or his repeated refusal to concern himself with Lolita's suffering, I think it better if they are primed for wariness and armed to resist Humbert's rhetoric from the outset. The ability to look from the viewpoint of those with less eloquence, confidence, or power is one that cannot be acquired too early, and learning how clearly Vladimir Nabokov manages to see from a position outside his narrator's offers a salutary lesson in imaginative and moral independence.

In part 1, chapter 10, Humbert has arrived in Ramsdale, hoping that as a lodger in the McCoo house he can take advantage of his proximity to twelve-year-old Ginny McCoo. When he discovers the McCoo home has burnt down, he has no reason to remain in Ramsdale but cannot escape being taken to the home of the McCoos' friend, Charlotte Haze. Every detail of the Haze home hardens his indifference into positive revulsion, until this:

> I was still walking behind Mrs. Haze through the dining room when, beyond it, there came a sudden burst of greenery—"the piazza," sang out my leader, and then, without the least warning, a blue sea-wave swelled

under my heart and, from a mat in a pool of sun, half-naked, kneeling, turning about on her knees, there was my Riviera love peering at me over dark glasses.

It was the same child—the same frail, honey-hued shoulders, the same silky supple bare back, the same chestnut head of hair. A polka-dotted black kerchief tied around her chest hid from my aging ape eyes, but not from the gaze of young memory, the juvenile breasts I had fondled one immortal day. And, as if I were the fairy-tale nurse of some little princess (lost, kidnapped, discovered in gypsy rags through which her nakedness smiled at the king and his hounds), I recognized the tiny dark-brown mole on her side. With awe and delight (the king crying for joy, the trumpets blaring, the nurse drunk) I saw again her lovely in-drawn abdomen where my southbound mouth had briefly paused; and those puerile hips on which I had kissed the crenulated imprint left by the band of her shorts—that last mad immortal day behind the "Roches Roses." The twenty-five years I had lived since then, tapered to a palpitating point, and vanished.

I find it most difficult to express with adequate force that flash, that shiver, that impact of passionate recognition. In the course of the sun-shot moment that my glance slithered over the kneeling child (her eyes blinking over those stern dark spectacles—the little Herr Doktor who was to cure me of all my aches) while I passed by her in my adult disguise (a great big handsome hunk of movieland manhood), the vacuum of my soul managed to suck in every detail of her bright beauty, and these I checked against the features of my dead bride. A little later, of course, she, this *nouvelle*, this Lolita, *my* Lolita, was to eclipse completely her prototype. All I want to stress is that my discovery of her was a fatal consequence of that "princedom by the sea" in my tortured past. Everything between the two events was but a series of gropings and blunders, and false rudiments of joy. Everything they shared made one of them.

I have no illusions, however. My judges will regard all this as a piece of mummery on the part of a madman with a gross liking for the *fruit vert*. *Au fond, ça m'est bien égal.* All I know is that while the Haze woman and I went down the steps into the breathless garden, my knees were like reflections of knees in rippling water, and my lips were like sand, and—

"That was my Lo," she said, "and these are my lilies."

"Yes," I said, "yes. They are beautiful, beautiful, beautiful!"   (39–40)

How does the passage work on us, from Humbert's viewpoint and from Nabokov's? How does it work as comedy? as romance? How do we respond to the gap between the mundane suburban setting and Humbert's extravagant expression of his feelings? How does Humbert's baroque style invite us into the privileged position of his private awareness and ask us to remain amused at the gap between his sense of the scene and Charlotte's and Lolita's inability to

perceive what he feels? How do the shifting tones of Humbert's rhetoric operate to shape our responses? What part do the sliding times play? (Successively,
Humbert with Annabel Leigh in 1923; first seeing Lolita in May 1947; the
imagined time of fairy tale; the immediacy of the moment's impact and the
protractedness of the attempt to convey it; the near "future," first Lolita curing
Humbert of all his aches, then replacing Annabel; the courtroom scene Humbert still expects as he writes this in late 1952; the 1947 "present" again.) What
role does fairy tale play here and elsewhere in the novel? How does Nabokov
work on us by inventing a scene with such pointed connections to other parts of
the book (in this case, especially via Lolita's precursor, Annabel) and by allowing
Humbert such conscious control over our responses?

After this discussion, I invite the students to draft a screenplay scene for this
first glimpse of Lolita. I ask them to consider how they might deal with the
possibility that the camera could show the scene quite differently from the way
Humbert presents it in prose. In the Stephen Schiff screenplay used by Adrian
Lyne for his 1998 movie, the scene takes only a hundred words. How much time
would you give it? What would you want Humbert's first glimpse of Lolita to
establish? (And what would you have already established, by this point in your
film, of Humbert's feelings toward young girls or nymphets?) Do you wish to
render the intensity of the moment for Humbert, and if so, how? Is it important
to establish his sense that Lolita is Annabel revived? How could you do this?
What attitude do you want viewers to take toward this meeting? How could you
keep the comedy of the disparity between Humbert's feelings and Charlotte's
unawareness of what has changed his mind?

I especially encourage students to think and script how we might see Humbert
and Lo talk to each other alone for the first time. In the Schiff screenplay such
a scene follows immediately and takes another hundred fifty words. How much
screen time would you allow for this scene? What would you want to establish in
their attitudes toward each other? What responses would you want the audience
to have to each character, overall and in this scene?

We then consider the two film versions, directed by Stanley Kubrick (1962)
and Lyne, to see what features of the scene have been dropped or added and
to see to what extent these differences can be attributed to the change of
medium from prose to film, to the aims of the filmmakers, or to the circumstances of production.

Kubrick in 1962, I explain, had good reason to be wary of film censors and
hence to minimize Lolita's youth, maximize her readiness for Humbert, and
yet minimize the sexual element of the relationship. How do these aims affect
his handling of the scene? How does the music contribute to the impact of
the moment? Lyne in 1998, by contrast, had little to fear from censors and
could maximize Lolita's youth, minimize her invitation to Humbert, and yet
maximize the sexuality of the scene. How are these possibilities reflected in
his version of the scene? And how do the conditions facing Kubrick in 1962

throw light on Nabokov's constraints, and his aims, in a novel begun more than a decade earlier?

Schiff wrote the published screenplay of the Lyne film, but Lyne had first hired others to draft it, including playwrights like Harold Pinter and David Mamet. Schiff incorporated a couple of scenes from Pinter, including the first conversation between Humbert and Lolita, which was to follow immediately in film time though not story time from Humbert's first seeing Lolita. The clothes-line and pinging pebbles come from Humbert's initial diary entry, in the chapter of the novel following his first vision of Lolita:

> HUMBERT.   Yes, yes. They are beautiful, beautiful. *(pause)* Uh, how much was the room?
> *The back porch—day   Lolita taking clothes off a clothesline. Humbert—casually dressed, shoes off—is watching her. It is obvious he has moved in. Lolita puts the clothes in a tub, lazily brings the tub to the porch, glances at him.*
> LOLITA.   Hi.
> *Sitting on the step of the porch, she scoops peaches out of a can with her hand, and eats them. The syrup drips.*
> HUMBERT.   You like peaches.
> LOLITA.   Who doesn't? You want one?
> HUMBERT.   No, no. I generally wait until after the sun goes down.
> LOLITA.   For what?
> HUMBERT.   Peaches.
> *He gazes at her bare arms. She begins to pick up pebbles with her feet and tosses them at the can. The sound of pebbles hitting the can: ping ping . . .*
> LOLITA.   How come?
> HUMBERT.   Keeps the lions away. I learned that in Africa.
> LOLITA.   Learned what?
> HUMBERT.   About peaches.
> *She looks at him and grins.*
> LOLITA.   You're nuts.   (13–15)

Since Schiff retained the scene and Lyne filmed it, although he excised it in the editing room, we can presume they had aims similar to Pinter's, at least in this scene. What do we infer of their sense of the relationship between Humbert and Lolita here? What aspects of Humbert and of Lolita in the novel does this illuminate or obscure?

We then look at the scene through one more lens, the most surprising of all. Nabokov traveled to Hollywood to write a screenplay for Kubrick in 1960, but his text was drastically rewritten at the end of the year by Kubrick and his producer, James B. Harris. Nabokov received full screenplay credit, nevertheless, so that his literary reputation could serve as yet another line of defense against the forces of censorship potentially massing over the horizon. In 1974 Nabokov published his original screenplay. There the scene of the first conversation between Lolita and Humbert takes six pages. Although it incorporates "She's a fright. And mean. And lame" from Humbert's first diary entry (41), Nabokov makes the action follow directly from Humbert's decision to move into the Haze home. The new scene shows us Humbert not as seen by himself, debonair, impassioned, dramatic, wry, but as seen from outside, creepily persistent, slyly circumspect, disconcertingly sleazy:

LOLITA.   Did you see the fire?

HUMBERT.   No, it was all over when I came. Poor Mr. McCoo looked badly shaken.

LOLITA.   You look badly shaken yourself.

HUMBERT.   Why, no. I'm all right. I suppose I should change into lighter clothes. There's a ladybird on your leg.

LOLITA.   It's a ladybug, not a ladybird.

She transfers it to her finger and attempts to coax it into flight.

HUMBERT.   You should blow. Like this. There she goes.

LOLITA.   Ginny McCoo—she's in my class, you know. And she said you were going to be her tutor.

HUMBERT.   Oh, that's greatly exaggerated. The idea was I might help her with her French.

LOLITA.   She's grim, Ginny.

HUMBERT.   Is she—well, attractive?

LOLITA.   She's a fright. And mean. And lame.

HUMBERT.   Really? That's curious. Lame?

LOLITA.   Yah. She had polio or something. Are you going to help me with my homework?

HUMBERT.   *Mais oui*, Lolita. *Aujourd'hui?*

Charlotte comes in.

CHARLOTTE. That's where you are.

LOLITA.   He's going to help me with my homework.

CHARLOTTE. Fine. Mr. Humbert, I paid your taxi and had the man take your things upstairs. You owe me four dollars thirty-five. Later, later. Dolores, I think Mr. Humbert would like to rest.

HUMBERT.   Oh no, I'll help her with pleasure.

Charlotte leaves.

LOLITA.   Well, there's not much today. Gee, school will be over in three weeks.

A pause.

HUMBERT.   May I—I want to pluck some tissue paper out of that box. No, you're lying on it. There—let me—thanks.

LOLITA.   Hold on. This bit has my lipstick on it.

HUMBERT.   Does your mother allow lipstick?

LOLITA.   She does not. I hide it here.

She indraws her pretty abdomen and produces the lipstick from under the band of her shorts.

HUMBERT.   You're a very amusing little girl. Do you often go to the lake shore? I shaw—I mean, I saw that beautiful lake from the plane.

LOLITA.   (*lying back with a sigh*) Almost never. It's quite a way. And my mummy's too lazy to go there with me. Besides, we kids prefer the town pool.

HUMBERT.   Who is your favorite recording star?

LOLITA.   Oh, I dunno.

HUMBERT.   What grade are you in?

LOLITA.   This a quiz?

HUMBERT.   I only want to know more about you. I know that you like to solarize your solar plexus. But what else do you like?

LOLITA.   You shouldn't use such words, you know.

HUMBERT.   Should I say "what you *dig*"?

LOLITA.   That's old hat.

Pause. Lolita turns over on her tummy. Humbert, awkwardly squatting, tense, twitching, mutely moaning, devours her with sad eyes; Lolita, a restless sunbather, sits up again.

HUMBERT.   Is there anything special you'd like to be when you grow up?

LOLITA.   What?   (*Novels* 707–08)

What is different—from the students' versions, the film versions, the Schiff-Pinter screenplay, and the novel—in Nabokov's screenplay? What are his aims in this scene? What does the scene suggest about his attitudes to Humbert and Lolita? How and why are these attitudes more difficult to infer from the novel? What does the difference between the screenplay and the novel suggest of Nabokov's attitude to the audiences for each form?

What do we gain, and what do we lose, from the screenplay's more objective view of Humbert? Although it is morally clearer—and may therefore help some of the more susceptible students not to succumb to Humbert's seductive style—it is also artistically thinner. Why? Students are encouraged to think about the purpose of the novel's rich diction, imagery, and narrative self-consciousness, about the purpose and value of its characterization of Humbert from within, about the role of its humor. Why does Nabokov himself change the effect of the scene so dramatically from novel to screenplay? Because of a change of medium? For a different imagined audience? Because of a new attitude toward the story? Does the screenplay scene make explicit what Nabokov would like his best readers to understand from the novel? Does it perhaps reflect his awareness that some readers had not inferred so well, that he had made Humbert even more persuasive than he intended?

How do we take the screenplay into consideration as evidence for reading the novel? Does it have the same evidentiary value as the Schiff screenplay or the

Kubrick and Lyne films? If not, why not? What does our answer suggest about authors and authorial intentions and our response to them? How does it throw light on the William Wimsatt–Monroe Beardsley notion of the intentional fallacy? How do Nabokov's changes (and he made others: minor ones for the Russian translation of *Lolita* he prepared between 1963 and 1965 and major ones during the novel's evolution from the 1939 Russian ur-*Lolita*, *The Enchanter*, to *Lolita*) affect our notion of the unity or finality of a work of art?

What does a comparison of these different versions of the first meeting and first conversation of Humbert and Lolita suggest about the way we should read the novel? Are there aspects of the novel that already prefigure the kind of reading of the scene, or of the relationship between Humbert and Lolita in general, that we infer from juxtaposing screenplay and novel? Or does reading with that kind of imaginative independence of Humbert prove almost impossible? If so, why has Nabokov made it so difficult?

What advantages are there of the more complex but potentially more misleading presentation of the novel over the less complex and perhaps less treacherous presentation in the film? Does it become a different story on page and screen? Should a story, to stay the same story, be transformed as it moves from one medium to the other? Does a story stay the same story when it is transformed in medium or emphasis? What creative potentials remain within the constraints of a given story or even a single scene?

Lolita in an American Fiction Course

Michael Wood

Vladimir Nabokov became an American citizen in 1945 and liked to say he was an American writer. He could be whimsical about this: "I am as American as April in Arizona" (*Strong Opinions* 98). "As apple pie" is the cliché waiting just offstage, and the joke is complicated. We might paraphrase Nabokov as implying something like, "I know that whatever I say, you will continue to see me as an exotic Russian writing in English, but think again. That too is one of the things an American writer can be. This is a land of immigrants and I am not Joseph Conrad."

This comment makes a good start on the question of what an American writer is, but I suggest something more direct and less civic: an American writer is one whose work is at home in American literature. In what follows I try to evoke two (among many possible) ways in which *Lolita* may be seen as being at home specifically in American fiction courses. The first way is largely, although not exclusively, thematic; the second, a mixture of the technical and the philosophical. In considerations of the first way, "America" is more or less synonymous with the United States. The second way involves a larger notion of America, in which Jorge Luis Borges, for example, is an unavoidable figure.

America appears on the second page of Humbert's text. His Aunt Sybil's husband is said to have "spent most of his time in America, where eventually he founded a firm and acquired a bit of real estate" (10). This is the "*oncle d'Amérique*" (27) who is the source of Humbert's later income and the reason for his transmigration to the United States. This America is already a fabulous elsewhere, since an American uncle, in the French idiom, is anyone who leaves you a lot of money. Humbert brilliantly reinforces this effect by his manner of telling us about the legacy. He appears to be merely describing his domestic life with his first wife, Valeria, how they eat, where they shop, their regular restaurant in Paris.

> And next door, an art dealer displayed in his cluttered window a splendid, flamboyant, green, red, golden and inky blue, ancient American estampe— a locomotive with a gigantic smokestack, great baroque lamps and a tremendous cowcatcher, hauling its mauve coaches through the stormy prairie night and mixing a lot of spark-studded black smoke with the furry thunder clouds.
> These burst. (26–27)

Humbert is going not only to America but also to a mythological, western, distance-stretching America. Much later, driving across and around the country with Lolita, Humbert describes himself as "putting the geography of the United States into motion" (152)—or locomotion, as he also says (174). And more than once he hears the train he saw in the print: "And sometimes trains would cry in the monstrously hot and humid night with heartrending and ominous plangency, mingling power and hysteria in one desperate scream" (146). There are trains in Europe too, and these instances owe something to Proust, and perhaps to Joyce, but the scream here comes from a combination of Humbert's guilt and a double idea (European and American) of the unpredictable loneliness of America.

It is not only Humbert who is putting geography into motion. Nabokov's own scene stretches from coast to coast, from Providence (189) to Alaska, where Lolita dies in childbirth. She mentions Juneau, where her husband's brother lives—Humbert in his perturbation hears it as Jupiter (275, 280). And Nabokov uses Humbert's descriptions of America to tell us something about Humbert as well as the country. Even in memory Humbert is triumphant and very funny about his first travels with Lolita. "This is royal fun," he says as he gets going on his witty account of the sights and sounds and motels of 1940s America (146). This is where a sign saying "VACANCY" becomes a sorry confession ("countless motor courts proclaimed their vacancy in neon lights" [116]) and where a sign saying "SLOW CHILDREN" becomes a description, not an instruction ("[w]e . . ..spared slow children" [219]). But in his darker moments he loses control of his prose and his geography. His wit runs out, and all he has to tell us about one place is its altitude and about another is that he and Lolita had a row on a street corner "facing Safeway, a grocery" (158). Humbert is falling apart, and his failure to find an ironic comment reflects Nabokov's sense of the limits of a busy mind.

A similar gap between Humbert and Nabokov opens up in one of the book's most famous passages, except that Humbert's imagination is now working too hard rather than fading:

> We had been everywhere. We had really seen nothing. And I catch myself thinking today that our long journey had only defiled with a sinuous trail of slime the lovely, trustful, dreamy, enormous country that by then, in retrospect, was no more to us than a collection of dog-eared maps, ru-ined tour books, old tires, and her sobs in the night—every night, every night—the moment I feigned sleep.   (175–76)

Humbert's repeatedly feigning sleep is as telling as Lolita's constant sobbing, and the repetition of "every night" produces an almost unbearable emphasis. His guilt has the size and shape of the United States. Lolita and America have lost their innocence through Humbert's intervention—this is both true and false, in ways more than a little too complicated to detail here. In the myth America is lonely and innocent, innocent because lonely. And because this idea (and this guilt) is so clearly Humbert's, we have to wonder what Nabokov's idea is and whether he has one. He is not going to tell, and we miss his irony entirely if we miss his disappearing act. But of course his disappearance does not abolish or even undermine the American allegory, the trail of European slime over the

American dream. It frames it as a question and links Nabokov to a whole tradition of American writers, from Henry James to F. Scott Fitzgerald and beyond. American innocence in this tradition is not a fact but a recurring fantasy, something no actual experience can ruin.

Space and innocence, trains in the night. Roads, cars, beaches, lakes, high mountain slopes. Advertising, popular music, movies, schools and headmistresses, summer camps, small towns, and much, much more, to borrow the last words of *Ada* (589). The America of *Lolita* is a closely observed place, the result of Nabokov's own watchful work and travels. I think of those "impaled guest checks" at American diners and "horribly experienced flies" on the sticky counter (155), and every reader of the novel will come up with his or her own favorite examples, images, or snatches of languages that seem shockingly familiar, all too real, often very funny. Creating these instances (that is, finding them and slightly tilting them) is part of what Nabokov means by "inventing America" ("On a Book" 312). But this same America is constantly in dialogue with American literature, at times quite consciously through Nabokov's own signals, at times because of preoccupations shared with writers in whom Nabokov had no interest and whom he perhaps never read.

Edgar Allan Poe is everywhere in *Lolita*, of course, and not only because of "Annabel Lee" and his thirteen-year-old bride. The whole novel climaxes in a parody of one of the Gothic mansions found so frequently in Poe. But Humbert also mentions an expedition to Pierre Point, Melville Sound, supposedly in "arctic Canada" (33), and Alfred Appel reports that Nabokov said, "When I was young I liked Poe, and I still love Melville" (Notes 331). These signals are an invitation to imagine *Lolita* at home in a course that studies the morbid American worlds of Poe (and Hawthorne) and the grander pathologies of Melville, but I suggest that *Lolita* is also relevant to any course in which varieties of American loneliness are explored, particularly in relation to those leaps of hope and desire that Europeans are supposedly (and sometimes actually) too tired to manage.

Jay Gatsby's disappointments are in direct proportion to the expectations his American world has led him to entertain, and William Faulkner's novels are full of founding energies that have ended in intricate melancholy, solitude, and despair. It is tempting to think of *Lolita* as also related to the novels of Mark Twain and the recurring theme of what Richard Poirier has called "a world elsewhere"; Morris Dickstein has aptly placed it in the genre of "road novels."

In all but the last of these instances we are looking backward in time, but that is not all we can do. Jack Kerouac's *On the Road* was published in 1957 and is a reminder that we can also situate Nabokov among his contemporaries. *Lolita* would be just as much at home in a course on midcentury American fiction as in a survey of the longer term. Saul Bellow's *Adventures of Augie March* appeared the year before *Lolita*, Flannery O'Connor's *A Good Man Is Hard to Find* in the same year, and Philip Roth's *Goodbye, Columbus*, in 1959. Joseph Heller's *Catch-22* was published in 1961. It would be absurd for me to try to summarize or conflate such different works or predict what will happen when we study them alongside *Lolita*, but it's not hard to imagine how productive a series of comparisons could be.

Gathering the preceding suggestions together, we might say *Lolita* is an American novel (and Nabokov therefore an American writer) because its narrator, and in one sense the book itself, dreams constantly of America and offers expert, detailed witness to the American dream, where that dream is not only the familiar belief in first and second chances (Humbert imagines Lolita's unborn child as "dreaming already in her of becoming a big shot and retiring around 2020 A.D." [277]) and not only the always deferred dream of Langston Hughes's well-known poem but also a dream that can die ("everything soiled, torn, dead" [185]), even, and especially, if every death is swallowed up in a new alluring vision of possibility. When Humbert says goodbye to Lolita for the last time, or rather when she chants "Good by-aye" in his version of her accent, he has four adjectives for her, unseparated by commas. She is his "American sweet immortal dead love" (280). In the vision we are pursuing, it is because she is American that she is sweet, dead, and immortal.

In *City of Words*, a pioneering study of contemporary American fiction, Tony Tanner writes that "the old geographies no longer obtain" (34). But the geographies in question are not those of the literal, continental United States so much as those of "reality" itself ("one of the few words which mean nothing without quotes," Nabokov says in "On a Book Entitled *Lolita*," [312]), the familiar human world unsettled by mischief, skepticism, or the restless imagination. Much of the most remarkable North American fiction of the second half of the twentieth century, whether we think of the work of John Barth, Donald Barthelme, Thomas Pynchon, or Don DeLillo, courts a kind of epistemological liberation that is also a form of panic; it finds a dizzying freedom from fact only to learn that fact is often lurking in unexpected places, like a madman escaped from a hospital or an assassin who has crossed an ocean to do his job.

I evoke these images from *Pale Fire*, because that is the novel that Tanner and other critics place at or near the origin of these tendencies, along with the stealthy stories of Borges. Borges and Nabokov, in this view, preside together over a whole series of fictions, sometimes thought of as paranoid, in which the mind discovers the terror and the wonder of its own power to dissolve the world. This is an American development, because it repeats the gesture of finding or founding a new world; but it goes beyond the United States and finds many echoes in the so-called Boom novels of Latin America, represented chiefly by the writing of Guillermo Cabrera Infante, Julio Cortázar, Carlos Fuentes, Gabriel García Márquez, and José Donoso. This writing in turn, especially García Márquez's *One Hundred Years of Solitude*, had a strong influence on Toni Morrison and other North American writers, for whom ghosts, for example, assumed a new force and a new respectability.

This form of fiction, these interests and preoccupations, are already present, and indeed richly displayed, in *Lolita*, making it a perfect candidate for a course on recent American fiction or metafiction. In *Pale Fire* we wonder how

real the quirky country of Zembla can be and who our narrator is, and critics
have been eager to imagine that one or other of the characters in this novel
invented all the rest. And in *Lolita* we are invited to ask similar questions. Who
is John Ray, Jr., the alternately eloquent and sanctimonious psychologist who
writes the foreword to Humbert's "strange pages" (3)? What sort of existence
do we ascribe to the person who is not Humbert Humbert but gives himself that
name, after passing over Otto Otto, Mesmer Mesmer, and Lambert Lambert?
"[F]or some reason," he says, "I think my choice expresses the nastiness best"
(308). For some reason? What reason? And why does he need a name that
sounds like a stutter? What else has he invented or switched in the course of
telling his story?

He says he started to write *Lolita* (his memoir) "fifty-six days" ago (308), and
a little arithmetic starts up all kinds of odd possibilities. Humbert died, John
Ray, Jr., tells us, on 16 November 1952. Humbert says he set out for his last visit
to Lolita on 22 September 1952, arriving the next day. He leaves in the after-
noon, returns to Ramsdale, and finds his way to Quilty's Gothic manor, where
he kills him. The date now is 25 or 26 September. Now even if Humbert died
on the very day of completing his manuscript, fifty-six days back puts us on 22
September. How can Humbert be in jail, as he says he is on his second page, for
a crime he has not yet committed? Maybe John Ray, Jr., or Humbert (or both)
are wrong about the dates. It is hard to see where that leaves us. It's not impossible that Humbert started to write his memoir as soon as he heard from Lolita
and went to see her, but then he would have to have added the Quilty plot at a
late stage and to have gone through his text inserting notations and apostrophes
("Ladies and gentlemen of the jury," "Gentlewomen of the jury," "Frigid gentlewomen of the jury" [9, 123, 132]) to make it look as if the whole thing were
written in prison. Another possibility is that he did not find Lolita and did not
kill Quilty and has fantasized his story's ending, his last encounter with Lolita,
and his ludicrously executed murder of his rival.

But then he could have fantasized the complete story, from the first page—all
we know for sure is that he has borrowed hundreds of elements from an America we recognize. He has certainly arranged the symmetries and coincidences
of his story—the matching number 342 for the Haze house, the hotel room at
the Enchanted Hunters, and the number of "hotels, motels and tourist homes"
Humbert stayed at when he was on the trail of Quilty (35, 118, 248)—to enhance
the sense of a plot against him, to make us see more clearly than he could at
the time (or can now) that what he thought was accidental reality was in fact a
conspiracy. He writes of the "chance memories that I have threaded through my
book with considerably more ostentation than they present themselves with to
my mind even now when I know what to seek in the past"—a riddling sentence
and a miniature theory of narrative (255). He pictures his second journey with
Lolita and his loss of her as a real-life play staged by the late-symbolist play-
wright Quilty (305). But what if he has invented Quilty out of nothing, treated
himself to the luxury of a full-blown Dostoevskian alter ego?

We ask what is real within the fiction and what it means to speak of reality in fiction, apart from the strict specifications of naturalism. One good answer in this context is that the fiction itself is real, or rather the fiction-making capacity that renders any world a potential new world, with uncertain relations to the old. "Almost immediately," Borges writes of a fantastic formation that is taking over the whole historical universe, "reality yielded on more than one account. The truth is that it longed to yield" (17). In Nabokov it's not that reality longs to give in but that it never settles down before distortions and modifications ruffle it ("I have camouflaged everything, my love," Humbert says [267]). It has always already been stylized by a creative imagination—manipulative in Humbert's case, transformative in Nabokov's—and so we suspect every word of being some sort of disguise, like Humbert's name itself. But a disguise has to be a disguise of something, and this hidden something is the eerie Nabokov effect, which we find richly echoed in Pynchon's V and Gravity's Rainbow and in DeLillo's Libra. We seem to glimpse, behind the art, a world that art did not make: a mother and a daughter who really die, for example, one in a freak accident (like Humbert's mother), the other in childbirth in Alaska.

Charlotte Haze's death in Lolita is a perfect example of what can be thought of as conspiracy fiction, where plots are not only made but unmade, like the American dream. Humbert heavily foreshadows the event—"the poor lady," "the doomed dear," "a bad accident is to happen quite soon" (37, 38, 79)—tempts us into thinking that "accident" is a euphemism, that he is going to murder Charlotte, and then gives us the details of a causal sequence so intricate that it amounts to chance: weeping in distress at her discovery of Humbert's snarling diary, Charlotte crosses the road and is hit and killed by a car whose driver is trying to avoid the dog we met on Humbert's arrival at Lawn Street. Humbert speaks of "precise fate, that synchronizing phantom" (103) but means only what we call chance. Chance is what we live, and fate is the same thing relived as an ordered story. And the ideal modern American fiction—a subject for discussion—will remember, will hint at, all the random pieces of the real that are lost when chance becomes fate and will celebrate fiction as much for what it misses or disguises as for what it magically conjures up.

Lolita: Law, Ethics, Politics

Dana Dragunoiu

Students are fascinated by *Lolita*'s publication history and the controversies sparked by its Paris debut and its subsequent publication in the United States. A brief account of *Lolita*'s reception history provides students with an overview of the legal and moral issues at the heart of the debates surrounding the novel. Students typically have no difficulty identifying the aspects of the novel that have generated these debates. Whereas some students argue that the novel seems to condone and perhaps even glorify pedophilia, others point out that the novel does not allow us to forget the pain and suffering Dolly experiences as a victim of sexual abuse. I use this debate to initiate a discussion about the novel's formal structure by asking students to consider the genre Nabokov has chosen for *Lolita*. We note that the novel is written as a confessional legal document intended to justify Humbert Humbert's murder of Clare Quilty to the jurors who will one day sit in judgment at his trial.

Conceived as part of Humbert's legal defense, *Lolita* makes explicit its connection to the law. The novel's formal structure invites readers to see themselves as engaged in legal deliberation: we are the "[l]adies and gentlemen of the jury" to whom Humbert turns for vindication (9). I tell students that if we are attentive to this legal framework, we have to assume the role of jurors in Humbert's hypothetical trial and assess the extent of his guilt in the murder of Clare Quilty and the sexual abuse of Dolly Haze. These questions prompt us to reflect further on the nature of the law and its relation to the political domain. Our discussions move through four related topics: the competing claims of positive and natural law, the relation between law and ethics, the limits and limitations of liberalism, and the conflict between civil rights and the public good.

In the first of these discussions we consider the legitimacy of Humbert's arguments in defense of his actions. We reconstruct Humbert's defense by noting that, despite freely admitting to the murder of Quilty, Humbert argues that Quilty's murder was a crime of passion and as such should be judged with leniency. To make this argument, however, Humbert must expose his relationship with Dolly, a relationship that opens him to the charge of rape and sexual abuse. Knowing that sexual intercourse with a child is a felony in the United States, Humbert must first defend his actions against Lolita before he can exonerate himself for the murder of Quilty.

I ask students to identify the ways in which Humbert justifies his actions. They usually single out for attention Humbert's claim that his passion for nymphets, his "nympholepsy," as he calls it, is a direct consequence of his childhood romance with Annabel Leigh. This first romance, Humbert tells us, cast a spell on him, interrupting his sexual development (13–14). Humbert portrays himself as the victim of a specific pathology, and he seeks to be acquitted on the ground that his actions were not taken from a position of autonomy. This line of argument highlights the way in which our legal system defines crime as an autonomous action, a subject that plays an integral part in our discussion of age-of-consent laws.

Some students also note that Humbert's most forceful and sustained defense of his conduct makes the claim that there is nothing intrinsically immoral about a grown man's sexual relations with an underage girl. Moral standards are culturally relative, Humbert argues, and this moral relativism is reflected in the arbitrariness of the law. As he points out on several occasions, the legal prohibitions against sex with minors are mere taboos (18, 264). I ask students to consider why Humbert is intent on identifying his actions with taboos. The distinction between a culturally relative taboo and a universally binding moral prohibition enables students to see the ethical implications of Humbert's line of defense. We examine some of the passages in which Humbert's eclectic invocation of the work of historians and anthropologists reveals that the legal and moral prohibition against pedophilia is only a recent phenomenon (19, 124, 150). Students begin to see that Humbert's most concerted self-defense turns on the idea that the law does not draw its sustenance from an absolute moral order but is socially and historically constructed.

The language of jurisprudence helps us articulate the larger implications of Humbert's position in this matter. Philosophers of law, I explain, refer to legal positivism as the doctrine that all law derives from the will of legislators. Legal positivists, I elaborate, argue that the law is made rather than discovered and that there is no intrinsic link between law and morality. I ask students to imagine themselves as a jury of legal positivists who must pass a verdict on Humbert's actions. This thought experiment is intended to enable students to see the interpretive consequences that emerge from judging Humbert according to a specific jurisprudential standard. Students begin to see that if they evaluate Humbert's actions from the perspective of legal positivism, they have to find Humbert guilty for defying the laws of the land. Since American law in the 1950s prohibited murder and sexual intercourse between children and adults, a legal positivist would convict Humbert on these grounds. A legal positivist, however, would have nothing to say about the moral dimension of Humbert's conduct. The legal positivist, who believes that there is no universal, absolute moral standard against which we can evaluate our laws, would have to acquit Humbert had he conducted an affair with Dolly in a culture in which sex with the underaged was permissible. A juror inclined to judge Humbert from the positivist perspective would have to agree with Humbert that his misfortune is to be a nympholept in twentieth-century Europe and the United States.

The discussion proceeds by asking if members of the class are satisfied with such a verdict. Some are not, arguing that the extent of Humbert's crime is greater than legal positivism allows. They point out that Humbert's confession also reveals him to be self-aware in ways that challenge the positivist claim that law and morality are unrelated and culturally contingent. They point to passages in which Humbert describes the pain he causes Dolly by conducting a sexual relationship with her (140, 282–83, 287). His remorse and his confession that he is not exempt from "universal emotions" undermine his argument that there is nothing intrinsically wrong in an adult man's sexual relationship with a twelve-year-old girl (287). I tell students that to declare Humbert's conduct impermissible in absolute terms, we must abandon legal positivism in favor of natural law. Natural law is a jurisprudential doctrine that sets itself in opposition to legal positivism by asserting that the law is discovered rather than made. The law is conceived as a system of justice common to all humankind, independent of sociopolitical contingencies, and derived from reason or nature. According to the natural law theorist, the law is ineluctably connected to morality. Humbert's guilt and remorse suggest that human beings, however corrupt and opportunistic, know the difference between right and wrong. A jury committed to natural law principles would convict Humbert not only on legal grounds but also on moral grounds for performing an action that is unconditionally wrong. By discussing Humbert's self-defense as a debate between natural and positive law, students begin to see that to hold Humbert categorically responsible for his conduct toward Dolly is to insist on a universally binding set of ethical and legal norms.

The second discussion problematizes the novel's allegiance to natural law by confronting students with the difficulties that bedevil any attempt to translate moral principles into legal statutes. We note that Humbert's opportunistic observations about the arbitrariness of the law are true when he points out that some laws vary from state to state (171–72) and that age-of-consent laws are inescapably random (18). I provide students with a table that illustrates the inconsistencies among age-of-consent laws from country to country, state to state, and sex to sex (see table).

Worldwide Ages of Consent

	Male-Female	*Male-Male*	*Female-Female*
Bahamas	16	18	18
France	15	15	15
Ireland	17	17	17
Madagascar	21	21	21
Puerto Rico	14	illegal	illegal
Saudi Arabia	must be married	illegal	illegal
Spain	13	13	13
UNITED STATES:			
Connecticut	16	16	16
California	18	18	18
Illinois	17	17	17
Nevada	16	18	18

I ask students to consider whether this variation supports Humbert's positivist argument that the law is arbitrary and therefore detached from moral constraints. Does this fact undermine the conclusion that *Lolita* stakes its ethical commitments in natural law? We begin answering this question by examining the principles that underwrite sexual consent laws. We take up once again the question of autonomy, the animating principle behind these laws, and note that age-of-consent laws seek to distinguish between those who can make informed decisions about their sexual conduct and those who cannot. The difficulty of identifying with precision when individuals become autonomous accounts for the inconsistency in such laws. These inconsistencies, however, do not invalidate the ethical principles that guide them.

The question of autonomy brings us to one of the most unsettling aspects of the novel. Humbert takes enormous satisfaction in telling the jury that Dolly first seduced him (132). He interprets Dolly's proposition as a form of consent: her unexpected words give him "the odd sense of living in a brand new, mad new dream world, where everything was permissible" (133). I ask the class to consider the validity of Humbert's interpretation by asking whether Dolly's invitation to sex is made from a position of autonomy. Students point out that despite her sexual precocity Dolly is not autonomous. Her proposition is largely fueled by her unreflective passion for Hollywood glamour magazines (49) and by her mistaken belief that sex with Humbert will be no different from sex with Charlie Holmes, her summer-camp paramour and coeval (133–34). When Dolly "seduces" Humbert, she does so from a position of naïveté and ignorance, something that Humbert knows but refuses to acknowledge. He also downplays the physical pain this sexual act inflicts on Dolly (141). Taken together, these passages reveal that Humbert has raped Dolly, something he admits in the final chapter of the novel when he sentences himself to "thirty-five years for rape" (308).

Lolita's exploration of the nature of autonomy extends to Dolly's relationship with Quilty. At fourteen, Dolly is no longer a child according to the law. Statutory rape, I tell the class, refers to sexual intercourse with a female below the age of consent but above the age of a child even if the act is consensual. Though most state laws in the United States designate fourteen as the end of childhood, they assert that girls below the legal age of consent continue to be incapable of agreeing voluntarily to sexual intercourse. The ambiguity of this legal predicament is reflected by events in the novel. Dolly seems much more capable of making informed choices at fourteen, even though her decision to abscond with Quilty is made against a backdrop of complete helplessness. Our discussion takes into account her lack of opportunities when she agrees to run off with Quilty, the false promises with which he lures her away from Humbert (276), and the fact that she claims to have "been crazy about" him (272). Dolly's affair with Quilty demonstrates that her capacity to determine her own actions increases as she gets older. Though her choices remain limited, Dolly's evolving maturity enables her to avoid the worst forms of tyranny and exploitation.

Lolita's probing inquiry into the nature of autonomy reveals the opportunism behind Humbert's critique of natural law. Though he is right that all law is infected by a degree of arbitrariness, this fact does not negate the claim made by proponents of natural law that the law can and ought to reflect universally binding moral principles. Age-of-consent laws are inconsistent because they are forced to correlate age with sexual autonomy, but they are also inspired by principles that reasonable people can agree to be valid.

Our third discussion focuses on *Lolita*'s investigation into the promises and limitations of liberalism. I remind students that Humbert is in prison for murdering Quilty and ask them why Humbert's sex-related felonies go undetected. Humbert's assessment of a fellow pedophile, Gaston Godin, suggests that the answer might be tied to the sociopolitical climate in which these events occur:

> There he was, devoid of any talent whatsoever, a mediocre teacher, a worthless scholar, a glum repulsive fat old invert, highly contemptuous of the American way of life, triumphantly ignorant of the English language— there he was in priggish New England, crooned over by the old and caressed by the young—oh, having a grand time and fooling everybody; and here was I.   (183)

I ask students to consider what this passage tells us about life in the United States and its citizens. Initial responses criticize Gaston's American neighbors for being blind, gullible, and slow-witted. But closer attention to detail also reveals in this passage a moving tribute to American openness and tolerance. Gaston escapes detection because he deceives his neighbors and because his neighbors do not automatically assume the worst of foreigners. His ignorance of the English language and his refusal to give up his European habits are in themselves no reason for suspicion. Like Humbert and Quilty, Gaston successfully conceals his crimes because he lives in a country that is committed to the protection of privacy and to the assumption of innocence.

Turning to the language of political theory, we begin to see that the crimes perpetrated by Humbert are abetted by his adoptive nation's constitutional protection of individual rights. According to the liberal formulation that underwrites the United States Constitution, the individual possesses certain inalienable rights that the state and others may not violate. These rights include freedom of speech, freedom to associate and organize, and freedom from arbitrary arrest and punishment. Most relevantly to *Lolita*, they also include rights that protect the private sphere, such as religious worship, artistic expression, and domestic relations. The novel depicts a nation that lives up to the rights and freedoms spelled out in the American Declaration of Independence. Humbert is relieved to discover that a speeding offense fails to elicit questions about his domestic relations (171). Though he often feels that he and Dolly "lived in a lighted house of glass" (180), his anxiety springs from paranoia rather than from society's intrusion into his personal affairs.

These examples showcase the problem that plagues all liberal societies in which a commitment to personal freedoms becomes complicit in the violation of the freedoms of others. As a citizen of a liberal nation, Dolly has state-sponsored rights, yet these rights are violated. Key moments in the novel indicate why the state's capacity to protect Dolly against the likes of Humbert is fatally circumscribed by the legal provisions designed to protect individuals from state interference. For instance, the social service monograph Humbert discovers during his covert legal inquiries shows the state in a passive relationship with those who depend on it (172). This relationship weakens the state's capacity to intercede effectively on Dolly's behalf, and Humbert draws comfort from the knowledge that even a modicum of discretion will enable him to act with impunity.

Humbert's crimes go undetected largely because he commits them in a country that puts a high premium on liberal values such as the right to privacy. One might say that Dolly's fate would have had a much greater chance of being averted in a dictatorship, where unlimited state power penetrates the private sphere without just cause. *Lolita*'s critique of liberalism serves as a useful counterpoint in a class that has already studied illiberal dystopias, such as Yevgeny Zamyatin's *We*, George Orwell's *1984*, Franz Kafka's *The Trial*, or Nadezhda Mandelstam's *Hope against Hope*. Familiarity with such literature helps frame the debate that closes our discussion of *Lolita*. I ask students if the novel endorses the abandonment of liberal values. Does *Lolita*'s portrayal of the enormous costs of liberalism suggest that liberalism is a flawed political ideal? We consider this question by turning to the "general lesson" John Ray, Jr., extracts from Humbert's narrative (5–6). In his preface to Humbert's confession, Ray suggests that a comprehensive machinery of surveillance is needed to aid the state and its representatives (its social workers, its educators) in identifying those in need of protection. This lesson conjures up visions of a society in which the presumption of innocence gives way to a climate of suspicion and of a citizenry willing to condone all kinds of injustice perpetrated in the name of the public good.

The class begins to see *Lolita*'s complex approach to liberal values. Though the novel acknowledges that liberal principles are complicit in tragedies such as Dolly's, it also suggests that liberalism is the only form of political organization that can protect us from tyranny. John Ray, Jr., is right when he says that to assure the security of victims such as Dolly Haze, the state must assume an expansion of its activities. But *Lolita* reminds us that such a project would erode the openness and tolerance that Americans like to claim as core values of their national identity. I remind students of Ellen Pifer's observation that Dolly's liberation occurs on the Fourth of July, America's annual celebration of its birth as a nation ("Nabokov's Discovery" 411). American gullibility abets Gaston's crimes, but it also helps Dolly escape from Humbert's tyranny when the Elphinstone hospital staff allows her to check out in the company of her

"uncle" without the permission of her ostensible father and primary guard-
ian. The yoking of the novel's legal and ethical preoccupations to its political
concerns alerts students to the dilemma we must confront as readers of *Lolita*:
if we are unwilling to sacrifice our civil rights for the sake of "bringing up a
better generation in a safer world" (6), we are indirectly delivering Dolly into
Humbert's clutches. If we are willing, however, to accept an erosion of our
rights for the sake of Dolly and others like her, we are taking the first steps
down a road that may lead to the dystopias imagined by Zamyatin and Orwell
or experienced firsthand by the victims of Nazism, Stalinism, and other dicta-
torships that claimed to subordinate the rights of the individual for the sake
of public profit.

Lolita and 1950s American Culture

David Clippinger

Humbert Humbert and Lolita's meanderings through 1950s America bring into sharp relief the American infatuation with popular culture, the codified gender roles of women and young girls, and the disdain of the academic and intellectual pursuits. Alongside Humbert Humbert and his captive Lolita, two other sets of travelers help illuminate the full contours of *Lolita's* cultural landscape: Véra and Vladimir Nabokov, who voyaged by car on their annual migration to the butterfly grounds spread throughout the United States, and Jean Baudrillard and the specter of his historical predecessor, Alexis de Tocqueville, who studied America from the windows of cars, trains, or carriages. Each of these sets of travelers shares a vital similarity: with the exception of Lolita, none is American by birth, and all are to various degrees outsiders to American culture. Through their sociocultural and rhetorical positions as mediated by their texts, each pair attempts to make sense of the nuances of the culture that they encounter. The American cultural landscape, viewed through the eyes of these travelers, yields a startlingly fresh perspective of the social forces operating in midcentury America and proves to be a cornerstone for any pedagogical discussion of the cultural history of America.

My approach to *Lolita* is concerned less with the primary narrative of the triangle of Humbert Humbert, Clare Quilty, and Lolita than with the 1950s cultural backdrop against which that narrative plays: namely, the suspicion of potential subversives from both the outside and the inside; the proliferation of popular culture as defining American taste; and the rigid gender roles prescribed and reinforced by cultural practices and institutions. Each of these elements contributes to Humbert Humbert's doomed quest for Lolita, and each accentuates Humbert Humbert's inability to comprehend Lolita and reinforces his position as a perennial outsider to American culture, which was, in the political climate of 1950s America, a dubious position.

In 1950, the United States government passed the Internal Security Act (also named the McCarran Act), which refueled the House Un-American Activities Committee's interrogation into potential subversive Communist activities in the United States. Although the cultural mood of the time was that of hyper-suspicion, when Vladimir Nabokov arrived in New York in May 1940, the "red scare" had yet to fully bloom. By the time he began writing, in 1947, the fear of Communism was beginning to escalate. Nabokov's vociferous disdain for Communists, who had ousted his family from its ancestral home, alleviated close scrutiny of his own possible connections, yet his novel, albeit in an indirect way, plays into the cultural anxieties of subversion. That fear in *Lolita*, though, has shifted from Communism to the domain of culture. As John Haegert observes:

Behind all the familiar oppositions of the book—the conflict between Lolita as demonic temptress and Lolita as prepubescent brat, the conflicts between art and nature and between imagination and reality—looms the greatest and most potent of American polarities: the legendary conflict between New World possibilities and Old World sensibilities.   (139)

The dialectic of Old World / New World might be reduced to Communist versus capitalist ideology. But, more poignant, certain European qualities of the Old World embedded in the character of Humbert Humbert escalate the clash with (what Nabokov coins as) the *poshlust* of Charlotte's and Lolita's New World. While Nabokov is quick to distance himself from his narrator of *Lolita*, he confesses that, like Humbert, he "loathe[s] popular pulp. I loathe go-go gangs, I loathe jungle music . . . I especially loathe vulgar movies— cripples raping nuns under tables, or near-naked girls' breasts squeezing against the tanned torsos of repulsive young males" (*Strong Opinions* 117). Humbert Humbert's taste clashes directly with Lolita's appetite for gangster movies and musicals. Nevertheless, the novel, in its rendering of these disparate cultural worlds, plays into a second order of fear—the disdain and distrust of the producers of the "cultural"—the various left-leaning and blacklisted American artists, filmmakers, writers, and intellectuals who fed into the general public's fear of being covertly influenced. While Humbert Humbert lacks the impetus to subvert American political culture, his position as a scholar and writer as well as his voiced disdain of popular culture challenges the 1950s Americana of Disneyland, *I Love Lucy*, Betty Crocker, Elvis, Hollywood surf movies, Grandma Moses, and the rise of paint by numbers. The novel includes two other cultural subversives—Gaston Godin, the homosexual European academic, and Clare Quilty, the writer-pornographer. Both represent high culture and are characteristic of what mainstream 1950s America regarded as corrosive moral forces.

Beyond these linkages of culture and perversion, whether political or sexual, the tension between the Old World and the New is clearly an obstacle in Humbert Humbert's relationship with both Charlotte and Lolita. As he remarks when he first visits the Haze household:

I could not be happy in that type of household with bedraggled magazines on every chair and a kind of horrible hybridization between the comedy of so-called "functional modern furniture" and the tragedy of decrepit rockers and rickety lamp tables with dead lamps.   (37–38)

Despite his initial rejection of the Haze household, which he refers to as a "white-frame horror" (36), Humbert's "Old-world politeness . . . obliged [him] to go on with the ordeal" (38). His aesthetic rejection, however, vanishes once he enters "the piazza" and spies his "Riviera love peering at [him] over dark glasses" (39). His idealized conception of his Old World love is grafted on the new. Whereas Humbert thinks that he has discovered a bridge between the worlds of his idealized European childhood and his American present, in fact he has located the aporia between his "ideal" world and "reality."

Clearly, the novel renders a chasm between the aesthetic and cultural worlds of Charlotte Haze and Humbert Humbert, wherein Charlotte exemplifies all the traits of middle-class American culture, with its magazines instead of books and functional furniture in lieu of objets d'art. Given the abyss that separates the "[o]ld-world politeness" and the New World gauche, it seems inevitable that Humbert's conquest of Lolita, the inheritor of American culture through her mother, is doomed to failure. And as the pair crisscross the United States, Humbert attempts to educate Lolita by visiting sites highlighted in the Baedeker's guide such as Magnolia Garden, the world's largest stalagmite, an obelisk commemorating the Battle of Blue Licks, Abraham Lincoln's birthplace, and other distinctively American sites, but Lolita remains uninterested. As he puts it, "To the wonderland I had to offer, my fool preferred the corniest movies, the most cloying fudge. To think that between a Hamburger and a Humburger, she would—invariably, with icy precision—plump for the former" (166).

The schisms between Humbert Humbert and Lolita are manifest most readily along cultural perspectives. Humbert's idealized conception of America is located in its geography and history, neither of which is easily reconciled with the popular culture and advertisements that define the New World. Such a perspective follows in the wake of another European visitor to United States soil, Tocqueville, who professed his admiration for the geography: "Those coasts, so admirably adapted for commerce and industry, those wide and deep rivers; that inexhaustible valley of the Mississippi; the whole continent, in short, seemed prepared to be the abode of a great nation, yet unborn" (28). Tocqueville envisions the potential of the American landscape for democracy, but the "reality" that emerges from the Industrial Revolution and dominates the landscape is more akin to the description given by Baudrillard, one hundred fifty years after Tocqueville. Baudrillard writes, "[T]he whole of America is a desert. Culture exists there in a wild state: it sacrifices all intellect, all aesthetics in a process of literal transcription into the real" (99). The natural potential Tocqueville speaks of has been squandered. What remains, as Baudrillard remarks, is a cultural vacuum: "It is a world completely rotten with wealth, power, senility, indifference, puritanism and mental hygiene, poverty and waste, technological futility and aimless violence" (73).

The naked potential for greatness has shifted from national culture to spectacle—the desert of advertisements, popular culture, and ever-shifting popular taste. "The confrontation between America and Europe," Baudrillard concludes, "reveals not so much a *rapprochement* as a distortion, an unbridgeable rift. There isn't just a gap between us, but a whole chasm of modernity" (73). That rift is clearly located in the figures of Lolita and Humbert Humbert. Just as the Old World is grafted onto Humbert Humbert, Lolita is described as "the ideal consumer, the subject and object of every foul poster" (148). The extended narrative passage concerning the realization of the American quality of Lolita's character is particularly revealing:

> Mentally, I found her to be a disgustingly conventional little girl. Sweet hot jazz, square dancing, gooey fudge sundaes, musicals, movie magazines and so forth—these were the obvious items in her list of beloved things. The Lord knows how many nickels I fed to the gorgeous music boxes that came with every meal we had! I still hear the nasal voices of those invisibles serenading her, people with names like Sammy and Jo and Eddy and Tony and Peggy and Guy and Patty and Rex, and sentimental song hits, all of them as similar to my ear as her various candies were to my palate. She believed, with a kind of celestial trust, any advertisement or advice that appeared in *Movie Love* or *Screen Land*. . . . She it was to whom ads were dedicated . . . and she attempted—unsuccessfully— to patronize only those restaurants where the holy spirit of Huncan Dines had descended upon the cute paper napkins and cottage-cheese-crested salads. (148)

Lolita's seemingly blind acceptance of the promise of various advertisements may be more developmental than the essence of her "disgustingly conventional" character. Yet Humbert Humbert's depiction of Lolita and especially his allusion to taste in his use of the word "palate" are significant. Lolita's taste irritates him, and he threatens to take Lolita into "exile for months and years if need be, [forcing her to study] under [him] French and Latin, unless her 'present attitude' changed" (149). In this way, Lolita's proclivities for popular culture and its language of taste would be supplanted by a European language smacking of high culture, the dead language of Latin. Through such an imposed exile, Humbert hopes to erase the remnants of the middlebrow and shape her into his own version of Dante's Beatrice or Edgar Allan Poe's Annabel Lee. The desert of American popular culture would be transformed into an oasis, and his transformation of Lolita into his "Riviera love" would be complete.

Since Humbert Humbert's attempts to acculturate Lolita fail miserably, he enrolls her in Beardsley School:

> [A]nything was better for Lo than the demoralizing idleness in which she lived. I could persuade her to do so many things . . . but no matter how I pleaded or stormed, I could never make her read any other book than the so-called comic books or stories in magazines for American females. Any literature a peg higher smacked to her of school . . . [and] she was quite sure she would not fritter away her "vacation" on such highbrow reading matter. (173)

If we accept the depiction of Lolita as a "disgustingly conventional young girl" with an aversion to academics, then Beardsley is indeed the perfect fit. Her proclivity for musicals, gangster movies, and westerns and her passion for the sugar-coated pop music of the 1950s have more than prepared her to excel within the less academically minded environment of Beardsley.

Humbert Humbert's encounter with Beardsley School and its "four D's" curriculum reveal to him aspects of the gendered landscape of 1950s America, embedded in headmistress Pratt's spiel about the school:

> We are not so much concerned, Mr. Humbird, with having our students become bookworms or be able to reel off all the capitals of Europe which nobody knows anyway, or learn by heart the dates of forgotten battles. What we are concerned with is the adjustment of the child to group life. This is why we stress the four D's: Dramatics, Dance, Debating and Dating. . . . To put it briefly, while adopting certain teaching techniques, we are more interested in communication than in composition. That is, with due respect to Shakespeare and others, we want our girls to *communicate* freely with the live world around them rather than plunge into musty old books.   (177)

The juxtaposition between the old and the new—the dead and the living—is further reinforced by the fact that Humbert chooses Beardsley precisely because he would have access to just such "musty old books," namely, J. G. Woerner's treatise "On the American Law of Guardianship" and publications by the United States Children's Bureau (173). (Ironically, Humbert writes scholarly tomes that are often relegated to dusty corners of university libraries, and he is emblematic of the "dead" worlds that Beardsley, its faculty, and its students eschew.) Pratt continues:

> We have done away with the mass of irrelevant topics that have traditionally been presented to young girls, leaving no place, in former days, for the knowledges and the skills, and the attitudes they will need in managing their lives and—as the cynic might add—the lives of their husbands.   (177–78)

Irrelevant material is what resides beyond the ken of the housewife's life; consequently, "the position of a star is important, but the most practical spot for an icebox in the kitchen may be even more important to the budding housewife" (178). Culture, history, and the arts are not the focal points for the school since devoting time to such academic topics would reduce the amount of valuable time to educate the girls in domesticity and, therefore, would diminish their potential worth as housewives.

Pratt's assessments and Beardsley's curriculum, unfortunately, ring true when viewed against the gendered landscape of 1950s America. As Karal Ann Marling notes, the daily lives of most women focused on fashion trends like the "New Look" inaugurated by Mamie Eisenhower, cooking and the phenomena of the good housewife proliferated by magazines and the Betty Crocker cookbook, as well as mastery of the modern kitchen with its appliances that accentuated the housewife's domain. The role of women was culturally prescribed and bound to the domestic sphere—and not the world of astronomy, history, literature, and geography.

Even before her domestic indoctrination at Beardsley, Lolita is clearly aware of the role that society forces on women: "My duty is—to be useful. I am a friend to male animals. I obey orders. I am cheerful. . . . I am thrifty and I am absolutely filthy in thought, word and deed" (114). Lolita sarcastically articulates her understanding that femininity is inscribed paradoxically as submissive and yet sexual—a familiar gender stereotype. Given the social norms that Lolita is expected to navigate, it is hardly surprising that she conceives of sexual acts as empty of emotion or as duties performed in exchange for goods. Humbert Humbert conceives of his misunderstanding of Lolita as his inability to recognize her prowess as an actress, but quite clearly, what he really miscalculates is the gender and cultural lessons that Lolita has keenly absorbed and bodies forth.

In short, the failure of Humbert Humbert to comprehend Lolita and the rigidly prescribed sociocultural world that she inhabits is directly implicated in the political and cultural landscape of 1950s America as well as the gap that Humbert attempts to bridge repeatedly and unsuccessfully. The shortcomings of Humbert Humbert, in this respect, are interwoven with his position as a cultural outsider and his inability to deal with American middlebrow taste, with its penchant for material goods and popular culture and its aversion or at least suspicion of the highbrow. Most interesting, the novel makes a rather compelling argument for that suspicion with its pantheon of morally bankrupt characters such as Clare Quilty and Humbert Humbert. In this respect, the cultural backdrop of the narrative unveils the socioeconomic forces that shape identity in 1950s America. Even though those forces linger at the periphery of the main story line, the "love story," they are central to the failures of Humbert Humbert, as is Lolita's saturation by American popular culture. In a final and fitting act of defiance of the American popular culture that he deplores, Humbert Humbert decides to "disregard the rules of traffic" and crosses to the left side of the highway to drive British style. Tellingly, Humbert confesses that "the feeling was good. It was a pleasant diaphragmal melting, with elements of diffused tactility" (306). And it is there, on the wrong side of the road, that his voyage ends.

"Dolorès Disparue": Reading Misogyny in *Lolita*

Sarah Herbold

In our post–John Ray, Jr., enlightened age, we teachers of literature may laugh at the "philistine[s]" (4) who would question whether *Lolita* belongs in the American literary canon. In particular, we might be tempted to scoff at feminist critics who accuse admirers of *Lolita* of turning a blind eye toward the novel's misogyny. Most obviously, that misogyny takes the form of anathematizing adult women and turning the sexual exploitation of pubescent girls into a joke—or a romance. Less obviously, it takes the form of scorning and excluding the female reader, for Vladimir Nabokov appears to direct his novel toward a male audience, whom he invites to join him in a literary sexcapade that is naughty and exhilarating partly because it seems to exclude women as readers (and writers). While experienced readers may have trained themselves to overlook *Lolita*'s hostility to women, students are likely to feel troubled by it and to worry (as they should) about whether enjoying the novel makes them complicit in it.

One way to foreground (rather than minimize) this issue is to offer the perspective of critics who argue that reading *Lolita* is tantamount to reading pornography (e.g., Blum; Kennedy). They contend that just as pornography works to unify a male pornographer with a male viewer and empower them through the medium of a victimized female body, so Humbert seeks to entrap and dominate a victimized Lolita while Nabokov seeks to subjugate the female reader, by showing her how powerless she is to do anything but meekly follow his lordly textual commands. Although this view might seem to be merely special-interest criticism, it is not; the text explicitly raises the question of how gender and genre are related and what the implications of such relations might be.

Claiming that *Lolita* is offensively pornographic does it less injury than allowing students to fall back on *Lolita*'s status as a masterpiece as a way of dodging—and therefore foreclosing—its difficult interpretive challenges, including the issue of its misogyny. A pedagogical short circuit occurs when the teacher informs students that through narrative irony, Nabokov clearly distances himself from Humbert, whom he indicts of child abuse, misogyny, and narcissism while embracing his poetic gifts (see, e.g., Alexandrov, *Nabokov's Otherworld* 163; Boyd, *American Years* 232). This solution to the novel's ambiguities does not really work, for reasons I elaborate below. More important, a teacher who deprives students of their opportunity—and responsibility—to decide for themselves whether, and how, Nabokov differentiates himself from his narrator may succeed in defanging the novel, but only by destroying much of its power as a teaching text. Nabokov exploits ambiguous representations of narrative point of view and of the text's imagined audience to place readers in interpretive quandaries that have serious moral implications and no easy solutions and that may also evoke intense pleasure and anguish. He challenges students to read more skillfully as they try to extricate themselves from *Lolita*'s narrative and moral ambiguities.

Thus I would define my topic not as whether *Lolita* is misogynistic but, rather, as what purpose is served (or what effect is produced) by the misogyny that is unquestionably present. I believe *Lolita* can demonstrate the mistaken assumptions that underlie a kind of misogyny that is cultural, and not simply individual, as well as its negative consequences. Moreover, the novel offers students the chance to discover that its imagined female reader, although she often seems implicitly excluded (and perhaps belittled), is the hidden fulcrum of meaning. Indeed, only after students account for the role of the imagined female reader can they fully appreciate the profound and irresolvable ambiguities that make *Lolita* worthy of serious consideration—and of a place on universities' (or anyone's) reading lists.

As I noted earlier, many critics (including some feminists) try to render *Lolita*'s problematic depictions of women unproblematic by claiming that Nabokov dissociates himself from Humbert's misogyny. In their reading, Humbert is clearly a villain and Lolita an innocent victim. American undergraduates (who are often excessively docile and—as Humbert expresses it—"standard-brained" [14]), will likely be only too willing to go along with this view, since it makes *Lolita* morally intelligible along conventional lines. But it is a gross oversimplification, which does little to make the novel less misogynistic, since Nabokov's ostensible disavowal of Humbert's flaws can easily be seen as too little, too late.

Admittedly, the standard interpretation does have some support, for Nabokov does seem ultimately to characterize Humbert as a criminal and Lolita as a victim. In summing up his tale, Humbert says he deserves to be sentenced to thirty-five years in prison for rape (308). He also acknowledges that Lolita's loss of her childhood is more "hopelessly poignant" than his own sorrow at having lost her (308). More generally, the Coalmont section of the novel seems to present a transformed Humbert who no longer simply lusts for Lolita but genuinely loves her. Humbert declares:

> What I used to pamper among the tangled vines of my heart, *mon grand pêché radieux*, had dwindled to its essence: sterile and selfish vice, all *that* I canceled and cursed. . . . I insist the world know how much I loved my Lolita, *this* Lolita, pale and polluted, and big with another's child, but still gray-eyed, still sooty-lashed, still auburn and almond, still Carmencita, still mine.   (278)

Humbert claims that he is no longer driven simply by sexual desire ("sterile and selfish vice"). Instead, he has learned how to love Lolita more profoundly: he adores even her "womanish" cleavage (273) and "adult, rope-veined narrow hands and her gooseflesh white arms, and her shallow ears, and her unkempt armpits" (277). Lolita herself is also transformed in the Coalmont section. No longer a devious nymphet, she is now (paradoxically) a Virgin Mary figure. Safely married off to a Joseph-like stand-in, she is "frankly and hugely pregnant"; her sexy, Annabel-like tan has given way to "pale-freckled cheeks" and "watered-milk-white arms" (269–70). Lolita has been sanctified: her baby, ostensibly a boy, is due at Christmas (266), and she stands "crucified" in the doorway as she admits Humbert to her humble home (270).

But Humbert's references in this scene to "my Lolita, . . . still Carmencita, still mine" undermine critics' claims that Humbert is morally transformed. Even though Lolita has declared her independence from him, Humbert still insists that she belongs to him and remains what he has made of her in his mind ("Carmencita"). Nor does he truly abjure his "crime"; he still wants Lolita to leave her husband and come away with him (280). Moreover, Humbert's apostrophes to Lolita make it impossible to draw a clear line between Nabokov and Humbert, because from the novel's opening phrases ("Lolita, light of my life") to its last words ("And this is the only immortality you and I may share, my Lolita"), Nabokov's voice and Humbert's are conflated in such a way as to foreground both men's claims that they own Lolita, whom they have invented. We could call this aspect of Humbert's/Nabokov's relation to Lolita the Pygmalion theme: male artistic subject and female aestheticized object. Coupled with the formal issue of the unstable relation between author and protagonist-narrator, this theme has led feminist critics to ask whether there really is a woman in the text, since Lolita exists only as Humbert's representation of her. But since Nabokov and Humbert cannot be clearly distinguished, it cannot be merely Humbert (as critics such as Kauffman argue) who is "misappropriating" Lolita. By implication, Nabokov, too, is guilty ("Quilty") of usurping and exploiting the Lolita whom the novel invites us to imagine as existing in her own right.

It is important to see, however, that Nabokov does not conceal this entrapment of Lolita within the fiction that bears her name. He emphasizes it in passages such as those just cited, in which "I" refers to both Nabokov and Humbert. "*Dolorès Disparue,*" a mock title Humbert gives his narrative after Lolita has vanished (253), refers to Marcel Proust's *Albertine disparue*, which chronicles the disappearance of the similarly autobiographical first-person narrator's lover. In using this allusion, Nabokov implies that a (male) writer who claims to possess the (female) character he has created is as deluded as a man who claims to possess wholly the woman he loves. Nabokov implies, that is, that once created, Galatea has a moral and existential integrity of her own, and the Pygmalions who fail to recognize and respect that autonomy are mistaken in thinking they can fully claim—or even know—the object of their desire. As Humbert discovers, this mistake is a factual as well as a moral error: Lolita had a life of her own, of which Humbert only caught glimpses. Given that Nabokov acknowledges this truth, by identifying his authorial voice with Humbert's narrative voice, we can say that there is a woman in the text, if only as a trace of the woman (or girl) who was—or could have been—present, but who can no longer truly be made present to author, narrator, or reader.

Even if Lolita is present only as a trace, *Lolita* should not be reduced to "a case study in child abuse" (Boyd, *American Years* 227) that describes only Humbert's obsessional version of "an entirely ordinary child" who is Humbert's victim (Wood 116; see also Kauffman). Because the novel is a first-person narrative, and especially because Nabokov often blurs the distinction between author and narrator (presumably to make the moral and formal complexities of *Lolita* greater), there is no objective reality in *Lolita* with which the reader could compare Humbert's possible distortions. This epistemological "no-exit" is especially notable in the later sections of the novel, where, as critics have pointed out, Nabokov almost taunts readers with their inability to tell what is Humbert's fantasy and what is "real" (see Connolly, "'Nature's Reality'"; Boyd, "'Even Homais Nods'"; Dolinin). The Lolita we see may not be the "real" Lolita, but students and teachers have no access to any other Lolita. Therefore, the Lolita we see is both provisional and, de facto, "real." But we should see that she is a layered character: levels of illusion and reality shift in her just as they do in the play Humbert and Lolita see in Wace, in which "a living rainbow" composed of "seven . . . pubescent girls . . . rather teasingly faded behind a series of multiplied veils" (220–21). From the beginning, the reader is given conflicting information concerning whether Lolita is dumb or smart, a virgin or sexually experienced, powerless or powerful, and students can readily understand that these ambiguities have significant interpretive value. It may be harder for them to see that these uncertainties cannot—and need not—be resolved, but that is one of the things *Lolita* can teach them.

Students can most easily be helped to articulate Lolita's "duplicity" in scenes such as the one on the "candy-striped davenport" (pt. 1, ch. 13), or in relation to *The Enchanted Hunters*, the play in which Lolita participates at Beardsley, in part 2. In these sections, two quite different versions of Lolita reveal themselves: one is the "ordinary child" so beloved by critics, who is all the more innocent, pitiable, and adorable because she mistakenly believes she is sophisticated. The other Lolita really is sophisticated, sexually and intellectually, so much so that she manages to be more ingenious in her plots than Humbert is in his. This Lolita is depicted not simply as Humbert's but also as Nabokov's equal or superior. Indeed, Lolita's special skill is the same as Nabokov's: she excels in creating fictions.

In the davenport scene, for example, students can be encouraged to see that it is not simply Humbert who turns Lolita into a series of virtuosic literary allusions (Eve, Snow White, Beauty, Emma Bovary, etc. [Couturier, "Nabokov" 410]); Lolita is "herself" donning these guises and using them to seduce Humbert / Nabokov / the apparently privileged male reader. When Lolita draws Humbert's attention to a magazine photo showing a version of Pygmalion and Galatea, she alludes to her role as an object of representation and desire. In so doing, she demonstrates her own ability to represent—and slyly comment on—that representation. The photo is a humorous *mise en abyme*: it shows "a surrealist painter relaxing, supine, on a beach, and near him, likewise supine, a plaster replica of the Venus di Milo, half-buried in sand" (58). That Lolita herself makes this coy reference to the Pygmalion theme reverses its apparent meaning. "Venus" becomes a dummy who is only pretending to be inert, and the "surrealist painter" is shown to be deceived in thinking that he is her lord and master. Naturally, Humbert responds by "whisk[ing] the whole obscene thing away" (58), for he does not want to realize the double implication of the image: first, that in appropriating Lolita to his own uses he is mortifying her, and, second, that she is neither unaware of the power dynamic between them nor as powerless in it as he imagines. Instead, Lolita is here appropriating Humbert to her own uses—one of which is to make him believe he is all-powerful. (Even Charlotte Haze, the most obvious target of Humbert's misogyny, is much more powerful than she seems; see Herbold, "'(I Have).'")

Similarly, while rehearsing *The Enchanted Hunters*, Quilty's play, at Beardsley, Lolita succeeds in creating a fictive illusion that completely enchants Humbert. With the help of Quilty and other actors, such as Mona Dahl ("my doll"), Lolita enacts a scenario of deception and betrayal whose real victim is Humbert. Thus she is not only naive and pseudosophisticated but artfully so. Students should be encouraged to articulate the paradox of Lolita's duplicity and to confront head-on its confusing implications. While Lolita can be seen as a victim, she must also be seen as a powerful agent, in whom erotic desire and creativity are as closely intertwined as they are for Humbert (and Nabokov).

I have been describing a related paradox: if we let students focus on Lolita's victimization to the exclusion of her agency, she becomes more of a victim of misogyny as well as less so. Similarly, if we do not invite students to discuss how Nabokov constructs readers according to their gender or how a female reader's reaction to the text might differ from a male's, they may well see *Lolita* as more misogynistic than it is. We should encourage students to notice, therefore, that Nabokov often signals that *Lolita* was written for men and seems to imagine female readers at best as trespassers on masculine territory. For example, Humbert/Nabokov sometimes specifically addresses a male reader ("himself" [4]; "his bald head" [48]; "a blond-bearded scholar" [226]). More generally, Humbert's/Nabokov's frequent allusions to other male writers' paeans to their beloveds suggest that *Lolita* is meant to be seen as the latest entry in a long line of literary contests among male poets, for whom the lady in question is only a pretext for a Harold Bloomian struggle with poetic tradition. The subplot involving Clare Quilty (which turns out not to be a subplot after all) corroborates the impression that the most important transactions, both within the text and outside it (that is, between its author and his audience), occur between men. Even when Nabokov does address female readers, they seem to be characterized as one-dimensional: they are principled citizens who will judge, but could not possibly derive pleasure from, Humbert's story (e.g., "ladies . . . of the jury" [9, 87]).

But we should also draw students' attention to the fact that Humbert/ Nabokov sometimes addresses women readers specifically when embarking on an erotic scene, such as the one at the Enchanted Hunters hotel ("Gentlewomen of the jury" [123]), or when presenting a shocking sexual revelation, such as that Lolita seduces Humbert rather than vice versa ("frigid gentlewomen of the jury" [132]). In addition, women are implicitly included—though not explicitly acknowledged—in frequent gender-neutral apostrophes to the reader:

> Knowing the magic of her own soft mouth, [Lolita] managed—during one schoolyear!—to raise the bonus price of a fancy embrace to three, and even four bucks. *O Reader! Laugh not, as you imagine me,* on the very rack of joy noisily emitting dimes and quarters, and great big silver dollars.
>
> (184; emphasis added)

The mock-elevated style and sentimental affect of "O Reader!" cite romantic fictions of an earlier era, which were typically addressed to a female readership or depicted a feminized hero. By adopting this persona and by not limiting his "joke" to an explicitly male reader (as he has sometimes done before), Nabokov hints that he imagines a female reader, too, laughing—and probably cringing—at the image of Humbert disgorging money as Lolita performs oral sex on him for ever-higher prices. By asking students how Nabokov "cues" the female reader here ("Well, Cue—they all called him Cue" [276]), we can help them see that the female reader is carefully characterized as duplicitous: on the one hand, she is absent or, if present, in a state of moral outrage or sentimental grief, and, on the other, she is present and slyly appreciative. Because she is represented even more schizophrenically than the male reader, her role is key to understanding how *Lolita's* textual dynamics intersect with its themes. That is, just as Lolita appears in alternate and conflicting guises, so the female reader periodically surfaces in alternative impersonations, in a text that mostly conceals her participation altogether. The female reader thus helps Nabokov at once distinguish between and confound the licit and the illicit. This double role is central to the text's moral and interpretive cruxes and is a key to its meaning (I construe "meaning" here not as a static message but as what happens when author and reader meet in a complex and unstable textual encounter).

As Nabokov himself hints by referring to a famous line in Dostoevsky's *The Brothers Karamazov*, *Lolita*'s ambiguous use of conventions of gender and genre to subvert the literary and social norms based on those conventions gestures toward an alluring—but terrifying—state of freedom in which "everything is permitted" (133; Dostoevsky, *Brothers* 764). *Lolita* challenges students not to shy away from exploring this enfranchisement, which is extended not only to a male reader but also, more provocatively, to a female reader. Because woman's textual power is partially concealed, it may seem inferior to the male narrator's, or author's, or reader's, but it is not. The veiled figure of a Galatea who is also a Pygmalion is the nexus for the formal and thematic ambiguity that is integral to Nabokov's most powerful novel.

Humbert's "Gendered" Appeals to the Jury Not of His Peers

Lisa Ryoko Wakamiya

Teaching *Lolita* within the context of a seminar devoted exclusively to the writings of Vladimir Nabokov raises specific questions about the novel's relation to the writer's other works. Students who have read much Nabokov by the time they read *Lolita* are wary of the coexistence of statements he has made such as "*Lolita* has no moral in tow" ("On a Book" 315) and *Lolita* is "a highly moral affair" (*Dear Bunny* 331) and are attuned to the writer's attitude toward the relation between art and social phenomena. These students are also prepared for the challenge of *Lolita* and understand the need to engage the novel, respond to it, and take responsibility for their response.

In such a course, it is constructive to view Humbert Humbert's narrative as an exercise in transgressing certain boundaries implicit in the cultural hierarchies represented in Nabokov's fictional worlds while maintaining others. Readers familiar with Nabokov's descriptions of the child's spontaneous creative acts in *Speak, Memory* and *The Gift* are struck by Humbert's paradoxical affirmation of child as muse. In my seminar, Humbert's brutal denial of childhood and diatribes against adult women turned class discussions toward the representation of gender in *Lolita*. Adopting the pedagogy described by James Phelan, which emphasizes readers' roles in recognizing authorial agency and textual phenomena while acknowledging their own, and other readers', experiences and perspectives of the novel, we contextualized gender among other rhetorical positions we had treated in connection with Nabokov's works.

Debates concerning the implications of the absence of childhood in *Lolita* raised questions about Nabokov's method: if Nabokov's other novels engage the reader in recognizing, and accepting, certain characteristic rhetorical and ethical positions on issues of art and life, why does *Lolita* challenge the reader to adopt such untenable positions? The reader accustomed to viewing Nabokov as an absolutist judge—"a rigid moralist kicking sin, scuffing stupidity, ridiculing the vulgar and cruel—and assigning sovereign power to tenderness, talent, and pride" (*Strong Opinions* 193)—is placed in the position of judge and jury while reading *Lolita*.

Humbert's frequent addresses to his "dear readers," "learned readers," the "ladies and gentlemen of the jury," "winged gentlemen of the jury," and "sensitive gentlewomen of the jury" frame the presentations of evidence in his journal and anticipate the reader's response to his appeals. While students immediately recognize that Humbert undermines his testimony by claiming to have a photographic memory that allows him to reproduce several weeks of entries from a diary destroyed five years hence (40), they should also sense that Humbert's appeals are rhetorically constructed in such a way as to make the reader complicit in his guilt.

It has been pointed out that Humbert "wants us to recognize how much we have in common with him" (Winston 427). Among the points of identification he creates between himself and the reader, points intended to encourage the reader to confirm Humbert's own pronouncements, are carefully constructed attitudes toward gender. As students readied for the challenge of judging Humbert based on his manipulative testimony, it was instructive to mention Sarah Herbold's observation that Humbert intends the reader to respond at times as a man and at other times as a woman ("Reflections" 149). The students, who were familiar with Nabokov's various criteria for "good" and "bad" readers (*Lectures on Literature* 2–6), were now asked to adopt the gender identities and roles Humbert assigns them, keeping in mind that the makeup of these identities shifts as Humbert modulates their responses to his narrative and they respond in kind.

The task of recognizing when one is asked to "read as a man" or "read as a woman" foregrounds the question of the stability of the implied reader's identity and underscores the role gender plays in Humbert's constructing (and our accepting) his pronouncements on issues of aesthetics and ethics. Is it the case, as Herbold proposes, that "Nabokov deliberately sexualizes different reading perspectives so as to pit them against each other—and sometimes, to allow them to meet" ("Reflections" 149)? If so, is the strategy of destabilizing the implied reader's identity exclusive to *Lolita*, or does it have further implications for reading Nabokov's other works?

To begin, I asked students to work in groups to reread specific passages that feature Humbert's addresses to the jury, directing particular attention toward his appeals to the "gentlemen of the jury" and "gentlewomen of the jury." They focused on the first time Humbert addresses the "gentlewomen":

> Gentlewomen of the jury! Bear with me! Allow me to take just a tiny bit of your precious time! So this was *le grand moment*. I had left my Lolita still sitting on the edge of the abysmal bed, drowsily raising her foot, fumbling at the shoelaces and showing as she did so the nether side of her thigh up to the crotch of her panties—she had always been singularly absent-minded, or shameless, or both, in matters of legshow.   (123)

This address, as Nomi Tamir-Ghez points out, follows "the novel's most delicate situation, which requires Humbert's most powerful rhetoric" ("Art" 33): Humbert has given Dolores a sleeping pill and wanders through the Enchanted Hunters hotel, waiting for the pill to take effect so that "by nine, when *his* show began, she would be dead in his arms" (116).

Several students observed that Humbert foresees the female implied reader's response and attempts to subdue it by framing her apprehension of the scene. They recognized Humbert's obfuscations as Herbold describes them:

> Lolita may be doing a little dance of seduction, or is she just absent-minded? Similarly, Humbert seems to be toying with the female reader, who cannot know what the truth is or how she is expected to react. Is this a rape scene, or is Lolita a little seductress?   (" '(I Have)' " 89)

Over the next several pages, students encountered many of Humbert's deliberately conflicting signals. He announces that his "only regret . . . is that [he] did not quietly deposit key '342' at the office, and leave the town, the country, the continent, the hemisphere,—indeed, the globe—that very same night" (123). Likewise, he "should have known . . . that nothing but pain and horror would result from the expected rapture" (125). Yet in the same pages, he proclaims that he "should have understood that Lolita had *already* proved to be something quite different from innocent Annabel" (124), presents the reader with a mental picture of her naked body described in disturbing detail (125), and admires another "nymphet" in the hotel lobby (126).

When he addresses the "frigid gentlewomen of the jury" again, it is to inform them not only that did he not expect to even dare to reveal himself to Dolores for months, or even years, but that the morning after he drugged her, it was she who seduced him (132). The mixed messages of the last several pages are brought into focus as Humbert enumerates his efforts to spare Dolores's purity, which, he argues, proved to have been "damaged" earlier at Camp Q (124). After one more reminder of his guilt, "this horror that I cannot shake off," Humbert declares, "Sensitive gentlewomen of the jury, I was not even her first lover" (135). Having painted Dolores as either "absent-minded, or shameless, or both," Humbert similarly divides his female implied reader (Herbold argues that the female reader participates in her own "immascula-tion," to use Judith Fetterley's term, in that she is "urged to acknowledge that she is a willing cocreator" and spectator of Humbert's more lurid scenes at the same time that she is invited to "refuse the position of excluded victim" [" '(I Have)' " 89, 92]). He repents and repels, expresses regret, then enrages—only to accuse the "frigid gentlewomen" of prudishness—and finally proclaims his innocence.

Students pinpointed each of Humbert's attempts to mediate the female read-er's response. Though several noted the degree to which they allowed them-selves to be seduced by Humbert, even while rereading these passages in class, all acknowledged Humbert's assumption that while reading as women they would be pulled in opposite directions by his rhetorical strategies and while reading as men they would share his attitudes toward women. When we turned our attention to Humbert's appeals to the "gentlemen of the jury," however, we determined that the rhetoric of the male-oriented passages produced complex responses that similarly divided the reader.

The first address to the "gentlemen of the jury" comes early in the novel: "my moaning mouth, gentlemen of the jury, almost reached her bare neck, while I crushed out against her left buttock the last throb of the longest ecstasy man or monster had ever known" (61). Linda Kauffman argues that here both the text and Dolores function "as an object of exchange between men. . . . The scene in which Humbert masturbates with Lolita on his lap is a good example of how the text makes what is male seem universal" (136). Kauffman's argument similarly applies to Humbert's next address to the "gentlemen of the jury," in which he describes the "torture," *"pavor nocturnus," "peine forte et dure,"* "'trauma,' 'traumatic event,' and 'transom'" of trying to "fit [Charlotte] into a plausible daydream," of "conjur[ing] up Charlotte as a possible mate," and bringing her breakfast so that he can eventually "have [his] way with her child" (70). Humbert's pleas for sympathy draw on a mainstay of the comic tradition: jokes about aging women. As Herbold observes, "virtually every adult woman whom Humbert describes is mercilessly lampooned as stupid, unattractive, and deluded" ("'(I Have)'" 74).

While these early addresses to the male implied reader demand complicity with Humbert's cruel sensibilities, it is precisely among the above-noted entreaties to the "gentlewomen of the jury" that Humbert calls to the "gentlemen" a third time: "I should have known . . . that nothing but pain and horror would result from the expected rapture. Oh, winged gentlemen of the jury!" (125). This confession is strategically placed between Humbert's earlier expressions of regret directed toward women and his explicit imaginings of Dolores's dimly lit naked body; the mixed messages of these passages may signal the narrative's continued reflection of, or initiate a significant break with, the male implied reader's responses.

When asked whether this address to the "gentlemen of the jury" could be read as an appeal to the male implied reader's sympathies, several students observed that Humbert, in making the implied reader complicit in his guilt, can simultaneously plead for exoneration and beg the male implied reader's attention as he imagines Dolores naked and "spread-eagled on the bed" (125). In other words, if every appeal to traditional cultural values is accompanied by subversion (Rampton 101 [St. Martin's]) and the male implied reader always is expected to uphold the former and always is guilty of the latter, the difference between them becomes difficult to discern. Similarly, if, in Humbert's view, the female implied reader travesties the former with excessive suspicion or prudishness and is obliged to protest the latter (though "it was she who seduced [him]"), Humbert has effectively destabilized the system of gendered discourse he created in the first place.

The reactions generated by Humbert's gendered rhetoric engaged students in what J. Hillis Miller calls an "ethical moment of reading," during which they recognized they must respond to the text (4). Humbert's construction of his male and female implied readers prompted students to evaluate their own responses to the novel. *Lolita*, we agreed, was a novel less about the violation of taboos than about the transgression and reinforcement of certain cultural values. As Susan Mizruchi observes, Humbert's construction of male desire demands complicity and thus requires readers to determine to what lengths they will go to continue to identify with his appeals to male fantasy, subversion, and traditional morality (643). At the same time, Humbert elicits strong responses on the part of the female implied reader, only to silence them with admonishments and parodies of their views as he imagines them. Is this female voice intended to reinforce, rather than challenge, a certain construction of female identity? With this, students began to consider the role of the female voice in Nabokov's work, as well as how the author might have responded to gendered readings.

Nabokov's disposition toward social movements that challenged hegemonic cultural values had been discussed in class in connection with *poshlust*, and certainly any kind of political or social advocacy would fall under its label (Leona Toker observes that Nabokov would have found appeals for solidarity with marginalized groups distasteful, if only because he considered such appeals self-evident ["Liberal Ironists"]). Perhaps for this reason, Nabokov's *Lectures on Literature* displays a complicated attitude toward gender and the role of the reader. Nabokov once admitted to being "prejudiced, in fact, against all women writers" (*Dear Bunny* 268) but came to appreciate and assign Jane Austen's *Mansfield Park* in his Masters of European Fiction course. Nevertheless, Joseph Frank notes, Nabokov "does his best to overcome what he senses would be the resistance of his students to her world" (237). One could add that Frank here implies the resistance of Nabokov's *male* students to her world: "In our dealings with Jane Austen we had to make a certain effort in order to join the ladies in the drawing room," Nabokov declares, seemingly addressing an exclusively male audience. "In the case of Dickens we remain at table with our tawny port" (*Lectures on Literature* 63).

Nabokov's proposal that readers can only appreciate *Mansfield Park* if "we adopt its conventions, its rules, its enchanting make-believe" suggests that the male reader should be attentive to Austen's style and her intertextual references, and perhaps, at times, they should read like a woman to enjoy "the work of a lady" (*Lectures on Literature* 10) and "have some degree of fun with her delicate patterns": "I have tried to be very objective. My objective method was, among other ways, an approach through the prism of the culture that her young ladies and gentlemen had imbibed" (*Lectures on Literature* 63). Among his examples, he mentions "The Sofa," by William Cowper, a poem cited by Austen's heroine and "a good example of the kind of thing that was familiar to the mind of a young lady of Jane's or Fanny's time and set" (*Lectures on Literature* 24). Though Nabokov concludes that "the fun was forced" and that when one reads Dickens "there is no problem of approach as with Jane Austen" (*Lectures on Literature* 63), such statements may attest to the experience of being confronted with a gendered narrative that requires readers to "slip into a certain mood," "focus [their] eyes in a certain way," and reappraise their own attitudes and roles.

The students in my seminar all agreed Nabokov would reject the label "feminist," but they stopped short of accusing him of patriarchal attitudes. Striving

to reconcile the splitting of male and female readers' identities that characterized *Lolita* with a position on gender compatible with their own, they proposed
diverse readings of the conclusion of Humbert's narrative. Some suggested that
Humbert's last visit to Dolores was redemptive and his contrition constituted
the novel's moral message; others remained suspicious of his "fancy prose" (9)
and argued that, while Humbert did not succeed in taking back Dolores, he
had successfully snared the naive reader; many claimed that the female voice
was still absent from the text and warranted the individual reader's response.
That the students remained divided after prolonged critical engagement with
the novel revealed that the absolutist positions they had often ascribed to
Nabokov while reading his other works served to demonstrate the degree to
which they had comfortably agreed with particular cultural values represented
in his writing when they might have challenged the representation, or absence,
of other values.

Azar Nafisi describes Nabokov's sense of morality as stemming from "his loy-
alty to the act of writing . . . his desire to imaginatively grasp and articulate what
is commonly called truth behind the ordinary interactions of men and women"
("Interview," par. 5). By identifying Nabokov's intent in gendered terms, Nafisi
foregrounds the absence of ordinary social interactions between the sexes in
many of Nabokov's works, an absence that, it seems, can be addressed productively through gendered readings, including Nafisi's own. Moving from Humbert's addresses to his male and female implied readers to the impossibility of
any kind of ordinary interaction between them, the class, in conclusion, revisited the notion of Nabokov's "good" reader. If, as Nabokov declared in *Nikolai
Gogol*, the genuine artist always creates his reader (Fanger 426), the properly
"Nabokovized" reader would not allow Humbert's appeals or pronouncements to
determine his or her attitudes toward gender identity. To be "of" the artist, rather
than on the bandwagon with him, entails the challenge of articulating that which
has been left unsaid, what Nabokov called those "subliminal co-ordinates by
means of which the book is plotted" that may be "skimmed over or not noticed,
or never even reached" ("On a Book" 316). Just as Anna Brodsky brings the
wartime frame of the novel into focus, Richard Rorty elucidates the story of the
deceased son of the barber of Kasbeam (214–17), Mizruchi identifies the details
that cause Dolores suddenly to drop her friend Eva Rosen, and countless readers endeavor to reclaim Dolores's voice, Nabokov's good readers are attentive to
his narrator's incuriosity and are prompted to investigate absence. Such reading
necessitates attention to detail and to other readers, responsibility, as well as
response. This last statement may be printed in course syllabi and reiterated on
introducing each of Nabokov's works in class, but it will always be *Lolita* that con-
firms its importance for understanding the implications of the act of reading and
why, despite the real challenges one faces when assigning and reading *Lolita*, it
is most productively experienced in the classroom setting.

Teaching *Lolita* at a Religious College

Marianne Cotugno

If *Lolita* remains a controversial text to teach in colleges and universities, nowhere might it be more controversial to teach than at a religious institution. While a professor at Mount Olive College, a liberal arts school affiliated with the Free Will Baptist Church, I taught the novel in the courses Major American Novels and American Literature II. This essay addresses some of the challenges and opportunities teaching the novel at a religious college offers; it also argues that teaching Vladimir Nabokov's novel alongside Azar Nafisi's *Reading* Lolita *in Tehran* at both secular and religious schools can reinvigorate frequently explored topics and raise new issues in class discussions of *Lolita*. The memoir accomplishes these goals by calling attention to the act and place of reading—place in the sense both of a physical space and of role or function.

In her best-selling memoir, Nafisi writes about her experiences in Iran meeting with a group of women in the mid-1990s to discuss forbidden works of Western literature after leaving her post as a university professor. Nafisi describes the space of her apartment and the living room in particular:

> More than any other place in our home, the living room was symbolic of my nomadic and borrowed life. Vagrant pieces of furniture from different times and places were thrown together, partly out of financial necessity, and partly because of my eclectic taste. Oddly, these incongruous ingredients created a symmetry that the other, more deliberately furnished rooms in the apartment lacked. (7)

The physical space contributed to the students' comfort and openness, because the mismatched, discordant furnishings resemble the unique gathering of students.

Nafisi emphasizes the importance of place as function:

> I formulated certain general questions for them to consider, the most central of which was how these great works of imagination could help us in our present trapped situation as women. We were not looking for blueprints, for an easy solution, but we did hope to find a link between the open spaces the novels provided and the closed ones we were confined to. (19)

These lines link physical and social space; the world within her home became a safe place where the women could question the expectations and rules that governed life outside that space. Paradoxically, within the confined space of a living room, the women felt freer than they did beyond those walls.

Nafisi calls this room "a place of transgression" (8). Galya Diment's review of *Reading* Lolita *in Tehran* suggests why: "Nafisi's book makes clear that where and when you read certain works can greatly influence your perception of them" ("Ayatollah"). Although this observation may seem like a truism, often it is taken for granted in college classrooms, where teachers frequently fail to examine the context into which they introduce a text. This aspect of Nafisi's work makes it particularly compelling for teaching her memoir alongside Nabokov's novel at a religious college where students may be more resistant than students at secular schools to think about how context affects their interpretations. Nafisi's book encourages teachers to ask their students to reflect on whether the circumstances of where and when they read a text shape their responses. The discussion can transform a classroom into a place of transgression where students and faculty members can question the assumptions, values, and beliefs that govern their everyday lives.

To dramatize how her home functioned as a place of transgression, Nafisi asks the reader to imagine her student Sanaz leaving the house on her way home: "You might notice that her gait and her gestures have changed. It is in her best interest not to be seen, not to be heard or noticed. She doesn't walk upright, but bends her head towards the ground and doesn't look at passersby" (26). This radical transformation occurs so that Sanaz can avoid the attention of the Blood of God, who "patrol the streets to make sure that women like Sanaz wear their veils properly, do not wear makeup, do not walk in public with men who are not their fathers, brothers or husbands" (26).

If I could follow my students back to their homes, I would probably observe similar changes in behavior and appearance. Many Mount Olive College students come from conservative, deeply religious communities, so (as it is for many college students) campus becomes a place to experience less social restraint and to rebel against parental and societal expectations. I have often noticed that many students became more animated, vocal, and outgoing outside the classroom, which might seem to be governed by the same rules that govern their lives at home. That our discussions of the novel occurred at a religious school made the idea of the classroom as a place of transgression a more challenging goal, because often students seemed to bring a more rigid set of beliefs about religion, gender, and nation—the very topics I hoped the pairing of texts would raise—to their reading. Some expected the classroom to reinforce those values, so conflicts, ranging from reluctance to speak to vocal dismissal of the novel, arose when it did not.

With this situation in mind, what was the place or function of *Lolita* for my students? Reflecting on my experiences teaching the novel has helped me appreciate how the place or role of the novel for us is intimately connected with the place of the classroom as a physical and social space. Although we could become involved in heated discussions in the classroom, generally students were respectful and polite—sometimes too polite for my taste. Our initial discussions of *Lolita* were muted. Students expressed reluctance to go over the details of the story but were not necessarily shy with their disgust for the basic plot. For every student who expressed a concern or objection to *Lolita*, I suspect that there were several more who shared those feelings but were afraid to state them. I also believe, and student writings support this, that many students had a more enthusiastic response to the novel than they were willing to articulate in class.

My students' reticence might be explained in several ways. I often felt that their reserve indicated their discomfort with the subject matter. For example, when looking at the infamous "couch scene" during which Humbert Humbert brings himself to orgasm with Lolita on his lap, several students expressed disgust that the scene occurs and refused to discuss the details. Reluctance on the part of students who enjoyed or appreciated the novel may have stemmed from worries about their peers' responses (i.e., they wouldn't be seen as good Christians if they seemed too interested in such a "dirty" book). Those students who strongly objected to the novel's content but still remained quiet may have been unwilling to talk openly because they did not want to be perceived as challenging me as an authority figure. In general, students may have been less likely to accept the novel's subject matter because of the expectations they brought to the classroom. After all, many came to a religious college or were sent there by their parents to avoid a cultural environment saturated with sex.

The physical space may have contributed to the atmosphere as well. Our classroom was in the middle of a hall bookended by a dean's office and the vice president for academic affairs's office. A monitoring device near the doorway allowed someone from a central location to listen in on the classroom. Installed as a way to protect the safety of teachers and students, it could also be viewed as Big Brother (although I was never aware that classes were monitored in this way). Therefore, what became the safest place for students to express their views of the novel was not the space of the classroom but the space of the written page. The students seemed far more open and receptive to *Lolita* in their writing than in classroom discussion. It was through these responses that I began to see how the classroom could be (or perhaps was!) a place of transgression.

In a capstone assignment, I encouraged students to think about both the situation the women of Tehran faced and their own lives at Mount Olive College by asking the following questions:

> Do you see any parallels between life in Iran and life here at Mount Olive College (or life at a religious school or within a religious community)? If not, what prevents life here from becoming like life there?
>
> How do you respond to Nafisi's statement about the novel: "The desperate truth of Lolita's story is not the rape of a twelve-year-old by a dirty old man but the confiscation of one individual's life by another. We don't know what Lolita would have become if Humbert had not engulfed her. Yet the novel, the finished work, is hopeful, beautiful even, a defense not just of beauty but of life, ordinary everyday life, all the normal pleasures that Lolita, like Yass, was deprived of" (33). Is it possible for religion to "confiscate one's life"? Explain why or why not.

One student saw a limited parallel between life in both places. She mentioned the required chapel attendance as well as limitations on how students dress, but she recognized that a student can choose to come to the college; in Iran there is no choice. This same student also mentioned how she believes Nafisi wants Iran to be wholly realized in the sense that *Lolita* is, so that the place will be (echoing Nafisi's words) "hopeful, beautiful even." Another student saw two types of oppressiveness existing at the college and in Iran, and, while recognizing that his and his classmates' situation is less serious than the Iranian people's, he acknowledged that an individual's personality is altered, if not confiscated, by being at the college. Yet another student asserted that religion cannot confiscate one's life because individuals have free will; he also stated that in Iran, it is not religion that confiscates lives but those responsible for forcing religious beliefs on the people. Most students acknowledged the possibility of religion's confiscating a life, and although I did not expect students to read Nafisi's memoir and then awaken to the startling realization that religion, through attendance at Mount Olive College, could take over their lives, I did want them to develop a stronger awareness of where they were and how that might affect what they believe. Their writings suggested that they were doing just that.

While religious or spiritual concerns probably do influence students' approaches to *Lolita*, a student does not need to attend a religious college or even identify himself or herself as religious to feel and express anxiety about the novel or to be shocked and repulsed by the story of an older man's sexual relationship with a twelve-year-old girl. In my classroom, several students believed that by proclaiming that the book portrays a repulsive or immoral relationship, they had engaged critically with the novel. Some students openly questioned why they should have to read such a text. One student came to me during office hours to object to the terrible language in the novel, but when prompted to show me examples, the student could not do so. Nafisi's memoir articulates far more eloquent responses to these students than I could offer.

To encourage my students to engage with Nafisi's approach, I asked them in the capstone writing assignment whether they were surprised that the women in Tehran chose to read *Lolita*. After all, as Nafisi points out, merely meeting together constituted a great risk. Some students were shocked that the women gathered under the conditions described to discuss any book. For most, *Lolita* was an unexpected choice. A few students saw the very act of reading this novel in Iran as an expression of rebellion. One student asserted that the novel possessed power for these women, because they saw themselves in situations similar to Lolita's—being controlled in their own country. Another student explained that she began to understand their interest in reading *Lolita* as a way of identifying with Lolita's sense of being deprived or imprisoned.

The clearest record I have of the impact of Nafisi's text is in students' answers to whether and how Nafisi's memoir affected the way they understood *Lolita*. Most students admitted that the memoir helped them see the novel differently. Often students pointed out that Nafisi helped them acknowledge Lolita more as a victim of Humbert than they had initially. Yet this sympathy was sometimes tempered; one student noted that she was not as confused about the novel as she had been, but she also did not feel as sorry for Lolita as she once had. This student felt that Lolita had opportunities for freedom that Nafisi's students did not possess. For this student, reading about the circumstances of life for Iranian women made Lolita's experiences seem far less horrific.

The juxtaposition of the texts also reenergizes the commonplace debate over whether Lolita is somehow complicit in her "seduction." When readers become aware of the very real circumstances that women (and girls) face in other countries, such judgments become more uncomfortable to make because their assessments of a fictional character might then be extended to include real people. Nafisi's text makes clear that in Iran girls of Lolita's age (or younger) are subject to marriage to significantly older men; after the revolution, the marriage age was lowered from eighteen to nine (43, 27). Thus, although students might be disturbed by Humbert and Lolita's illegal relationship, Nafisi's text helps these readers appreciate that the circumstances in the novel are very close to legal situations in other countries. This recognition might not lessen students' repulsion toward the subject matter of the book (in fact, it might increase it), but it might at least encourage students to develop a more sophisticated response to the story.

Pairing the texts also creates an opportunity for exploring topics not typically spoken about when dealing with Nabokov's novel. For example, my students' responses to the women in the memoir often reminded us of our ignorance and misconceptions about Iran, its people, Islam, and the entire region. By facilitating discussion of these topics, Nafisi's story helps the classroom function as a place where students can challenge their preconceptions about the novel and the Middle East. The knee-jerk reaction by some students to *Lolita* parallels the knee-jerk reaction by some students to anything connected with the Middle East and Islam. By reading selections from Nafisi's text, students observe women living in a society about which they know little. Students see educated, independent women struggling under an oppressive regime but maintaining individual identities that Nafisi takes care to demonstrate. For fundamentalist Christian students, some of whom have been taught that Islam is the enemy of Christianity, their encounters with these women can be jarring.

Although creating a place of transgression in the classroom of a religious institution may pose more obvious challenges than in a secular school, I believe that the opportunities for radical, transformative dialogue are, because of that, more plentiful. The experience of reading student responses, which were written after our discussion of the novel and memoir had ended, demonstrated to me the many potential venues that I left unexplored. *Reading* Lolita *in Tehran* offers students and teachers of Nabokov's novel a fresh approach to a highly regarded but still controversial novel and encourages students to experience the classroom, regardless of its affiliation, as a place of transgression where complicated issues of sexuality, gender, religion, nation, and one's core beliefs can be explored.

Being Read by *Lolita*

Leona Toker

Lolita can provide a test case for the study of the ethics of literary form. The artistic merit of this novel is a matter of consensus, but the combination of stylistic and structural sophistication with the theme of pedophilia has caused much uneasiness. Like the literature of atrocities (tellingly, Humbert Humbert spends the years of World War II in psychiatric institutions), this novel puts its readers on the spot, making us ask why we enjoy it, whether we can be satisfied with aesthetically oriented explanations of this enjoyment, whether the self-evident agenda of condemning Humbert's pedophilia is not our attempt to normalize our own attitudes in atonement for the voyeurism of which we may suspect ourselves at one or another point. If in my 1989 book on Vladimir Nabokov I attempted to deal with the experience of the "implied reader" (see Rimmon-Kenan 86–89) of *Lolita*, in teaching this novel I have been thinking rather in terms of the "implicated reader" (cf. Lehman 4): *Lolita* demands that we turn back on ourselves and examine not only our attitudes to the narrative but also the wider ethical implications of these attitudes.

To reconcile the ideologically tinged question of the ethics of literary form with Nabokov's preference for artistic detail over general ideas, it helps to start the study of the novel by a close text analysis—our only insurance (and even that with limited coverage) against bending the text. This involves the nomenclature of structuralist poetics—the point of view, voice and focus, temporal and spatial ordering, semic and cultural codes (Barthes, S/Z), recurrent images and motifs, figurative language, reflexivity, heteroglossia (cf. Tammi). We analyze these aspects of narrative technique in terms of their functions, their effect on the readers, which leads to the discussion of reader response. The ethics of literary form is, to a large extent, the ethics of the relationship between the text and the reader.

Reader-response criticism no longer privileges the with-the-grain type of reading or bases the pursuit of intersubjectivity on the assumption of ideal laboratory conditions prominently including a postulated normative reader, which in the early days of the discipline was conceptualized as "the informed reader" (Fish, "Literature"), or "the model reader" (Eco 8), akin to the notion of the ideal observer in ethical theory (see Toker, *Eloquent Reticence* 10–12). Details of the texts are "events" that happen to the reader (Fish, "Literature" 125), "instructions" about concretizing the fictional world (Iser 64), or "stumbling blocks" that demand readjustments (Harrison, "Gaps"), but one no longer expects the same textual units to gain the same prominence in or exert the same influence on every reader's attention. Instead, one is reminded of the effect of specialized ideological sensibilities of what Stanley Fish aptly called "interpretive communities" (*Is There a Text*) as well as of the need to read texts not only with but also against the grain, resisting their rhetoric (see Fetterley).

Wayne Booth, whose *The Rhetoric of Fiction* had given the major impetus for anglophone narratology, has, more recently, provided a helpful concept for theorizing the diversity of reader responses without giving up common ground: a dynamic response to the work can be stimulated by conversation with other readers (not least in classroom situations). By analogy with induction and deduction, Booth calls this process "co-duction" (*Company* 70–77). Far from renouncing the aspiration to cultivate the erudite sensibility of a bias-free reader, the idea of coduction welcomes specialized sensitivities associated with class, gender, racial, or national consciousness. In the process of coduction the "mainstream" reader comes to recognize that these formerly marginalized sensitivities may lead to enriching insights that are not readily available to him or her or may even yield new overall interpretations for which one can enlist a fair amount of textual evidence. The mainstream reader (if such exists) does not merely learn more of the semantic load borne by details of the text but may also recombine the layers of meaning for which the text creates the conditions. The reader with specialized sensitivities can likewise recognize the validity of the canonical readings: the sympathy with another view can go both ways.

The result of this process is that we do not emerge from the reading unchanged. As Bernard Harrison argues in *Inconvenient Fictions*, in addition to knowledge as amenity, great novels offer dangerous knowledge, which not merely fine-tunes but substantially changes our attitudes. If we become conscious of this change, turn away from the text to ourselves, and ask what in our own response calls for a revision, then we have performed a reflexive twist, allowing the text to read ourselves and not only be read by us. *Lolita* can vex the reader into such a twist during the one-on-one interaction with the text; but the stimulus can also come from coduction, whether involving secondary sources or live discussion.

Student responses to *Lolita* are, indeed, an unfailing channel of coduction. They often testify to the troubling effect of this novel, which is, I believe, associated with the temporary sympathy for Humbert, even after it becomes clear that his pursuits are criminal. Narratives often make us sympathize with criminals when they turn into objects of manhunt or retribution. On the first reading of *Lolita*, however, we catch ourselves sympathizing with the pedophile while he is still on the prowl. When we shake off the spell, we may want to strike out against the author who has exposed us to this trial—or else turn on ourselves and ask what made us fall into his trap.

The answers to this last question may be couched in notions that reflect our training. Narratologically trained graduate students will note the almost automatic convention of sympathy with a focal character, especially one who narrates his story in the first person, starts with "all that David Copperfield kind of crap" (Salinger 1), and engages in a challenging endeavor obstructed by legal, social, or moral barriers. They may also note that we find ourselves expecting an erotic heightening because our attention is constantly diverted from the realistic picture of an eleven- or twelve-year-old schoolgirl to an imaginary (solipsized and fetishized) eidolon. Those with a training in Renaissance literature may note that this failure in the consistency of our imaginative construction of Dolly Haze's portrait is associated with Humbert's use of the technique of blazon—the segmentation of her image into separate itemized features, colors, body parts. Explanations of our misplaced sympathy with Humbert are also found in one or another of his techniques of persuasion (see Tamir-Ghez, "Art").

Another stimulus for the self-reflexive twist may be given by the handling of dates in *Lolita*: after the discovery of Elizabeth Bruss (145–46) and of Christina Tekiner that the dates mentioned in the novel suggest that the Coalmont episode and the murder of Quilty may be read as having happened only in Humbert's imagination, readers have been forced not only to take positions on the subject but also to evaluate the implications of these positions. Each interpretive stance taken on this issue (cf. Dolinin; Connolly, "'Nature's Reality'"; Boyd, "'Even Homais'") faces forking options, each pertinent to a different set of ethical or cultural issues: readers must situate their own attitudes among them, taking the responsibility for the way they construct the alternative possible worlds.

Students with interest in ethical criticism are keenly receptive to the points made (some a little hastily) in Richard Rorty's chapter on Nabokov in *Contingency, Irony, and Solidarity*. Rorty notes the formerly unperceived connection between two details of the novel, Charlotte's mourning for a dead son and the bereavement of a briefly encountered hairdresser:

> In Kasbeam a very old barber gave me a very mediocre haircut: he babbled of a baseball-playing son of his, and, at every explodent, spat into my neck, and every now and then wiped his glasses on my sheet-wrap, or interrupted his tremulous scissor work to produce new paper clippings, and so inattentive was I that it came as a shock to realize as he pointed to an easeled photograph among the ancient gray lotions, that the mustached young ball player had been dead the last thirty years.   (213)

Here the comedy of misunderstandings and incongruities deflects our sympathy from the old man, whose grief for his son has translated itself into prideful discourse about him. In *The Theory of Moral Sentiment* Adam Smith has noted that we tend to sympathize with other people's small joys and great sorrows—not vice versa (no wonder Jane Austen underplayed the jackpot happiness of the heroines at the end of her novels). By contrast, the Kasbeam episode shows how even great sorrow can be denied acknowledgment and "conditional sympathy" (Smith 16): as the account of Humbert's paranoia and his desperate endeavors to keep Dolly to himself distracts us from the signals of an irrelevant character's grief, we reenact Humbert's own single-mindedness; we also neglect to connect this episode with Humbert's earlier reference to Charlotte's mourning her son. The emotionally handicapped protagonist of Nabokov's *Defense* would leaf through journals in search of chess problems without pausing at the pictures of famine victims. Newspapers we peruse in search of the weather forecast also report on genocide, famine, AIDS, and political persecutions in the global village; do we acknowledge their claim on our attention? What are the threshold points at which great sorrows (individual or communal) cease to draw sympathy?

A different take on the issue of the individual and the communal was presented in Nabokov: The American Years, a graduate course offered at the Hebrew University of Jerusalem in fall 2003, by Hanan Abu Dalu, an observant Muslim woman and an experienced and highly intelligent teacher of English. The presentation dealt with Azar Nafisi's *Reading* Lolita *in Tehran.* Having conceded the possible justice of Nafisi's analogy between Humbert's "solipsizing" of Dolly Haze and the mullahs' solipsistic regulative images of Muslim women, who have an intense inner life of their own, Abu Dalu went on to say that Nafisi erred in her choice of the book: what ethical value, for example, can be derived from the famous couch scene in Ramsdale? Abu Dalu objected not to Nafisi's liking the book but to her teaching it. The point was countered by Moira Feinsilver, a middle-aged American-born observant Jewish student, who said that while she too "was not crazy" about *Lolita*, she remembered the censorship debates in the United States and restated the classical Voltairian principle, "I disapprove of what you say, but I will defend to the death your right to say it."

In answer, Abu Dalu denied that she favored censorship unconditionally. She noted (and later explained more fully) that Islam encourages guarding oneself physically, spiritually, and morally; the three aspects are integrated and influence one another. If any persons choose not to abide by this teaching, Islam urges the individuals to keep this to themselves and not to talk in public about their interest in alcohol, adultery, or pornography. Censorship over texts that would contribute to normalizing such interest must be primarily individual—a self-censorship. If this self-censorship fails, it is the society's responsibility to take certain measures in accordance with Koranic teaching, in order that such phenomena should not become widespread. "As a Muslim educator," she added, "I wouldn't include *Lolita* in my teenage students' literature program. Nevertheless, talking professionally about the existence of such practices in society, how to deal with, face, and prevent them with Islamic guidance is a religious obligation."

The response of a younger student was, "Do you mean that one should not publicize this book because some of its readers will think, 'Wow, what a good idea, let's go after little girls'?" Abu Dalu answered that things hardly worked that way but that, nevertheless, the problem was that *Lolita* "made the unthinkable thinkable." Though that argument was easily countered by "newspapers are full of child-molestation cases, anyway," Abu Dalu's formula gave everyone pause: do media accounts of the crimes raise consciousness or produce copycat crimes by normalizing what used to be "unthinkable"? A careful reader of *Lolita* feels the tension between the normality and the abnormality in the novel—suffice it to recollect Dolly's touching attempt to achieve normality at the cost of reverse class mobility by marrying the symbolically deaf working-class war veteran. Although this narrative can be variously underread or misread in the ratings marketplace (the scene of Dolly's orgasm in Adrian Lyne's film is one example), the humanities-student audience—in New York, Jerusalem, or Tehran—is an intellectual, elite readership that can be trusted, or trained, to avoid misreadings.

Abu Dalu's special sensitivity gave the idea of coduction an almost eschatological edge. But that particular class ended on an unexpected psychological point raised by the usually quiet Elena Kulazhko, a young immigrant from Belarus. At issue were Humbert's memories of Avis Byrd and her father:

> Suddenly, as Avis clung to her father's neck and ear while, with a casual arm, the man enveloped his lumpy and large offspring, I saw Lolita's smile lose all its light . . . and the fruit knife slipped off the table and struck her with its silver handle a freak blow on the ankle which made her gasp, and . . . then, jumping on one leg, her face awful with the preparatory grimace which children hold till the tears gush, she was gone—to be followed at once and consoled in the kitchen by Avis who had such a wonderful fat pink dad and a small chubby brother, and a brand-new baby sister, and a home, and two grinning dogs, and Lolita had nothing.   (286)

While Avis thinks that Dolly is driven to tears by the hurt from the fruit knife, Humbert, and most of the readers, associate her distress with the comparison between Avis's conventionally healthy and normal "pink dad" and the grim parody of the father in Dolly's life; the Iranian student whom Nafisi calls Nassrin contributes the poignant comment that, surprisingly, "Nabokov, who is so hard on poshlust, [makes] us pity the loss of the most conventional forms of life" (50). Rorty's coductive addition to the reading of this scene is the recollection that Dolly too once had "a small chubby brother" and may long for him as well as for an idealized Charlotte whose grief for her son should not have been dismissed any more than the grief of the Kasbeam barber (163). When Rorty's implicit reproach calls our attention to these connections, our construction of Dolly's personality emerges as but a small improvement on Humbert's own.

Kulazhko went further than this—to suggest the possibility of an *alternative* rather than a *better* construction of Dolly's inner life. Perhaps, she said, Dolly's "smile lose[s] all its light" because Byrd's "casual arm" enveloping Avis makes her suspect that the relationship between those two is not as placid as it seems—that it may be a version of her own relationship with Humbert. Echoing the debates on the lasting psychological aftereffects of trauma—and resisting the contrary evidence of Humbert's style—Kulazhko maintained that the emotionally wounded Dolly could all too automatically misread the perfectly normative parent-child intimacy. This possibility opened further interpretive options: should one see Dolly as mortified by what she suspects to be Avis's plight or by a compunction about having had this suspicion?

Being read by *Lolita* does not mean trying to account for the response of other readers (Abu Dalu or Feinsilver; or Kulazhko; or Nafisi, Tekiner, or Toker) by specific cultural influences—reality is more complex than semiological labeling might allow. Being read by any great book means performing a self-reflexive twist, turning to oneself to question the sources and the implications of one's own responses. A demand for such a twist, built into the narrative of *Lolita*, is more troubling than the milder invitations in more classical fiction. A possible reason for numerous first-time readers' hostility to this novel may lie in a resistance to this demand.

Vivian Darkbloom:
Floral Border or Moral Order?

Lisa Sternlieb

In "On a Book Entitled *Lolita*" Vladimir Nabokov notes that "despite John Ray's assertion, *Lolita* has no moral in tow" (315). Indeed, the novel does not pull a moral along behind it; instead, the moral of this apparently immoral novel might be embedded in every line and, most important, in every word of the book. But how do we help students discover this? I begin with one of Nabokov's obsessions, the anagram, to show how the clever reordering of letters can open up the novel in dozens of ways and take us from aesthetic self-indulgence to ethical awareness. At the same time, by focusing on this endlessly resonant anagram, I help students unconvinced by any possible moral reading of the novel find the value of Nabokov's "aesthetic bliss" ("On a Book" 314).

I taught *Lolita* in freshman writing courses at Wake Forest University. After students had finished reading the book, we spent a class working on how to generate ideas for their papers. I never assigned paper topics. Many freshmen believe that they must begin with large, general ideas and end with something specific. I helped them see why starting with something tiny and seemingly insignificant can lead to broad and often unexpected readings of literature. *Lolita* was the last text of the semester. By this time they were well-versed in the idea of starting small and getting somewhere important. I started using the Vivian Darkbloom approach to teaching *Lolita* in an upper-level English class at Princeton University in 1995 and continue to use this method with majors at Penn State. Each time I teach the novel, whether to a freshman or a senior English major, a student discovers something that I had never noticed before about her endlessly fascinating name.

I begin by writing VIVIAN DARKBLOOM on the board and asking students what they notice.[1] With some gentle persuasion students should be able to see that her name is an anagram for the author's and points to the novel's concern with orthography. We discuss other ways in which spelling has both moral and aesthetic implications, such as the relation between "the rapist" and "therapist." We analyze the difference between Our Glass Lake and Hourglass Lake and note that the lake with the fantasy spelling has the initials o-g-l, obviously an appropriate place to ogle Lolita, whereas the actual spelling describes Charlotte's curvaceous figure and points to her impending death. Humbert misspells Hourglass Lake until he goes there with Charlotte, although he obviously knows how to spell the lake by the time he writes *Lolita*, demonstrating one of the many ways he uses spelling to play games with retrospection. The anagram also points to the centrality of metamorphosis in the novel. Vladimir Nabokov is transformed into Vivian Darkbloom as Dolores is into Lolita as Lolita is into

Charlotte, and so on. We may also read Vladimir Nabokov and Vivian Darkbloom as doubles, like Quilty and Humbert or Dolores and Annabel Leigh or
the novel's many twins. Doubling is, of course, crucial to understanding the
novel's obsession with solipsism. Does this anagram speak to the fact that Humbert is constantly bumping into mirrors or that Nabokov cannot get away from
himself as he creates his maniac narrator? Playing with hidden authorship was
more than a game for the novelist who had to consider the possibility that his
masterpiece would be published anonymously. Yet Vivian's name is a key route
to understanding the novel's game playing. Like the names in the hotel registers, hers is a text in itself. She reminds us of how words engender other words,
how names engender other names. No name in this novel should remain unexamined. As John Ray, Jr., tells us, the heroine's surname only rhymes with Haze
(3–4). One could no doubt write a dissertation on the various possible interpretations this clue presents. Is Dolores going through a phase? Is she caught in a
maze? Is she John Ray's?

Within Vivian's name Nabokov gestures to his place in modern literature. If
"bloom" points us to *Ulysses* and her "heart of darkness" to Conrad, her first
name is *The Enchanter*, the ur-*Lolita*. Bloom also hints at her Jewishness and
the novel's subtle reminders of both American and European anti-Semitism.
Her darkness suggests her connection to Humbert (umber), and both must be
seen in contrast to Clare (*clair*). Her initials lead us to both the sublime and the
ridiculous, both Nabokov's beloved father and venereal disease. Her last name
explains her appropriateness for Quilty. It evokes female genitalia as well as a
photographer's darkroom and a cinema. Does her heart of darkness counteract
the life-affirming nature of "Vivian" and "bloom"? Or does her oxymoronic
name prove that Nabokov's effort to bring forth life from all the death in the
novel is successful? Her association with Quilty goes on after his death in her
biography of him, *My Cue*. This title should point us to the cues and clues with
which the novel's master plotter (Quilty) establishes his superiority over the
novel's conscientious recorder (Humbert). Quilty's and Darkbloom's fruitful
coauthorship prepares us for the relationship maintained among John Ray, Jr.,
Humbert, and Nabokov. As Nabokov insists that he impersonates John Ray
and possibly impersonates himself (311), Vivian reminds us of the difficulty of
determining who is the author, who is the subject, who is the doctor, who is
the patient.

Humbert is deceived by Lo because he cannot listen, because he cannot pay
enough attention to notice sexual identity, to remember that Vivian is the man,
Clare the woman. In the final epiphanic moment on the mountaintop Humbert is finally able to hear. But, of course, this moment is not the epiphany we
have longed for but another deception. Humbert has played fast and loose
with chronology, leading us to believe that this is the final event of his narrative rather than one that has taken place years before he has tried to get Lolita
back, years before he has murdered Quilty. This reordering of events has been
Humbert's signature style. If the anagram requires us to read both forward

and backward, so does *Lolita* itself. But while retrospection as sleight of hand has been primarily clever or humorous (e.g., in the diary entry "[b]eginning perhaps amended" [42]), it is here potentially devastating. As a name Vivian Darkbloom is not simply the funny or clever rearrangement of letters; it is the figure for the moral manipulation allowed by ordering and reordering. We first discover Vivian's name in Ray's appalling misreading of Humbert's manuscript, in which the fate of Mrs. Richard F. Schiller follows Louise's and Mona Dahl's and is wedged between Rita's and Vivian Darkbloom's (4). Nabokov mocks the social scientist's need to prioritize and categorize, yet his novel may suggest the moral implications of order, chronology, and arrangement. If we want to train our students to be better readers than John Ray, Jr., if we want them to reject his easy sociological reading, then we should help them see that the placement of Vivian's name here indicates both Ray's obtuseness and his unwitting brilliance, both Nabokov's devilish sense of humor and his pervasive sense of tragedy. If Vivian's name reminds us that we should not trust art to lead us to moral transcendence, her character points to *Lolita*'s delicious paradox, that sometimes kitsch provides the only hope of redemption. For she, like the authors Lo reads, writes "trash for young people" (286), and only when Humbert puts down his Dante, Petrarch, and Poe and picks up the story of the "gloomy girl Marion" (286) does he realize what his "power of imagination" (287) has never revealed, that he has failed as parent, teacher, lover, and, finally, artist. Vivian Darkbloom, one of the unnamed "nerves of the novel," helps us understand why even Humbert's extraordinarily beautiful writing cannot compensate us for the loss of "pale, pregnant, beloved, irretrievable Dolly Schiller" ("On a Book" 316).

Vivian Darkbloom is barely a character. Yet even this rearrangement of letters reminds us that human beings are not simply patterns. Is she male or female? Does she write kitsch or art? Is she Quilty's lover or only his collaborator? Does she, like Mona and Louise, merely not belong in the same paragraph with Mrs. Richard F. Schiller, or is she actually more crucial than the title character? Is Vivian Darkbloom the creator of John Ray, Jr., and Humbert, or is she merely, like a chess piece, at their will to position her wherever they prefer? Her uncategorizable instability reminds us that no matter how detestable, predictable, or ideologically uninteresting human beings may appear to an artist, they are all, even John Ray, Jr., wonderful surprises. John Ray stands for everything Nabokov loathes. He is a bad reader and a pretentious, bad writer. His interpretation lacks all literary merit and instead relies on the legalistic, the sociological, and worst of all the Freudian. And yet if Humbert, Nabokov's Adam, is given the power to name himself Humbert Humbert and Dolores Lolita, it is John Ray Jr., who has apparently created and assigned the names in quotation marks in his foreword: Louise Windmuller, Mona Dahl, Mrs. Richard F. Schiller, and the most gorgeous of all the names in the book, Vivian Darkbloom. John Ray is to Nabokov what John Farlow is to Humbert, the man he has sized up, reduced to nothing, been bored by thoroughly, and analyzed to death. Eventually Humbert will be forced to confront Farlow's unpredictable uniqueness. Our reading of Vivian Darkbloom forces us to reassess John Ray, Jr. His naming Vivian Darkbloom is to my mind one of the great moments of aesthetic bliss in the novel. It is the writer of "second-rate symphonies" who composes this most resonant piece of music (265). Like Humbert's encounter with the barber of Kasbeam or his sudden outburst, "Charlotte, I began to understand you!" (149), this is a moment in which a great artist is made to appreciate the beauty and humanity of what he detests.

But, as one of my students wrote, there is no evidence that John Ray, Jr., is anyone other than Humbert Humbert. The maniac has not died, but metamorphosed into the outside editor of his own novel. After all, why would Mr. Windmuller of Ramsdale know anything about Rita? Wouldn't this metamorphosis explain why Humbert could not have been writing for fifty-six days if he received the letter from Dolores on 22 September and died on 16 November? Vivian's name thus reminds us that in *Lolita* Nabokov overturns the most basic of novelistic conventions, the reader's ability to distinguish between one character and another. By turns he makes it virtually impossible to distinguish between Vivian and Quilty, Quilty and Humbert, Humbert and John Ray, Jr., Annabel and Lolita, Lolita and Charlotte, and himself and Vivian Darkbloom.

I do not want my students to rank the many meanings embedded within Nabokov's great anagram. Instead, I want them to see how entangled with and inseparable from one another they are. Rather than impose order on the text, Vivian Darkbloom points out the dangers and impossibilities of valuing art more than kitsch, the grand passion of a poet more than the panting lust of a frustrated housewife. While Humbert's nostalgia for and re-creation of gardens lost rivals Milton's, Vivian also blooms among Charlotte Haze's lilies. I want students to love this novel because it explores the origins and nature of sin and because it shows the magical beauty of a suburban backyard.

After years of teaching this approach to *Lolita*, I recently encountered the most skeptical class I have ever taught. Many students rejected the possibility that Nabokov could be this clever and that language could be this resonant. Some students accused me of being as paranoid as Humbert himself. My experience of reading Vivian's name, they said, mirrors Humbert's experience of reading the hotel registers. I had so thoroughly gotten inside a madman's head that what I saw as clues were merely my own paranoid projections. (I am prepared to accept their attacks on me as compliments to Nabokov.) Another student, however, countered that their unwillingness to entertain my reading illustrated her classmates' myopia. Their desire to read literature to reaffirm their own views, their unwillingness to admit that Nabokov could be that much smarter than anything they had imagined, simply illustrated another example of Nabokovian solipsism. This same class realized that Humbert's manipulation of language is best summed up several sentences after Humbert first drops Vivian Darkbloom's name in the closing words of part 1, chapter 8: "Guilty of killing Quilty. Oh, my Lolita, I have only words to play with!" (32). I hope this exercise teaches my students that Nabokov also has his readers to play with. Like a clue from Edgar Allan Poe's "The Purloined Letter," the opaque and the transparent are hidden in plain sight.

By starting with the small and the seemingly insignificant, I show my students that it is virtually impossible to overread *Lolita*. I get extraordinary papers on *Lolita* because students learn to approach the novel as Nabokovians, through its "nerves" rather than its groin. I am astonished by the large arguments they are able to make by following the logic of tiny details to their surprising conclusions. For example, one student picked up on the detail that while Dolores rarely speaks, she makes plenty of noise by slamming doors throughout the book. This student showed how Humbert's melodious language is countered by this cacophony of slamming doors and that a novel ostensibly celebrating language eventually ends up slamming it. Another student began with the purported inspiration for the novel, the story of the ape in the Jardin des Plantes. He explored the vast amount of animal imagery and constructed a reading of the novel as a massive zoo. A third student, fascinated by the colors used in the scene in which Dolores first sits on Humbert's lap, showed the correspondence between these colors and those used in the scene of the murder of Quilty. She made surprising connections between these two crimes. A bilingual student showed how French words become characters' names. The gooey, baked apple French pastry *charlotte* becomes the mother who is in stark contrast with her daughter, *le fruit vert*. The French word for "ass," *cul*, becomes the nickname of the novel's twin pedophile. No name in *Lolita* turns out to be coincidental.

Students have written remarkable papers by beginning with stars, butterflies, the weather, dogs, numbers, parentheses, tennis, and ringing telephones. After our class on Vivian Darkbloom, freshmen came to the next class prepared to discuss their paper ideas. By sharing these ideas with one another, they came to realize how easily they would be able to generate their own takes on *Lolita*. The Vivian Darkbloom class simultaneously overwhelms students with Nabokov's brilliance and empowers them to come up with their own approaches to the novel.

NOTE

[1] Here is an example of the kind of list the Vivian Darkbloom exercise generates: anagrams, orthography, retrospection, metamorphosis, doubles, solipsism, hidden authorship, games, names, anonymity, *Ulysses*, *Heart of Darkness*, *The Enchanter*, anti-Semitism, darkness, the sublime and the ridiculous, Nabokov's father, venereal disease, genitalia, darkroom, cinema, oxymorons, cues and clues, plotter, recorder, coauthorship, impersonation, listening, sexual identity, order, chronology and arrangement, art, kitsch, patterns, chess, instability, John Ray, Jr., surprises, aesthetic bliss, novelistic conventions, flowers, gardens, sin, *Paradise Lost*, magic, paranoid projections, myopia, manipulation of language, opacity and transparency.

Humor and *Lolita* in the Classroom

Paul Benedict Grant

Humor has long been recognized as a highly effective educational tool. Research has shown that it functions as a positive aid to teaching and a persuasive means of learning, creating a relaxed atmosphere in the classroom, reducing stress, lengthening attention spans, increasing motivation levels, encouraging creativity and problem solving, and aiding the retention of key concepts. Teachers who consistently use humor record high levels of student performance, and surveys show that students respond positively to humor when it appears in a classroom context. Simply put, if students find their teacher humorous, they are more likely to attend class regularly and to engage more readily with the texts they study—positive effects that will only increase if humor is used as the main topic of discussion when approaching set texts.

As a university professor, Vladimir Nabokov certainly recognized the value of humor as a learning tool; as Brian Boyd records, his "sense of humor was a key to the charm of his lectures" (*American Years* 180). At Wellesley College, Cornell University, and elsewhere, he had a reputation as a "flamboyant, funny lecturer," playing pranks, cracking jokes, and doubling himself and his students up with laughter (V. Nabokov, *Strong Opinions* 128). Indeed, à la Pnin, he was often overcome to the point where he lost control of himself:

> Occasionally he would find something so uproarious in Gogol or Dickens or Flaubert that his laughter would infiltrate his lecturing until his wife would have to signal to him from her front-row seat that no one could understand what he was saying. (Boyd, *American Years* 181)

Nabokov delivered his last academic lectures in 1959, and they were full of his trademark humor: a reporter was present to snap photographs of his students "grinning, laughing, and applauding his latest phrase" (Boyd, *American Years* 376). Academe's loss was literature's gain, but Nabokov's approach proves that the serious study of language and literature—indeed, of all fields of learning—need not exclude, and can only benefit from, humor. In published reminiscences, his students frequently emphasize this aspect of his teaching; many retained the facts they learned in his classes into adulthood and believe that his teaching methods helped foster a lifelong appreciation of literature (see, e.g., Wetzsteon).

The book that prompted Nabokov's exit from academe (and accounted for the presence of that reporter) was *Lolita*, a novel known, among other things, for its humor. As well as being one of the book's greatest attractions, humor is one of its most troublesome aspects and a root source of its unease: it is, to say the least, unsettling to find oneself laughing along with a pedophile and a murderer. It poses an enormous challenge for many student readers and places some complicated demands on their sensibilities; for both reasons, it warrants close analysis in the classroom. As Tony Sharpe notes, "notwithstanding its dark elements, [*Lolita*] is extremely funny; and recognition of its humor is essential to understanding its achievement" (71).

To underline how crucial humor is to the novel, teachers should recommend that their students read passages from its "prototype," *The Enchanter* (V. Nabokov, "On a Book" 311). The basic plot is essentially the same, but Nabokov's treatment of the theme differs radically from the approach he would take in *Lolita*. *The Enchanter* is told in the third person, which distances the reader from the action; just as important, it lacks the humor that lights up the later work. The protagonist, unlike Humbert, is humorless. We should not underestimate the importance of this characteristic as a governing factor in our response. David Rampton makes this point when comparing the respective seduction scenes (a comparison that proves constructive in class):

> The greater physical explicitness of [*The Enchanter*] makes the whole encounter repulsive in a way that the scene in the novel is not, and shows how Nabokov needs the comedy, the voice that articulates it, and the idea of a complex identity defining itself in the gap between decision and action.
> (92 [Macmillan])

While lacking in humor, the protagonist of *The Enchanter* knows that it would help him fulfill his desires: when he first finds himself alone with the girl, "[h]e tried to make her laugh, and chat with her as he would have with an ordinary child" (48). He sees his predicament as a bad joke and wishes he could dispose of the mother "so that the child might at last be aware of the joke and he might be rewarded by their having a good laugh together, by being able to take disinterested care of her, to meld the wave of fatherhood with the wave of sexual love" (49). When finally free of the mother, he realizes that humor could be an important tool in the process of seduction, a means of persuading the girl to surrender to his advances under the pretext of having fun: "[I]t would be easy, by means of pet names and jokes . . . to divert a normal girl's attention . . . so as to prepare a painless transition from a world of semiabstractions . . . into the everyday reality of pleasant fun" (72–73). These fantasies are never realized, and the story ends with his death by suicide after the bungled seduction. His death does not elicit sympathy, because he has also failed to seduce the reader. By contrast, Humbert, despite having the same vice, manages to retain the reader's sympathy for long stretches of the novel. No matter how nasty he gets, his humor makes him hard to hate. As Boyd writes, "He ruins one person's life and ends another's, and yet he makes us laugh: he is tragic hero, tragic villain, and court jester all in one" (*American Years* 228–29).

Like *The Enchanter*'s protagonist, Humbert recognizes the value of humor as a means of camouflaging his motivations, but he is more adept in its practice. One night, he, Charlotte, and Lolita are seated in close proximity on the piazza. To take advantage of the situation, writes Humbert, "I launched upon a hilarious account of my arctic adventures. . . . I chuckled at my own jokes, and trembled, and concealed my tremors, and once or twice felt with my rapid lips the warmth of her hair as I treated her to a quick nuzzling, humorous aside" (45–46). This situation mirrors the method Humbert takes with his readers. Humor is his main means of persuasion, the method by which he seeks to seduce two juries: the fictional jury within the novel and his general readership (for although he claims that he does not intend to use his notes at his trial, he begins with that intention). As a sometime teacher himself, Humbert is acutely aware that humor is a potential means of manipulation and uses it in an attempt to deflect our attention from his less attractive traits and from what he has done to Dolores and Quilty. It is a cunning ploy: in our amusement, it is easy for us to forget that there is "a cesspoolful of rotting monsters behind his slow boyish smile" and only retrospectively register the repugnant reality (44). By analyzing the humor in *Lolita*, students come to understand this rhetorical strategy and recognize the enormous power humor has to entice, create a collective empathy, and cause moral myopia.

Nabokov had already experimented with the complexities of first-person narration and the ethical consequences of group laughter in *Pnin*, but they reach perhaps their most disconcerting form in *Lolita*, where the subject matter makes the moral stakes much higher. Surrendering to Humbert's seduction has a number of unflattering ramifications: in becoming complicit in his laughter, we become unwitting collaborators in his actions. In *Le rire*, Henri Bergson describes how this process of inclusion works:

> You would hardly appreciate the comic if you felt yourself isolated from others. Laughter appears to stand in need of an echo . . . it is something which would fain be prolonged by reverberating from one to another. . . . Our laughter is always the laughter of a group. . . . However spontaneous it seems, laughter always implies a kind of secret freemasonry, or even complicity, with other laughers, real or imaginary. (64)

Sigmund Freud also touches on this subject in *Jokes and Their Relation to the Unconscious*, where he notes that a joke "bribe[s] the hearer with its yield of pleasure into taking sides . . . without any very close investigation" (147). Consulting both of these passages in conjunction with *Lolita* helps students arrive at a better understanding of how Humbert's humor functions in the novel.

Quilty's murder is perhaps the most potent example in *Lolita* of how humor can cloud our moral sense. It also cements the affinities between Humbert and Quilty with respect to their use of humor. Humbert admits to having "thoroughly studied" Quilty's humor (217), which, "at its best at least . . . had affinities with [his] own" (249): like the incarcerated Humbert who writes the novel, Quilty is looking death in the face and tries to joke his way out of the situation, and thus he "reflects Humbert's strategy of combatting his enemies with laughter" (Wallace 85). The tactic works—at least temporarily: as Ronald

Wallace notes, "undercut by the comedy" (86), Humbert is initially unable to shoot Quilty, a situation that replicates the reader's difficulty in condemning Humbert. The entire episode serves as a valuable blueprint for students in their interpretation of Humbert's humorous rhetoric.

In *Lolita*, this rhetoric operates on a number of levels. The following sub-headings (which are far from exhaustive) are followed by representative passages that exemplify each technique and would benefit from close analysis in the classroom. These passages are followed by questions that teachers could then pose to their students.

Familiarity

The scale of Nabokov's achievement in *Lolita* is in many ways dependent on reader identification—a remarkable accomplishment, given the perverted nature of his narrator. Critics often accord the humor special praise, without comprehending the manner in which it taps into our own experiences and forces us to confront our own value systems. In this sense, we do not really read *Lolita*; *Lolita* reads us. One of the novel's earliest critics, F. W. Dupee, recognized this:

> *Lolita* is very funny . . . but the supreme laugh may be on the reviewers for failing to see how much of everyone's reality lurks in its fantastic shadow play. . . . The images of life that *Lolita* gives back are ghastly but recognizable. If Mr. Nabokov's methods are the usual methods of comedy, they are here carried to new extremes.   ("Coming" 118–19)

Although Humbert's sexual preferences are abnormal, many of the situations he finds himself in are not. Many students, for example, will have experience with incompatible partners and difficult parent-child relations, and this familiarity may mitigate their reaction to Humbert's satirical treatment of Valeria and Charlotte—and perhaps even to aspects of his relationship with Lolita. As Dupee writes, "the grim sexual comedy of the Charlotte episode" is "a desperately common experience," and the "perverse partnership of Humbert and Lolita reflects some of the painful comedy of family relations in general" (129). Humbert's satirical descriptions of America's motels (paper-thin walls, cascading toilets, etc.) and the rampant consumerism that Dolores delights in are also sure to strike an empathetic chord. Representative passages include Humbert's relationship with Charlotte (35–97), his uncomfortable night at the Enchanted Hunters (129–32), and his description of the cultural delights on offer during his two cross-country trips with Lolita (145–58, 210). Teachers should ask their students, What kind of person is Humbert writing for? Are they disgusted that he addresses the reader as his "[b]ruder" (262), or are they flattered to be taken into his confidence? Is this a narrator they could relate to if the nature of his crime were different?

Iconoclasm

In common with many comics, Humbert has a problem with authority figures (e.g., psychiatrists, doctors, dentists, policemen, teachers). Many readers (especially student readers) will be able to relate to this and revel vicariously in his rebellion; in his acidulous attacks, he is appealing to the anarchic elements in our natures that rejoice at his license. Freud's theory of "tendentious jokes" should be consulted in relation to this topic and is especially interesting given Humbert's (and Nabokov's) scorn for psychoanalysis:

> By making our enemy small, inferior, despicable or comic, we achieve in a roundabout way the enjoyment of overcoming him . . . tendentious jokes are especially favoured in order to make aggressiveness or criticism possible against persons in exalted positions who claim to exercise authority. The joke then represents a rebellion against that authority, a liberation from its pressure. (*Jokes* 147, 149)

Representative passages for analysis include Humbert's disparagement of Freudian psychoanalysis (34–35, 125); his mocking of his Ramsdale doctor (94–95), of Camp Mistress Holmes (110), and of the hotel porters (118); his interviews with Headmistress Pratt (177–78, 193–97); his treatment of the doctors and nurses at the hospital in Elphinstone (240–47); his interview with Quilty's Uncle Ivor (291–92); and his deliberately driving on the wrong side of the road and running red lights (306). Questions for students may include the following: Is Humbert's dismissal of Freud a trap for those who would automatically arrive at a Freudian explanation for his actions, or does it imply a genuine psychological malady? Humbert's comic insurrection may be appealing, but is it nothing more than a liberation from pressure, as Freud suggests? Furthermore, is it wise, given that he is appealing to a group of authority figures (the jury) who have the power to influence the course of his life?

Malice

It would be easy to condemn Humbert's malicious humor, but it would be hypocritical to contend that we have not, at some point, indulged in it ourselves. Bergson addresses this subject at the close of *Le rire*, where he mentions the "spark of spitefulness" in human nature that draws us instinctively toward this type of humor, often despite ourselves (188–89). In *Lolita's* foreword, John Ray, Jr., asserts that Humbert's "mixture of ferocity and jocularity" is "not conducive to attractiveness" (5), but this aspect of his personality *does* make him more appealing. In addition to the above passage from Bergson, students should consult chapter 8, section 13, of Thomas Hobbes's *On Human Nature*, in which he expresses his so-called superiority theory of humor: "the passion of laughter

. . . is nothing else but sudden glory arising from some sudden conception of some eminency in ourselves, by comparison with the infirmity of others" (qtd. in Morreall 20). Also recommended is Freud's short paper "Humour" (1927), in which the author expands on his relief theory. For Freud, humor represents "the victorious assertion of the ego's invulnerability" but functions as a means of evading troublesome facts (162). These theories could be analyzed in relation to the following passages: Humbert's account of Valeria's fate (30–31), his nastiness toward Charlotte (see above), his description of fooling the Farlows (98–101), his visit from Beale (102–03), his conversation with Mrs. Chatfield (289–90), his meeting with Richard Schiller (273–75), and his interview with Ivor (see above). Questions for students may include the following: Does Humbert's sense of superiority mask his powerlessness and desperation? Do all the victims of his satire deserve his treatment? Do we feel guilty laughing along—and if so, how does that guilt influence our feelings toward him? Just as important, what does it tell us about ourselves?

Self-Deprecation

While Humbert's humor is rarely free of animus, he is also adept in the art of self-deprecating humor, a fail-safe tool in the comic's arsenal that makes us more willing to side with him when he goes on the attack. As Wallace writes:

> We have to identify with Humbert as a comic hero who criticizes himself while undercutting the pretensions of stuffy ladies and pompous dentists. . . . Humbert thinks that by smiling at his own actions and by persuading the reader to smile, he will be able to overcome any objections to his behavior.   (76, 85–86)

Representative passages include the following: Humbert's mistaking an old man for a nymphet while masturbating (20, 264), his betrayal by Valeria (27–30), his description of himself in drag (66), his hesitation over the wording of the telegram to the Enchanted Hunters (109), and his feelings of inadequacy during his night at the Hunters (128–32) and when tracking Quilty (247–51). Questions for students may include the following: Why does Humbert choose to divulge these embarrassing moments? In what context do they appear? Should they be seen as signs of sincerity or self-preservation?

Honesty

There is a candor to Humbert's account of himself that engenders a certain amount of empathy for this otherwise despicable character. The passages relating Humbert's late declaration of love for Lolita (277–78) and his remorse over his actions toward her (282–87, 307–08) must be read with a due amount of skepticism, but they are among the most powerful moments in the book. Students may be asked, Are you moved by Humbert's declaration and affected by his remorse? Why has Humbert chosen to place these particular passages at the end of his tale? Does the *absence* of humor in these passages contribute to their authenticity—that is, is this the "real" Humbert talking, and does the preceding humor merely mask a tortured and repentant soul?

Humbert appeals to us in a seemingly direct fashion when he is on the verge of raping a drugged Lolita in the Enchanted Hunters: "Imagine me; I shall not exist if you do not imagine me; try to discern the doe in me, trembling in the forest of my own iniquity; let's even smile a little. After all, there is no harm in smiling" (129). There is, of course, if one is sharing that smile with someone like Humbert, for by doing so one becomes complicit in his designs and implicitly condones his actions. Students should certainly not be discouraged from laughing at the humor in *Lolita* and made to feel in any way abnormal for doing so—as Gladys Clifton remarks, the invitation to smile "is surely Nabokov's as well as Humbert's. And if one has indeed fully imagined Humbert's plight, it is impossible not to smile at its ludicrous aspect" (153). But an understanding of humor's complexities and rhetorical strategies enables students to analyze passages like this with a greater awareness of their import and helps them navigate their way through this challenging, disconcerting, and very funny novel.

NOTES ON CONTRIBUTORS

Brian Boyd is University Distinguished Professor in the Department of English at the University of Auckland. He is the author of *Nabokov's Ada: The Place of Consciousness* (1985, 2001), *Vladimir Nabokov: The Russian Years* (1990), *Vladimir Nabokov: The American Years* (1991), *Vladimir Nabokov's Pale Fire: The Magic of Artistic Discovery* (1999), and the editor or coeditor of *Vladimir Nabokov: Novels and Memoirs, 1941–1974* (1996), *Nabokov's Butterflies* (2000), *Words That Count: Early Modern Authorship* (2004), and *Verses and Versions* (2008).

David Clippinger is visiting professor at the University of Pittsburgh, Pittsburgh. He is the author of *The Mind's Landscape: William Bronk and Twentieth-Century American Poetry* (2006), *The Body of This Life: Reading William Bronk* (2003), and *Bursts of Light: Collected Later Poems of William Bronk* (2006).

Julian W. Connolly is professor of Slavic languages and literatures at the University of Virginia. He is the author of *Ivan Bunin* (1982), *Nabokov's Early Fiction: Patterns of Self and Other* (1992), and *The Intimate Stranger: Meetings with the Devil in Nineteenth-Century Russian Literature* (2001). He edited *Nabokov's "Invitation to a Beheading": A Critical Companion* (1997), *Nabokov and His Fiction: New Perspectives* (1999), and *The Cambridge Companion to Nabokov* (2005).

Marianne Cotugno is assistant professor of English at Miami University. She has published articles on American and British poetry and is working on "On the Road with *Lolita*," a study of more than two dozen sites visited by Humbert and Lolita during their cross-country journeys.

Galya Diment is professor and chair in the Department of Slavic Languages and Literatures at the University of Washington, Seattle, where she teaches literature and film. She is the author of *Pniniad: Vladimir Nabokov and Marc Szeftel* (1997) and *The Autobiographical Novel of Co-consciousness: Goncharov, Woolf, and Joyce* (1993). She edited *Goncharov's Oblomov: A Critical Companion* (1998) and coedited *Between Heaven and Hell: The Myth of Siberia in Russian Culture* (1993).

Dana Dragunoiu is associate professor at Carleton University, where she teaches literature and intellectual history. She has published articles on Nabokov, Hemingway, Coetzee, and film in *Nabokov Studies, Modern Fiction Studies, Journal of Modern Literature, Contemporary Literature, Critique, Film Criticism*, and the *Journal of Commonwealth Literature*. Her current project is a book on Nabokov's politics.

Marilyn Edelstein is associate professor of English at Santa Clara University, where she teaches contemporary American literature, feminist theory, and critical theory. She has published articles and book chapters on Nabokov, contemporary American fiction, and feminist theory. She is working on a book on the intersections and ethics of feminism, postmodernism, and multiculturalism.

Paul Benedict Grant is assistant professor of English at Memorial University of Newfoundland, Sir Wilfred Grenfell College, where he teaches nineteenth- and twentieth-century literature. He is currently preparing a book on Nabokov's humor.

Sarah Herbold is lecturer in the Department of Comparative Literature at the University of California, Berkeley. She has published articles in *Approaches to Teaching Rousseau's* Confessions and Reveries of the Solitary Walker (2003), *Eighteenth-Century Studies*, *Nabokov Studies*, and *Signs: A Journal of Women in Culture and Society*. She is working on a study of *Jane Eyre*.

Zoran Kuzmanovich, professor of English at Davidson College, teaches American literature, literary criticism, and film studies. In 2004 he received Davidson's most prestigious teaching award, the Hunter-Hamilton Love of Teaching. He writes on the relations among arts, ethics, and politics. Since 1996, he has served as the editor of *Nabokov Studies*.

Jason Merrill is assistant professor of Russian at Michigan State University. He has published articles on intertextuality in the works of Fedor Sologub and on religion, politics, and literature in the films of Larisa Shepit'ko. He is the author of *Russian Folktales: A Student Reader* (2000). He is working on a book on Sologub's dramas.

Priscilla Meyer is professor of Russian language and literature at Wesleyan University. She has published a monograph on Vladimir Nabokov's *Pale Fire*, *Find What the Sailor Has Hidden*; coedited, with Jane Grayson and Arnold McMillin, *Nabokov's World*, and written articles on Pushkin, Lermontov, Gogol, Dostoevsky, Tolstoy, Nabokov, and Soviet prose of the 1960s and 1970s. Her book *How the Russians Read the French: Lermontov, Dostoevsky, Tolstoy* is forthcoming.

Claudia Moscovici teaches philosophy and arts and ideas at the University of Michigan, Ann Arbor. She is the author of five scholarly books and has published poems and chapters of her first novel, *The Cubic Planet*, in *Portland Magazine*, *Enigma Magazine*, the *Palo Alto Review*, the *Fairfield Review*, *WINGS*, *Outsider Ink*, *Nanny Fay Poetry Magazine*, the *Poetic Matrix*, *Three Cup Morning*, *Slate and Style*, and *Möbius*.

Eric Naiman is associate professor in the Departments of Comparative Literature and Slavic Languages and Literature at the University of California, Berkeley. He is the author of *Sex in Public: The Incarnation of Early Soviet Ideology* (1997) and articles on Nabokov, published in *Comparative Literature*, *Ulbandus*, and *Nabokov Studies*. He is working on "Nabokov, Perversely," a book about Nabokov and his readers.

Dale E. Peterson is Eliza Clark Folger Professor of English and Russian at Amherst College. He is the author of *The Clement Vision: Poetic Realism in Turgenev and James* (1975) and *Up from Bondage: The Literatures of Russian and African American Soul* (2000), which won the Best Book in Literary and Cultural Studies Award from the American Association of Teachers of Slavic and Eastern European Languages.

Ellen Pifer is professor of English and comparative literature at the University of Delaware, Newark. She is the author of *Nabokov and the Novel* (1980), *Saul Bellow against the Grain* (1990), and *Demon or Doll: Images of the Child in Contemporary Writing and Culture* (2000). She edited *Critical Essays on John Fowles* (1986) and *Vladimir Nabokov's* Lolita: A Casebook (2003). Other publications include two dozen essays and articles on Nabokov. Her current project is a book on American identity from a transatlantic literary perspective.

Tania Roy is assistant professor in the Department of English Language and Literature at the National University of Singapore, where she teaches courses on psychoanalysis and literature, critical theory, and modernism and modernity in South and Southeast Asia. She has published articles on the aesthetics in colonial India, Vivan Sundaram, and the Frankfurt school and Theodor W. Adorno.

Corinne Scheiner is Maytag Associate Professor of Comparative Literature at Colorado College. She has published articles on Nabokov, literary translation, bilingualism, and Samuel Beckett. She is working on the book "Writing Dualities: Literary Bi-discursivity, Self-Translation, and Themes of Doubleness in the Novels of Samuel Beckett and Vladimir Nabokov."

Samuel Schuman is chancellor emeritus of the University of Minnesota, Morris. His books on literature and education include *Vladimir Nabokov: A Reference Guide* (1979) and *Old Main: Small Colleges in Twenty-First Century America* (2005). His particular focus in Nabokov has been the writer's use of Shakespeare and Shakespearean materials.

Lisa Sternlieb is associate professor of English at Pennsylvania State University, University Park. She is the author of *The Female Narrator in the British Novel: Hidden Agendas* (2002) and has published on Joyce, Charlotte Brontë, Hardy, and Stoppard. She is working on "Old Maids: Redundant Women in Victorian Literature and Culture."

Leona Toker, professor of English at the Hebrew University of Jerusalem, is the author of *Nabokov: The Mystery of Literary Structures* (1989), *Eloquent Reticence: Withholding Information in Fictional Narrative* (1993), and *Return from the Archipelago: Narratives of Gulag Survivors* (2000). She is the editor of *Commitment in Reflection: Essays in Literature and Moral Philosophy* (1994) and of *Partial Answers: A Journal of Literature and the History of Ideas*.

Lisa Ryoko Wakamiya is assistant professor of Russian literature at Florida State University. She has published numerous articles on contemporary Russian writers, including Vassily Aksyonov, Eduard Limonov, and Sasha Sokolov. Her forthcoming monograph, *Locating Contemporary Russian Writing: The Rhetoric of Exile and Return*, is a study of writers exiled in the last decades of the Soviet period who have since returned to Russia.

John Whalen-Bridge is associate professor in the Department of English Language and Literature at the National University of Singapore. He is the author of *Political Fiction and the American Self* (1998) and articles on twentieth-century and contemporary American writers, among them Norman Mailer, Donald Barthelme, and Charles Johnson. His current project is a series of books on literary orientalism and "Buddhist Renaissance" in postwar American writings.

Michael Wood is professor of English and comparative literature at Princeton University. He is the author of *The Magician's Doubts: Nabokov and the Risks of Fiction* (1994), *Children of Silence: On Contemporary Fiction* (1998), *The Road to Delphi: The Life and Afterlife of Oracles* (2003), and *Literature and the Taste of Knowledge* (2005). He writes on film and literature for the *London Review of Books* and the *New York Review of Books*.

SURVEY PARTICIPANTS

We wish to thank the following scholars, who answered our questions and shared their classroom experience, wisdom, relevant materials, and suggestions on how best to teach *Lolita*.

Matthew Beedham, *Malaspina University College*
Kevin Birmingham, *Harvard University*
Tom Bontly, *University of Wisconsin, Milwaukee*
Brian Boyd, *University of Auckland*
Marsha Bryant, *University of Florida*
Suzanne Churchill, *Davidson College*
David Clippinger, *Pittsburgh University, Pittsburgh*
Julian W. Connolly, *University of Virginia*
Maurice Couturier, *University of Nice–Sophia Antipolis*
Marianne Cotugno, *Miami University, Middletown*
Dana Dragunoiu, *Carleton University*
Marilyn Edelstein, *Santa Clara University*
Charles H. Fischer, *University of Washington, Seattle*
Dennis Foster, *Southern Methodist University*
Paul Benedict Grant, *Memorial University of Newfoundland, Sir Wilfred Grenfell College*
Jaqueline Hamrit, *University of Lille*
Rebeca Helfer, *University of California, Irvine*
Jennifer Hendzlik, *Brentwood Library, Springfield, MO*
Sarah Herbold, *University of California, Berkeley*
Constance E. Holmes, *University of South Florida, Tampa*
Harriet Hustis, *The College of New Jersey*
Gary Levine, *Ashland University*
Christopher Link, *Boston University*
Micihyo Maruyama, *Ritsumeikan University*
Heather Meakin, *Case Western Reserve University*
Jason Merrill, *Michigan State University*
Priscilla Meyer, *Wesleyan University*
Tim Morris, *University of Texas, Arlington*
Claudia Moscovici, *University of Michigan, Ann Arbor*
Nick Mount, *University of Toronto*
Eric Naiman, *University of California, Berkeley*
Lara Suzanne Narcisi, *New York University*
Alan Michael Parker, *Davidson College*
Dale E. Peterson, *Amherst College*
Ellen Pifer, *University of Delaware, Newark*
Randall J. Pogorzelski, *University of California, Santa Barbara*
D. Matthew Ramsey, *Denison University*
Eric Rothstein, *University of Wisconsin, Madison*

Tania Roy, *National University of Singapore*
Corinne Scheiner, *Colorado College*
Karen Schneider, *Western Kentucky University*
Samuel Schuman, *University of New Mexico, Albuquerque*
Savely Senderovich, *Cornell University*
Lisa Sternlieb, *Pennsylvania State University, University Park*
Leona Toker, *Hebrew University of Jerusalem*
Lisa Ryoko Wakamiya, *Florida State University*
John Whalen-Bridge, *National University of Singapore*

WORKS CITED

Print Resources

Abrams, M. H. *The Mirror and the Lamp: Romantic Theory and the Critical Tradition.* Oxford: Oxford UP, 1953.
———. *Natural Supernaturalism: Tradition and Revolution in Romantic Literature.* New York: Norton, 1971.
Adorno, Theodor W., and Max Horkheimer. "The Culture Industry or Enlightenment as Mass Deception." *Dialectic of Enlightenment.* New York: Continuum, 1976.
Albee, Edward. *Lolita: A Play.* New York: Dramatists' Play Service, 1984.
Alexandrov, Vladimir, ed. *The Garland Companion to Vladimir Nabokov.* New York: Garland, 1995.
———. *Nabokov's Otherworld.* Princeton: Princeton UP, 1991.
Alvarez, Alfred. "London Letter: Exile's Return." *Partisan Review* 26 (1959): 284–89.
Amis, Kingsley. Rev. of *Lolita*, by Vladimir Nabokov. *Spectator* 6 Nov. 1959: 635–36.
Appel, Alfred, Jr. "In Memoriam." *In Memoriam: Vladimir Nabokov, 1899–1977.* Ed. Harold W. McGraw, Jr., et al. New York: McGraw, 1974. 7–10.
———. Introduction. V. Nabokov, *The Annotated* Lolita xvii–lxvii
———. "*Lolita*: The Springboard of Parody." Dembo 106–43.
———. *Nabokov's Dark Cinema.* New York: Oxford UP, 1974.
———. Notes. V. Nabokov, *Annotated* Lolita 319–457.
———. "Remembering Nabokov." Quennell 11–33.
Appel, Alfred, Jr., and Charles Newman, eds. *Nabokov: Criticism, Reminiscences, Translations, and Tributes.* Evanston: Northwestern UP, 1970.
Aristotle. *Poetics.* Trans. Leon Golden. Richter 42–64.
Bader, Julia. *Crystal Land: Artifice in Nabokov's English Novels.* Berkeley: U of California P, 1972.
Bakhtin, Mikhail. *Problems of Dostoevsky's Poetics.* Trans. and ed. Caryl Emerson. Minneapolis: U of Minnesota P, 1984.
Balestrini, Nassim. "Nabokov Criticism in German-Speaking Countries: A Survey." *Nabokov Studies* 5 (1998–99): 185–234.
"Ban on Lolita Lifted." *Times* [London] 21 Sept. 1959: 9.
Barthes, Roland. *Mythologies.* Paris: Seuil, 1957.
———. *S/Z.* Paris: Seuil, 1970.
Baudrillard, Jean. *America.* Trans. Chris Turner. New York: Verso, 1988.
Bellino, Mary. "The Student's Nabokov." *Nabokov Studies* 9 (2005): 209–15.
Benjamin, Walter. "Paris, Capital of the Nineteenth Century." *Reflections: Essays, Aphorisms, Autobiographical Writings.* Trans. Edmund Jephcott. Ed. and introd. Peter Demetz. New York: Harcourt, 1978. 146–62.
Berberova, Nina Nikolaevna. *Nabokov et sa "Lolita."* Arles: Actes Sud, 1996.
Bergson, Henri. *Le rire.* 1900. *Comedy.* Ed. Wylie Sypher. Baltimore: Johns Hopkins UP, 1994. 61–190.
Berlin, Isaiah. *The Roots of Romanticism.* Princeton: Princeton UP, 1999.
Bloom, Harold, ed. *Lolita.* New York: Chelsea, 1993.
———, ed. *Vladimir Nabokov's* Lolita. New York: Chelsea, 1987.

Blum, Virginia. "Nabokov's *Lolita* / Lacan's Mirror." *Hide and Seek: The Child between Psychoanalysis and Fiction*. Chicago: U of Chicago P, 1995. 201–45.

Booth, Wayne. *The Company We Keep: An Ethics of Fiction*. Berkeley: U of California P, 1988.

Borges, Jorge Luis. "Tlön, Uqbar, Orbis Tertius." *Labyrinths*. Trans. James E. Irby. New York: New Directions, 1964.

———. *The Rhetoric of Fiction*. Chicago: U of Chicago P, 1961.

Bowlby, Rachel. "*Lolita* and the Poetry of Advertising." Bowlby, *Shopping* 46–71.

———. *Shopping with Freud*. London: Routledge, 1993.

Boyd, Brian. "'Even Homais Nods': Nabokov's Fallibility; or, How to Revise *Lolita*." *Nabokov Studies* 2 (1995): 62–86.

———. "Nabokov, Literature, and Lepidoptera." Boyd and Pyle 1–31.

———. "Nabokov's Manuscripts." Alexandrov, *Garland Companion* 340–45.

———. *Vladimir Nabokov: The American Years*. Princeton: Princeton UP, 1991.

———. *Vladimir Nabokov: The Russian Years*. Princeton: Princeton UP, 1990.

Boyd, Brian, and Robert Michael Pyle, eds. *Nabokov's Butterflies: Unpublished and Uncollected Writings*. Boston: Beacon, 2000.

Brodsky, Anna. "Nabokov's *Lolita* and the Postwar Émigré Consciousness." *Realms of Exile: Nomadism, Diasporas, and Eastern European Voices*. Ed. Domnica Radulescu. Lanham: Lexington, 2002. 49–66.

Brooks, Peter. *Troubling Confessions: Speaking Guilt in Law and Literature*. Chicago: U of Chicago P, 2000.

Bruss, Elizabeth W. *Autobiographical Acts: The Changing Situation of a Literary Genre*. Baltimore: Johns Hopkins UP, 1976.

Bryer, Jackson R., and Thomas J. Bergin, Jr. "Vladimir Nabokov's Critical Reputation in English: A Note and a Checklist." Dembo 225–76.

Bullock, Richard H. "Humbert the Character, Humbert the Writer: Artifice, Reality, and Art in *Lolita*." *Philological Quarterly* 63 (1984): 187–204.

Butler, Diana. "Lolita Lepidoptera." *New World Writing* 16 (1960): 58–84.

Centerwall, Brandon S. "Hiding in Plain Sight: Nabokov and Pedophilia." *Texas Studies in Literature and Language* 32 (1990): 468–84.

Certeau, Michel de. *The Practice of Every-day Life*. Trans. Stephen Rendall. Berkeley: U of California P, 2002.

Clegg, Christine, ed. *Vladimir Nabokov,* Lolita: *A Reader's Guide to Essential Criticism*. Trumpington: Icon, 2000.

Clifton, Gladys M. "Humbert Humbert and the Limits of Artistic License." Rivers and Nicol 153–70.

The Confessions of Victor X. Ed. and trans. Donald Rayfield. New York: Grove, 1985.

Connolly, Julian W., ed. *The Cambridge Companion to Nabokov*. Cambridge: Cambridge UP, 2005.

———. "Madness and Doubling: From Dostoevsky's *The Double* to Nabokov's *The Eye*." *Russian Literature Triquarterly* 24 (1991): 129–39.

———. "'Nature's Reality' or Humbert's 'Fancy'? Scenes of Reunion and Murder in *Lolita*." *Nabokov Studies* 2 (1995): 41–61.

Corliss, Richard. *Lolita*. BFI Film Classics Series. London: British Film Inst., 1994.

Couturier, Maurice, ed. *Lolita*. Paris: Autrement, 1998.

———. "Nabokov and Flaubert." Alexandrov, *Garland Companion* 405–12.

———. *V. Nabokov:* Lolita. Paris: Didier-Erudition–CNED, 1995.

Cummins, George L. "Nabokov's Russian *Lolita*." *Slavic and East European Journal* 21 (1977): 354–65.

Dembo, L. S., ed. *Nabokov: The Man and His Work*. Madison: U of Wisconsin P, 1967.

Dickstein, Morris. *Leopards in the Temple: The Transformation of American Fiction, 1945–1970*. Cambridge: Harvard UP, 2002.

Diment, Galya. "Ayatollah Humbert: Reading Azar Nafisi's Memoir." *Stranger* 5–11 June 2003. 4 Apr. 2007 <http://www.thestranger.com/2003-06-05/books.html>.

———. "Nabokov at Cornell University: A View of the Outsider." *Russian Studies in Literature* 35.4 (1999): 7–15.

———. *Pniniad: Vladimir Nabokov and Marc Szeftel*. Seattle: U of Washington P, 1997.

Dolinin, Alexander. "Nabokov's Time Doubling: From *The Gift* to *Lolita*." *Nabokov Studies* 2 (1995): 3–40.

Dostoevsky, Fyodor. *The Brothers Karamazov*. Trans. David Magarshack. Harmondsworth: Penguin, 1958.

———. *Crime and Punishment*. Ed. George Gibian. Trans. Jessie Coulson. New York: Norton, 1989.

———. *The Devils*. Trans. and ed. Michael R. Katz. Oxford: Oxford UP, 1992.

——— "A Gentle Creature." Trans. David Magarshack. Dostoevsky, *Great Short Works* 669–714.

———. *Great Short Works of Fyodor Dostoevsky*. New York: Harper, 2004.

———. "Notes from the Underground." Trans. David Magarshack. Dostoevsky, *Great Short Works* 263–377.

Dunne, J. W. *An Experiment with Time*. London: Faber, 1939.

Dupee, F. W. "'Lolita' in America." *Encounter* 65 (1959): 30–35.

———. "A Preface to *Lolita*." *Anchor Review* 2 (1957): 1–13. Rpt. as "The Coming of Nabokov." *The King of the Cats*. Chicago: U of Chicago P, 1984. 117–31.

Eco, Umberto. *The Role of the Reader: Explorations in the Semiotics of Texts*. Bloomington: Indiana UP, 1979.

Edmunds, Jeff. "Nabokov, ou le vrai et l'invraisemblable." *Nabokov Studies* 3 (1996): 151–210.

Falk, Pasi, and Colin Campbell. *The Shopping Experience*. London: Sage, 1997.

Fanger, Donald. "Nabokov and Gogol." Alexandrov, *Garland Companion* 420–28.

Fetterley, Judith. *The Resisting Reader: A Feminist Approach to American Fiction*. Bloomington: Indiana UP, 1978.

Field, Andrew. *Nabokov: A Bibliography*. New York: McGraw, 1973.

———. *Nabokov: His Life in Art*. Boston: Little, 1967.

Fippinger, Andrew L. "Discussion Topic for Nabokv-L." Online posting. 18 Jan. 2003. Nabokv-L. 12 June 2005 <http://listserv.ucsb.edu/lsv-cgi-bin/wa?A2=ind0301&L=nabokv-l&P=R37018>.

Fish, Stanley. *Is There a Text in This Class? The Authority of Interpretive Communities*. Cambridge: Harvard UP, 1980.

———. "Literature in the Reader: Affective Stylistics." *New Literary History* 2 (1970): 123–62.

Flaubert, Gustave. *Madame Bovary*. New York: Bantam, 1982.

Frank, Joseph. "Lectures on Literature." Alexandrov, *Garland Companion* 234–58.

Freeman, Elizabeth. "Honeymoon with a Stranger: Pedophilliac Picaresques from Poe to Nabokov." *American Literature* 70 (1998): 863–97.

Freud, Sigmund. "Humour." *The Standard Edition of the Complete Psychological Works of Sigmund Freud.* Ed. and trans. James Strachey. Vol. 21. London: Hogarth, 1981. 159–66.

———. *Jokes and Their Relation to the Unconscious.* 1905. Ed. and trans. James Strachey. Harmondsworth: Penguin, 1983.

Friedan, Betty. *The Feminine Mystique.* New York: Norton, 1991.

Frosch, Thomas R. "Parody and Authenticity in *Lolita.*" Rivers and Nicol 171–87.

Gardner, John. *On Moral Fiction.* New York: Basic, 1978.

Gilliat, Penelope. "Nabokov." *Vogue* Dec. 1966.

Girodias, Maurice. "Lolita, Nabokov, and I." *Evergreen Review* Sept. 1965: 44+.

———. "Pornologist on Olympus." *Playboy* Apr. 1961: 56+.

Gogol, Nikolai. "A May Night, or The Drowned Maiden." *The Complete Tales of Nikolai Gogol.* Ed. Leonard J. Kent. Trans. Constance Garnett. Vol. 2. Chicago: U of Chicago P, 1985. 49–76.

Gordon, John. "Current Events." *Sunday Express* [London] 29 Jan. 1956: 6.

"A Gothic Lolita Style Identification Guide." 3 May 2007 <http://www.lerman.biz/asagao/gothic_lolita.html>.

Gould, Stephen Jay. "No Science without Fancy, No Art without Facts: The Lepidoptery of Vladimir Nabokov." *I Have Landed: The End of a Beginning in Natural History.* New York: Harmony, 2002. 29–53.

Grayson, Jane. *Vladimir Nabokov.* Overlook Illustrated Lives. London: Overlook, 2003.

Grayson, Jane, Arnold McMillin, and Priscilla Meyer, eds. *Nabokov's World.* 2 vols. New York: Palgrave, 2005.

Green, Martin. "The Morality of *Lolita.*" *Kenyon Review* 28 (1966): 352–77.

Greene, Graham: "Books of the Year-I." *Sunday Times* [London] 25 Dec. 1955: 4.

———. "The John Gordon Society." *Spectator* 10 Feb. 1956: 182.

Haegert, John. "Artist in Exile: The Americanization of Humbert Humbert." Pifer, *Vladimir* 137–54.

Harington, Donald. *Ekaterina.* New York: Harcourt, 1993.

Harrison, Bernard. "Gaps and Stumbling-Blocks in Fielding: A Response to Cerny, Hammond and Hudson." *Connotations* 3 (1993–94): 142–72.

———. *Inconvenient Fictions: Literature and the Limits of Theory.* New Haven: Yale UP, 1991.

Henderson, Bill, and André Bernard, eds. *Pushcart's Complete Rotten Reviews and Rejections.* New York: Norton, 1998.

Herbold, Sarah. "'(I Have Camouflaged Everything, My Love)': *Lolita* and the Woman Reader." *Nabokov Studies* 5 (1998-1999): 71–98.

———. "Reflections on Modernism: *Lolita* and Political Engagement; or, How the Left and the Right Both Have It Wrong." *Nabokov Studies* 3 (1996): 145–50.

Highsmith, Patricia. *The Price of Salt.* New York: Norton, 2004.

Hollander, John. "The Perilous Magic of Nymphets." *Partisan Review* 23 (1956): 557–60.

Hudgins, Christopher C. "Lolita 1995: The Four Filmscripts." *Literature Film Quarterly* 25 (1997): 23–29.

Hunt, Lynn, ed. *The Invention of Pornography: Obscenity and the Origins of Modernity, 1500–1800.* New York: Zone, 1996.

Iser, Wolfgang. *The Act of Reading: A Theory of Aesthetic Response.* Baltimore: Johns Hopkins UP, 1978.

Ivanits, Linda. *Russian Folk Belief*. Armonk: Sharpe, 1989.

Johnson, Kurt, and Steve Coates. *Nabokov's Blues: The Scientific Odyssey of a Literary Genius*. New York: McGraw; Cambridge: Zoland, 1999.

Jones, Nancy J. *Molly*. New York: Crown, 2000.

———. "Vladimir Nabokov's *Lolita*: A Survey of Scholarship and Criticism in English, 1977–95." *Bonner Beitrage* 54.2 (1997): 129–47.

Juliar, Michael. *Vladimir Nabokov: A Descriptive Bibliography*. New York: Garland, 1986.

Kant, Immanuel. "First Book: Analytic of the Beautiful." Trans. J. H. Bernard. Richter 257–80.

———. *Groundwork of the Metaphysics of Morals*. Trans. and ed. Mary Gregor. Cambridge: Cambridge UP, 1998.

Karges, Joann. *Nabokov's Lepidoptera: Genre and Genera*. Ann Arbor: Ardis, 1985.

Kauffman, Linda S. "Framing Lolita: Is There a Woman in the Text?" Bloom, *Vladimir Nabokov's* Lolita 149–68. Rpt. in *Refiguring the Father: New Feminist Readings of Patriarchy*. Ed. Patricia Yaeger and Beth Kowalski-Wallace Carbondale: Southern Illinois UP, 1989. 131–52.

Kennedy, Colleen. "The White Man's Guest; or, Why Aren't More Feminists Reading *Lolita*?" *Narrative and Culture*. Ed. Janice Carlisle and Daniel R. Schwartz. Athens: U of Georgia P, 1994. 46–53.

Kincaid, James R. *Child-Loving: The Erotic Child and Victorian Culture*. New York: Routledge, 1992.

Kinsey, Alfred C., et al. *Sexual Behavior in the Human Female*. 1953. Bloomington: Indiana UP, 1998.

———. *Sexual Behavior in the Human Male*. 1948. Bloomington: Indiana UP, 1998.

Kobel, Peter. "Nabokov Won't Be Nailed Down Onscreen." *New York Times* 22 Apr. 2001. <http://www.nytimes.com/2001/04/22/arts/22KOBE.html>.

Kurganov, Efim. *Lolita i Ada*. Saint Petersburg: Zvezda, 2001.

Kuzmanovich, Zoran. "Strong Opinions and Nerve Points: Nabokov's Life and Art." Connolly, *Cambridge Companion* 11–30.

Kuzmanovich, Zoran, et al. "*Lolita* A–Z." *Post Road* 7 (2003): 151–69.

Le Guin, Ursula K. "The Ones Who Walk away from Omelas." *The Wind's Twelve Quarters*. New York: Harper, 1975. 275–84.

Lehman, Daniel W. *Matters of Fact: Reading Nonfiction over the Edge*. Columbus: Ohio State UP, 1997.

Lerner, Alan Jay. *Lolita, My Love*. 1971.

Maar, Michael. *The Two Lolitas*. Trans. Perry Anderson. London: Verso, 2005.

Maddox, Lucy. *Nabokov's Novels in English*. Athens: U of Georgia P, 1983.

Marling, Karal Ann. *As Seen on TV: The Visual Culture of Everyday Life in the 1950s*. Cambridge: Harvard UP, 1996.

McCrum, Robert. "A Life in the Margins." *New Yorker* 11 Apr. 1994: 46–55.

Miller, J. Hillis. *The Ethics of Reading*. New York: Columbia UP, 1987.

Mizruchi, Susan. "*Lolita* in History." *American Literature* 75 (2003): 629–52.

Moore, Anthony R. "How Unreliable Is Humbert in *Lolita*?" *Journal of Modern Literature* 25.1 (2001): 71–80.

Morreall, John, ed. *The Philosophy of Laughter and Humor*. New York: State U of New York P, 1987.

Mulvey, Laura. *Visual and Other Pleasures*. Bloomington: Indiana UP, 1989.

Nabokov, Dmitri. "A Few Things That Must Be Said on Behalf of Vladimir Nabokov." Rivers and Nicol 35–42.

———. "In Memoriam." McGraw et al 41–42.

———. "On a Book Entitled *The Enchanter*." Afterword. V. Nabokov, *Enchanter* 79–144.

———. "On Revisiting Father's Room." Quennell 126–36.

———. "Things I Could Have Said." *Cycnos* 1 (1993): 75–79.

Nabokov, Vladimir. *Ada, or Ardor: A Family Chronicle*. New York: Vintage, 1990.

———. *The Annotated* Lolita. 1970. Ed. Alfred Appel, Jr. New York: Vintage, 1991.

———. "The Aurelian." V. Nabokov, *Stories* 248–58.

———. "Christmas." V. Nabokov, *Stories* 131–36.

———. *Conclusive Evidence*. New York: Harper, 1951.

———. *Dear Bunny, Dear Volodya: The Nabokov-Wilson Letters, 1940–1971*. Ed. Simon Karlinsky. Rev. ed. Berkeley: U of California P, 2001.

———. *The Defense*. Trans. Michael Scammell and Nabokov. New York: Vintage, 1990.

———. *The Enchanter*. 1986. Trans. Dmitri Nabokov. New York: Vintage, 1991.

———. *The Eye*. Trans. Dmitri Nabokov and Nabokov. New York: Vintage, 1990.

———. *The Gift*. 1935–37. Trans. Michael Scammell and Nabokov. New York: Vintage, 1991.

———. *Krug*. Ed. N. I. Tolstaia. Leningrad: Khudozhestvennaia, 1990.

———. *Laughter in the Dark*. New York: Vintage, 1989.

———. *Lectures on* Don Quixote. New York: Harcourt, 1984.

———. *Lectures on Literature*. Ed. Fredson Bowers. New York: Harcourt, 1980.

———. *Lectures on Russian Literature*. Ed. Fredson Bowers. New York: Harcourt, 1981.

———. "Lilith." *Poems and Problems*. New York: McGraw, 1970. 55.

———. *Lolita*. 1955. New York: Vintage, 1997.

———. *Lolita* [Russian-language version]. New York: Phaedra, 1967.

———. "*Lolita* and Mr. Girodias." *Evergreen Review* Feb. 1967: 37–41.

———. *Lolita: A Screenplay*. New York: McGraw, 1974.

———. *Mary*. New York: Vintage, 1989.

———. *Nikolai Gogol*. New York: New Directions, 1961.

———. *Novels, 1955–1962*. Ed. Brian Boyd. New York: Lib. of Amer., 1996.

———. "On a Book Entitled *Lolita*." V. Nabokov, *Lolita*, Vintage 311–17.

———. *Pale Fire*. New York: Vintage, 1989.

———. *Perepiska s sestroi*. Ann Arbor: Ardis, 1985.

———. *Pnin*. New York: Doubleday, 1984.

———. "The Return of Chorb." V. Nabokov, *Stories* 147–54.

———. "Rowe's Symbols." V. Nabokov, *Strong Opinions* 304–07 [1990].

———. *Speak, Memory: An Autobiography Revisited*. New York: Vintage, 1989.

———. *Stikhotvoreniia*. Saint Petersburg: Akademicheskii proekt, 2002.

———. *The Stories of Vladimir Nabokov*. New York: Vintage, 1995.

———. *Strong Opinions*. New York: Vintage, 1990.

———. "The Vane Sisters." V. Nabokov, *Stories* 619–31.

———. *Vladimir Nabokov: Selected Letters, 1940–1977*. Ed. Dmitri Nabokov and Matthew J. Bruccoli. New York: Harcourt, 1989.

Nafisi, Azar. "Interview with Azar Nafisi." *Samarkand Quarterly* 3-4 (2003-2004): 6 pars. 5 Apr. 2007 <http://staffweb.library.vanderbilt.edu/libtech/stringer/samarkand.html>.

———. *Reading* Lolita *in Tehran: A Memoir in Books*. New York: Random, 2004.

Nakhimovsky, Alexander D., and S. Paperno. *An English-Russian Dictionary of Nabokov's* Lolita. Ann Arbor: Ardis, 1982.

Nelson, Thomas Allen. "Kubrick in Nabokovland: *Lolita*." *Kubrick: Inside a Film Artist's Maze*. Bloomington: Indiana UP, 1982. 54–78.

Nosik, Boris. *Pionerskaia Lolita (Dobrye povesti dobrykh starykh vremen)*. Saint Petersburg: Zolotoi vek–Diamant, 2000.

Nussbaum, Martha. *Love's Knowledge: Essays on Philosophy and Literature*. Oxford: Oxford UP, 1992.

———. *Poetic Justice: The Literary Imagination and Public Life*. Boston: Beacon, 1997.

———. *Upheavals of Thought: The Intelligence of Emotions*. Cambridge: Cambridge UP, 2001.

O'Connor, Katherine Tiernan. "Rereading *Lolita*, Reconsidering Nabokov's Relationship with Dostoevskij." *Slavic and East European Journal* 33 (1989): 64–77.

Oddie, William. "Why This Loathsome *Lolita* Must Be Banished." *Daily Mail* 26 Aug. 1996. 5 Apr. 2007 <http://listserv.ucsb.edu/lsv-cgi-bin/wa?A2=ind9608&L=nabokv-l&P=R2506>.

Olsen, Lance. Lolita*: A Janus Text*. New York: Twayne, 1995.

Page, Norman, ed. *Nabokov: The Critical Heritage*. Boston: Routledge, 1982.

Parker, Stephen Jan. "Nabokov in the Margins: The Montreux Books." *Journal of Modern Literature* 14.1 (1987): 5–16.

———. "Nabokov's Montreux Books: Part II." *Cycnos* 1 (1993): 107–11.

———. *Understanding Vladimir Nabokov*. Columbia: U of South Carolina P, 1987.

Patnoe, Elizabeth. "Discourse, Ideology, and Hegemony: The Double Dramas in and around *Lolita*." *Discourse and Ideology in Nabokov's Prose*. Ed. David M. J. Larmour. London: Routledge, 2002. 111–36.

Pera, Pia. *Lo's Diary*. Trans. Ann Goldstein. Pref. Dmitri Nabokov. New York: Foxrock, 1999.

Peterson, Dale E. "Nabokov and Poe." Alexandrov, *Garland Companion* 463–72.

———. "White (K)nights: Dostoevskian Dreamers in Nabokov's Early Stories." *Nabokov's World*. Grayson, McMillin, and Meyers 2: 59–72.

Phelan, James. "Authorial Readers, Flesh and Blood Readers, and the Recursiveness of Rhetorical Reading." *Reader* 43 (2000): 65–69.

Pifer, Ellen. *Nabokov and the Novel*. Cambridge: Harvard UP, 1980.

———. "Nabokov's Discovery of America: From Russia to *Lolita*." *The American Columbiad: "Discovering" America, Inventing the United States*. Ed. Mario Materassi and Maria Irene Ramalho de Sousa Santos. Amsterdam: Vrije Universiteit UP, 1996. 407–14.

———, ed. *Vladimir Nabokov's* Lolita: *A Casebook*. New York: Oxford UP, 2003.

Plato. Book 10. *Republic*. Trans. Benjamin Jowett. Richter 21–29.

Podhoretz, Norman. "'Lolita,' My Mother-in-Law, the Marquis de Sade, and Larry Flynt." *Commentary* Apr. 1997: 23–35.

Poe, Edgar Allan. *The Complete Tales and Poems*. New York: Mod. Lib., 1938.

———. "Ligeia." *Complete Stories and Poems*. New York: Doubleday, 1966. 97–108.

Poirier, Richard. *A World Elsewhere: The Place of Style in American Literature*. New York: Oxford UP, 1966.

Prager, Emily. *Roger Fishbite*. New York: Random, 1999.

Preissler, Brigitte. "Lolita, Lollipops und Lollobrigida." *Die Welt* 14 May 2004. 5 Apr. 2007 <http://www.welt.de/data/2004/05/14/277475.html>.

Proffer, Carl R. *Keys to* Lolita. Bloomington: Indiana UP, 1968.

———. "Nabokov's Russian *Lolita.*" *Russian Literature and American Critics: In Honor of Deming B. Brown*. Ed. Kenneth N. Brostrom. Ann Arbor: U of Michigan P, 1984. 249–63.

———. "Profit without Honor." *Time* 21 Dec. 1970: 44.

Pushkin, Aleksandr. *Eugene Onegin*. Trans. Vladimir Nabokov. 4 vols. New York: Random, 1964.

———. *Rusalka. Boris Godunov and Other Dramatic Works*. Trans. James E. Falen. Introd. Caryl Emerson. New York: Oxford UP, 2007. 177–201.

Pyle, Robert Michael. "Between Climb and Cloud: Nabokov among the Lepidopterists." Boyd and Pyle 32–76.

Queneau, Raymond. *Zazie in the Metro*. Trans. Barbara Wright. New York: Riverrun, 1982.

Quennell, Peter, ed. *Vladimir Nabokov: A Tribute*. New York: Morrow, 1980.

Raguet-Bouvart, Christine. Lolita: *Un royaume au-delà des mers*. Bordeaux: Presses Universitaires de Bordeaux, 1996.

Rampton, David. *Vladimir Nabokov*. London: Macmillan; New York: St. Martin's, 1993.

Rembar, Charles. *The End of Obscenity: The Trials of* Lady Chatterly, Tropic of Cancer, *and* Fanny Hill. New York: Random, 1968.

"Remembering Nabokov: Cornell Colleagues and Others [Recollections by Alison Bishop, Meyer Abrams, J. Milton Cowan, William L. Brown, Jr., John G. Franclemont, Peter Kahn, Ephim Fogel]." *The Achievements of Vladimir Nabokov*. Ed. George Gibian and Stephen Jan Parker. Ithaca: Center for Intl. Studies, Cornell U, 1984. 215–33.

"Reminiscences" [Recollections by Lucie Léon Noel, Nina Berberova, Morris Bishop, Ross Wetzsteon, Julian Moynahan, Ellendea Proffer, Stanley Elkin]." *For Vladimir Nabokov on His Seventieth Birthday*. Ed. Charles Newman and Alfred Appel, Jr. *TriQuarterly* 17 (1970): 209–65.

Richter, David H., ed. *The Critical Tradition: Classic Texts and Contemporary Trends*. 2nd ed. New York: Bedford, 1998.

Rimmon-Kenan, Shlomith. *Narrative Fiction: Contemporary Poetics*. London: Methuen, 1983.

Rivers, J. E., and Charles Nicol, eds. *Nabokov's Fifth Arc: Nabokov and Others on His Life's Work*. Austin: U of Texas P, 1982.

Rorty, Richard. *Contingency, Irony, and Solidarity*. Cambridge: Cambridge UP, 1989.

Rowe, William Woodin. *Nabokov's Deceptive World*. New York: New York UP, 1971.

Salinger, J. D. *The Catcher in the Rye*. Boston: Little, 1951.

Schakovskoy, Zinaïda. *V poiskakh Nabokova*. Paris: Libre, 1979.

Schiff, Marjorie A. "To Impress an Admissions Officer, Read Something Worth Writing About." *Chronicle of Higher Education* 6 Feb. 2004: B15.

Schiff, Stacy. *Véra (Mrs. Vladimir Nabokov): Portrait of a Marriage*. New York: Random, 1999.

Schiff, Stephen. Lolita: *The Book of the Film*. Fwd. Jeremy Irons. Pref. Adrian Lyne. New York: Applause, 1998.

Schuman, Samuel. *Vladimir Nabokov: A Reference Guide*. Boston: Hall, 1979.

Shakespeare, William. *Midsummer Night's Dream*. *Riverside Shakespeare*. Boston: Houghton, 1974. 217–49.

———. *Shakespeare's Sonnets*. Ed. Stephen Booth. New Haven: Yale UP, 1977.

Shapiro, Gavriel. "*Lolita* Class List." *Cahiers du monde russe* 37 (1996): 317–36.

———, ed. *Nabokov at Cornell*. Ithaca: Cornell UP, 2003.

Sharpe, Tony. *Vladimir Nabokov*. London: Arnold, 1991.

Shattuck, Roger. *Forbidden Knowledge: From Prometheus to Pornography*. New York: St. Martin's, 1996.

Shelley, Percy Bysshe. "A Defence of Poetry." Richter 339–56.

Sidney, Philip. *An Apology for Poetry*. Richter 131–59.

Sinclair, Marianne. *Hollywood Lolita: The Nymphet Syndrome in the Movies*. London: Plexus, 1988.

Smith, Adam. *The Theory of Moral Sentiment*. London: Bohn, 1853.

Steiner, George. "Extraterritorial." *Triquarterly* 17 (1970): 119–27.

Steinle, Pamela. *In Cold Fear: The Catcher in the Rye Censorship Controversies and Postwar American Character*. Columbus: Ohio State UP, 2000.

Storey, John. *Cultural Consumption and Everyday Life*. New York: Arnold, 1999.

Stringer-Hye, Suellen. "CoLOlations." *Zembla*. 5 June 2005 <http://www.libraries.psu.edu/nabokov/colo.htm>.

Tamir-Ghez, Nomi. "The Art of Persuasion in Nabokov's *Lolita*." Pifer, *Vladimir* 17–37.

———. "Rhetorical Manipulation in *Lolita*." *The Structural Analysis of Narrative Texts*. Ed. Andrej Kodjak and Krystyna Pomorska. Columbus: Slavica, 1980. 172–95.

Tammi, Pekka. *Problems of Nabokov's Poetics: A Narratological Analysis*. Helsinki: Soumalainen Tiedeakatemia, 1985.

Tanner, Tony. *City of Words: American Fiction, 1950–1970*. New York: Harper, 1971.

Tekiner, Christina. "Time in *Lolita*." *Modern Fiction Studies* 25 (1979): 463–69.

Tocqueville, Alexis de. *Democracy in America*. Trans. Henry Reeve. New York: Knopf, 1994.

Toker, Leona. *Eloquent Reticence: Withholding Information in Fictional Narrative*. Lexington: UP of Kentucky, 1993.

———. "Liberal Ironists and the 'Gaudily Painted Savage': On Richard Rorty's Reading of Vladimir Nabokov." *Nabokov Studies* 1 (1994): 195–206. <http://www.libraries.psu.edu/nabokov/tokerp1.htm>.

———. *Nabokov: The Mystery of Literary Structures*. Ithaca: Cornell UP, 1989.

Tolstoy, Leo. *What Is Art?* Trans. Almyer Maude. Indianapolis: Bobbs, 1978.

Trainer, Russell. *The Lolita Complex: A Clinical Analysis*. New York: Citadel, 1966.

Trilling, Lionel. "The Last Lover: Vladimir Nabokov's *Lolita*." *Griffin* 7 (1958): 4–21.

Wallace, Ronald. "No Harm in Smiling: Vladimir Nabokov's *Lolita*." *The Last Laugh: Form and Affirmation in the Contemporary American Comic Novel*. Columbia: U of Missouri P, 1979. 65–89.

Weil, Irwin. "Odyssey of a Translator." *Triquarterly* 17 (1970): 266–83.

Wetzsteon, Ross. "Nabokov as Teacher." Appel and Newman 240–46.

Wimsatt, William K., Jr., and Monroe C. Beardsley. "The Intentional Fallacy." 1946. *The Norton Anthology of Theory and Criticism*. Ed. Vincent B. Leitch et al. New York: Norton, 2001. 1374–87.

Winston, Matthew. "*Lolita* and the Dangers of Fiction." *Twentieth Century Literature* 21 (1975): 421–27.

Wood, Michael. *The Magical Doubts: Nabokov and the Risks of Fiction.* Princeton: Princeton UP, 1994.

Wordsworth, William. *Preface to the Lyrical Ballads.* Copenhagen: Rosenkilde and Bagger, 1957.

"Worldwide Ages of Consent." *Avert.* 5 Apr. 2007 <http://www.avert.org/aofconsent.htm>.

Wyllie, Barbara. "Nabokov and Cinema." Connolly, *Cambridge Companion* 215–31.

——. *Nabokov at the Movies: Film Perspectives in Fiction.* Jefferson: McFarland, 2003.

Zimmer, Dieter E. *A Guide to Nabokov's Butterflies and Moths.* Hamburg: Zimmer, 2001.

——. "Nabokov Filmography." *Zembla.* Pennsylvania State U. Mar. 2001. 3 May 2007 <http://www.libraries.psu.edu/nabokov/zembla.htm>.

——. *Vladimir Nabokov: Bibliographie des Gesamtwerks.* Privatdruck: Rowohlt, 1963.

Audiovisual Materials

Bauer, Evgenii, dir. *Grezy* [Daydreams]. Khanzhonkov Studios, 1915. *Evgenii Bauer.* Early Russian Cinema 7. VHS. Milestone Films, 2002.

——, dir. *Posle smerti* [After Death]. Khanzhonkov Studios, 1915. *Mad Love: The Films of Evgenii Bauer.* DVD. Milestone Films, 2003.

——, dir. *Smert' na zhizn'* [Death for Life]. Khanzhonkov Studios, 1914. Early Russian Cinema 9. VHS. Milestone Films, 2002.

——, dir. *Umiraiushchii lebed'* [Dying Swan]. Khanzhonkov Studios, 1916. *Mad Love: The Films of Evgenii Bauer.* DVD. Milestone Films, 2003.

——, dir. *Za schast'em* [For Happiness]. Khanzhonkov Studios, 1917. *End of an Era.* Early Russian Cinema 10. VHS. Milestone Films, 2002.

Kubrick, Stanley, dir. *Lolita.* MGM and Seven Arts, 1962.

Lyne, Adrian, dir. *Lolita.* Pathe, 1998. Showtime, 1997.

Mendes, Sam, dir. *American Beauty.* Dream Works, 1999.

Nabokov, Vladimir. *Great Writers of the Twentieth Century: Vladimir Nabokov.* Clark Television for BBC Worldwide Television, London. 1998.

——. *Half an Hour with Nabokov.* Interview with Peter Duval Smith and Christopher Burstall. *Bookstand.* BBC, London. July 1962.

——. *Lolita.* Read by Jeremy Irons. Audiocassette. Random, 1997.

——. *Lolita.* Read by James Mason. Audiocassette. Caedmon, 1998.

——. Lolita *and Poems.* Read by Vladimir Nabokov. Audiocassette. Spoken Arts, 1980.

——. *Vladimir Nabokov.* Interview with Robert Hughes. Natl. Educ. Television, New York. 1965.

Solondz, Todd, dir. *Happiness.* Good Machine–Killer Films. October Films, 1998.

INDEX

Modern Language Association of America
Approaches to Teaching World Literature
Joseph Gibaldi, series editor

Achebe's Things Fall Apart. Ed. Bernth Lindfors. 1991.
Arthurian Tradition. Ed. Maureen Fries and Jeanie Watson. 1992.
Atwood's The Handmaid's Tale *and Other Works*. Ed. Sharon R. Wilson,
   Thomas B. Friedman, and Shannon Hengen. 1996.
Austen's Emma. Ed. Marcia McClintock Folsom. 2004.
Austen's Pride and Prejudice. Ed. Marcia McClintock Folsom. 1993.
Balzac's Old Goriot. Ed. Michal Peled Ginsburg. 2000.
Baudelaire's Flowers of Evil. Ed. Laurence M. Porter. 2000.
Beckett's Waiting for Godot. Ed. June Schlueter and Enoch Brater. 1991.
Beowulf. Ed. Jess B. Bessinger, Jr., and Robert F. Yeager. 1984.
Blake's Songs of Innocence and of Experience. Ed. Robert F. Gleckner and
   Mark L. Greenberg. 1989.
Boccaccio's Decameron. Ed. James H. McGregor. 2000.
British Women Poets of the Romantic Period. Ed. Stephen C. Behrendt and
   Harriet Kramer Linkin. 1997.
Brontë's Jane Eyre. Ed. Diane Long Hoeveler and Beth Lau. 1993.
Emily Brontë's Wuthering Heights. Ed. Sue Lonoff and Terri A. Hasseler. 2006.
Byron's Poetry. Ed. Frederick W. Shilstone. 1991.
Camus's The Plague. Ed. Steven G. Kellman. 1985.
Cather's My Ántonia. Ed. Susan J. Rosowski. 1989.
Cervantes' Don Quixote. Ed. Richard Bjornson. 1984.
Chaucer's Canterbury Tales. Ed. Joseph Gibaldi. 1980.
Chaucer's Troilus and Criseyde *and the Shorter Poems*. Ed. Tison Pugh and
   Angela Jane Weisl. 2006.
Chopin's The Awakening. Ed. Bernard Koloski. 1988.
Coleridge's Poetry and Prose. Ed. Richard E. Matlak. 1991.
Collodi's Pinocchio *and Its Adaptations*. Ed. Michael Sherberg. 2006.
Conrad's "Heart of Darkness" and "The Secret Sharer." Ed. Hunt Hawkins and
   Brian W. Shaffer. 2002.
Dante's Divine Comedy. Ed. Carole Slade. 1982.
Defoe's Robinson Crusoe. Ed. Maximillian E. Novak and Carl Fisher. 2005.
DeLillo's White Noise. Ed. Tim Engles and John N. Duvall. 2006.
Dickens' David Copperfield. Ed. Richard J. Dunn. 1984.
Dickinson's Poetry. Ed. Robin Riley Fast and Christine Mack Gordon. 1989.
Narrative of the Life of Frederick Douglass. Ed. James C. Hall. 1999.
Early Modern Spanish Drama. Ed. Laura R. Bass and Margaret R. Greer. 2006
Eliot's Middlemarch. Ed. Kathleen Blake. 1990.
Eliot's Poetry and Plays. Ed. Jewel Spears Brooker. 1988.

Shorter Elizabethan Poetry. Ed. Patrick Cheney and Anne Lake Prescott. 2000.

Ellison's Invisible Man. Ed. Susan Resneck Parr and Pancho Savery. 1989.

English Renaissance Drama. Ed. Karen Bamford and Alexander Leggatt. 2002.

Works of Louise Erdrich. Ed. Gregg Sarris, Connie A. Jacobs, and
    James R. Giles. 2004.

Dramas of Euripides. Ed. Robin Mitchell-Boyask. 2002.

Faulkner's The Sound and the Fury. Ed. Stephen Hahn and Arthur F. Kinney. 1996.

Flaubert's Madame Bovary. Ed. Laurence M. Porter and Eugene F. Gray. 1995.

García Márquez's One Hundred Years of Solitude. Ed. María Elena de Valdés and
    Mario J. Valdés. 1990.

Gilman's "The Yellow Wall-Paper" and Herland. Ed. Denise D. Knight and
    Cynthia J. Davis. 2003.

Goethe's Faust. Ed. Douglas J. McMillan. 1987.

Gothic Fiction: The British and American Traditions. Ed. Diane Long Hoeveler
    and Tamar Heller. 2003.

Grass's The Tin Drum. Ed. Monika Shafi. 2008.

Hebrew Bible as Literature in Translation. Ed. Barry N. Olshen and
    Yael S. Feldman. 1989.

Homer's Iliad *and* Odyssey. Ed. Kostas Myrsiades. 1987.

Ibsen's A Doll House. Ed. Yvonne Shafer. 1985.

Henry James's Daisy Miller *and* The Turn of the Screw. Ed. Kimberly C. Reed and
    Peter G. Beidler. 2005.

Works of Samuel Johnson. Ed. David R. Anderson and Gwin J. Kolb. 1993.

Joyce's Ulysses. Ed. Kathleen McCormick and Erwin R. Steinberg. 1993.

Works of Sor Juana Inés de la Cruz. Ed. Emilie L. Bergmann and Stacey Schlau.
    2007.

Kafka's Short Fiction. Ed. Richard T. Gray. 1995.

Keats's Poetry. Ed. Walter H. Evert and Jack W. Rhodes. 1991.

Kingston's The Woman Warrior. Ed. Shirley Geok-lin Lim. 1991.

Lafayette's The Princess of Clèves. Ed. Faith E. Beasley and
    Katharine Ann Jensen. 1998.

Works of D. H. Lawrence. Ed. M. Elizabeth Sargent and Garry Watson. 2001.

Lessing's The Golden Notebook. Ed. Carey Kaplan and Ellen Cronan Rose. 1989.

Mann's Death in Venice *and Other Short Fiction.* Ed. Jeffrey B. Berlin. 1992.

Marguerite de Navarre's Heptameron. Ed. Colette H. Winn. 2007.

Medieval English Drama. Ed. Richard K. Emmerson. 1990.

Melville's Moby-Dick. Ed. Martin Bickman. 1985.

Metaphysical Poets. Ed. Sidney Gottlieb. 1990.

Miller's Death of a Salesman. Ed. Matthew C. Roudané. 1995.

Milton's Paradise Lost. Ed. Galbraith M. Crump. 1986.

Milton's Shorter Poetry and Prose. Ed. Peter C. Herman. 2007.

Molière's Tartuffe *and Other Plays.* Ed. James F. Gaines and
    Michael S. Koppisch. 1995.

Momaday's The Way to Rainy Mountain. Ed. Kenneth M. Roemer. 1988.
Montaigne's Essays. Ed. Patrick Henry. 1994.
Novels of Toni Morrison. Ed. Nellie Y. McKay and Kathryn Earle. 1997.
Murasaki Shikibu's The Tale of Genji. Ed. Edward Kamens. 1993.
Nabokov's Lolita. Ed. Zoran Kuzmanovich and Galya Diment. 2008.
Pope's Poetry. Ed. Wallace Jackson and R. Paul Yoder. 1993.
Proust's Fiction and Criticism. Ed. Elyane Dezon-Jones and
    Inge Crosman Wimmers. 2003.
Puig's Kiss of the Spider Woman. Ed. Daniel Balderston and Francine Masiello.
    2007.
Pynchon's The Crying of Lot 49 *and Other Works.* Ed. Thomas H. Schaub. 2008.
Novels of Samuel Richardson. Ed. Lisa Zunshine and Jocelyn Harris. 2006.
Rousseau's Confessions *and* Reveries of the Solitary Walker. Ed. John C. O'Neal
    and Ourida Mostefai. 2003.
Shakespeare's Hamlet. Ed. Bernice W. Kliman. 2001.
Shakespeare's King Lear. Ed. Robert H. Ray. 1986.
Shakespeare's Othello. Ed. Peter Erickson and Maurice Hunt. 2005.
Shakespeare's Romeo and Juliet. Ed. Maurice Hunt. 2000.
Shakespeare's The Tempest *and Other Late Romances.* Ed. Maurice Hunt. 1992.
Shelley's Frankenstein. Ed. Stephen C. Behrendt. 1990.
Shelley's Poetry. Ed. Spencer Hall. 1990.
Sir Gawain and the Green Knight. Ed. Miriam Youngerman Miller and
    Jane Chance. 1986.
Song of Roland. Ed. William W. Kibler and Leslie Zarker Morgan. 2006.
Spenser's Faerie Queene. Ed. David Lee Miller and Alexander Dunlop. 1994.
Stendhal's The Red and the Black. Ed. Dean de la Motte and Stirling Haig. 1999.
Sterne's Tristram Shandy. Ed. Melvyn New. 1989.
Stowe's Uncle Tom's Cabin. Ed. Elizabeth Ammons and Susan Belasco. 2000.
Swift's Gulliver's Travels. Ed. Edward J. Rielly. 1988.
Thoreau's Walden *and Other Works.* Ed. Richard J. Schneider. 1996.
Tolstoy's Anna Karenina. Ed. Liza Knapp and Amy Mandelker. 2003.
Vergil's Aeneid. Ed. William S. Anderson and Lorina N. Quartarone. 2002.
Voltaire's Candide. Ed. Renée Waldinger. 1987.
Whitman's Leaves of Grass. Ed. Donald D. Kummings. 1990.
Wiesel's Night. Ed. Alan Rosen. 2007.
Woolf's To the Lighthouse. Ed. Beth Rigel Daugherty and Mary Beth Pringle. 2001.
Wordsworth's Poetry. Ed. Spencer Hall, with Jonathan Ramsey. 1986.
Wright's Native Son. Ed. James A. Miller. 1997.